EXPLORING THE MARGINS

EXPLORING THE MARGINS

CASTE, CLASS AND GENDER IDENTITY

SURESH KUMAR

Vitasta

Published by
Renu Kaul Verma
Vitasta Publishing Pvt Ltd
2/15, Ansari Road, Daryaganj
New Delhi-110 002
info@vitastapublishing.com

ISBN 978-93-90961-66-5

First Edition 2022

MRP ₹ 695

Edited by Renu Arya
Cover and Layout by Somesh Kumar Mishra
Printed by Chaman Enterprises, New Delhi

CONTENTS

PREFACE

Dalits, in India are considered the most contaminating beings since time immemorial. Positioned at the lowest rung of caste hierarchy, Dalits are socially segregated, economically, educationally destitute, and politically and geographically marginalised. They are stigmatised and marred by the long revered religio-cultural ideological structures and the fiats of caste which expose them to exploitation, humiliation, physical violence and perpetual impecuniousness. Divested of rights and dignity, Dalits have led lives of sub-human beings for centuries as they were traditionally denied voice and coerced to silently observe the edicts of caste. It was only with the advent of Bhimrao Ramaji Ambedkar that the distress, indignation, and resistance of Dalits found a systematic expression at a pan-India level, though, before him also some Dalit intellectuals such as Jyotirao Govindrao Phule, Iyothee Thass, Periyar, Narayana Guru, Harichand, Guruchand Thakur and others had also voiced their protest against caste-based oppression. As the champion of rights and emancipation of the deprived sections, Ambedkar awakened Dalits and organised them to speak against dominant socio-economic forces. It was evidently because of Ambedkar that the radical anti-caste groups such as Dalit Panthers subsequently fought against the high caste establishments and dominant power structures in post-independence India. The Dalit Panthers not only organised Dalits to protest against caste, class and gender-based disparities but also encouraged Dalit literary production which began sporadically in the 1950s in some regions of India.

Dalit literature, as an unconventional form of writing, strongly builds on anti-caste views expressed by Ambedkar and other Dalit intellectuals and stands steadfast for social, economic, political, cultural parities, and justices. It records Dalit voices of distress, dissent and resistance, expresses their will, desire, agency and demands structural transformation in existing power structures. The discriminatory socio-economic, political and religio-cultural conventions and institutions are frequently discussed and condemned in this literature. It is because the Dalit writers believe that they are the source of caste based discrimination which they have been subjected to for centuries. Dalit writers select non-traditional subjects such as caste based disparities and exploitation and shun traditionally meditated and practised themes such as gods and religions. Dalit literature rejects traditional aesthetics, language, symbols and images to assert their autonomy and register their protest against the hegemony of the high castes in literary spheres. Dalit writers have devised their own symbols and images to extol their culture and ridicule the sanskritised one.

The present volume is an attempt to examine how contemporary Dalit writings depict caste and how they perceive and respond to it. It also seeks to survey how selected Dalit writers voice their rebellion and strategize to abrogate caste and ultimately emancipate Dalits. The volume offers authentic reflections on the nature, purpose, aims and significance of Dalit literature. It also attempts to describe how Dalit literature explores social, economic, political, cultural and geographical margins, how it counters injustices and strives to initiate a just and egalitarian system where Dalits may be treated as equal human beings regardless of their caste, class, gender and identity.

The idea of this book was conceived after the completion of my PhD thesis when I started reading Dalit writings to enhance my insight on certain unexplored aspects of their life and literature. Texts such as Manoranjan Byapari's *Interrogating My Chandal Life*, Manohar Mouli Biswas's *Surviving in My World*, Balbir Madhopuri's *My Caste-My Shadow*, Kamal Dev Pall's *Days Will Come Back,* Kancha Iliah's *From a Shepherd to an Intellectual* and Meena Kandasamy's *When I Hit You Or, a Portrait of the Writer as a Young Wife* enabled me to apprehend the current facets of caste and Dalits' struggle for liberation. These texts detail how Dalit writings are rejected and condemned in caste dominated literary circles and how critical assumptions, socio-cultural circumstances and ideologies are hostile to them. They also suggest that education, which is considered to be the most powerful apparatus to empower Dalits and women, is also unable to save them from the stigma of caste. Even the highly educated Dalits and women are considered inferior and polluting and they too are suppressed, and tortured by casteist and patriarchal forces. The experiences, vision, perspectives, strategies and alternatives recorded and suggested by Dalit writers in their respective writings are so strong, insightful, constructive and significant that I felt duty-bound to critically examine and present them collectively to readers in the form of a book. The purpose of this book is to survey the textual representation of caste, class and gender identity and to disseminate Dalit voices to a wide readership so that they can address their issues and mobilise a strong mass opinion against caste, class and gender.

Though *Exploring the Margins* has been in the making for an inexcusably long span of time but working on it was an enriching, enlightening and elevating experience. While writing this book, I received help and support from many corners and people. I am thankful to all those who extended their help during the course of this book. It is with an extreme sense of debt that I record my sense of gratitude to my mentor Prof Meenakshi F Paul who not only initiated me into the subject but also taught, inspired, motivated and encouraged me. She not only readily helped me when I got into trouble with certain concepts, but also offered her scholarly comments and suggestions despite her busy schedule. It is because of her constant support, guidance and affection that I could complete this book. She is the beacon of my life in every possible way. But to write much about her is to minimise her importance.

I would also like to thank Prof Raj Kumar of Delhi University for his selfless help, support and intellectual suggestions. Millions of thanks and a bagful of appreciation to Dalit scholar, critic and former Professor of History, Dr Raj Kumar Hans, for reading the manuscript and giving suggestions. The innumerable rounds of discussion with him not only enhanced my understanding of Dalit issues but also cleared many doubts. I wish to thank Balbir Madhopuri, Kamal Dev Pall, Prof TC Ghai, Dr Sunetra Mitra, Dr Ujjwal

Jana of Pondicherry University, Dr R Uma Maheshwari of JNU, Dr Vikas Kumar and Dr Ajay Kumar of BR Ambedkar University Lucknow, Dr Vinod Verma of Delhi University and Rati Agnihotri for their support and suggestions to improve my manuscript. I also thank the staff members of the Indian Institute of Advanced Study, Shimla for their help in numerous ways. In addition, I would like to express my appreciation and gratitude to a number of my friends and close relatives who kept my motivation alive and supported me.

Finally, I would like to express my deep regard to my parents and brothers who always supported and encouraged me in all my endeavours. I feel short of words to express my gratitude to them. My wife Dr Monika has always been a constant support and encouragement. She not only read the manuscript and offered suggestions but also patiently helped me during my long engagement in writing the book. I thank my sister-in-law Sunita Kashyap for her support and help. I am thankful to little Shreyansh who cheered me up during the hard hours of stress. I would also like to thank my Publisher Renu Kaul Verma, Editor Renu Arya, Aman Ujjwal and the entire team at Vitasta Publishing for their help in bringing out this book.

I sincerely apologise to all those who may have felt offended by any omission or any unintended remark that I may have made in the pages ahead. I assure that I did not intend to hurt or misrepresent anyone.

—Suresh Kumar

INTRODUCTION

EMERGENCE, GROWTH and proliferation of Dalit literature is one of the most significant events of the twentieth century. Dalit literature is an awakened and collective response from Dalits to their social segregation, economic deprivation, political marginalisation, religio-cultural stigmatisation, and all forms of exploitation unleashed on them over the centuries. Dalit writers have used literature to induce caste and class consciousness among impoverished Dalits and to mobilise them against the hegemonic socio-economic forces that possess unrestrained social privileges and also control economic resources. Dalit literature voices a systematic rebellion against the long preserved system of caste that exploited and promoted numerous discernments against them. The precept of caste denies them basic humanity and subjects them to an unending, unbridled thraldom to the high castes who humiliate and exploit them in numerous ways on account of their caste and economic vulnerability. Examining the implications of caste in Dalit lives, Arjun Dangle writes, "The living conditions of these untouchables were shameful. They had no land to till nor could they follow any profession. They did menial work ordered by the high castes. Treated like animals, they lived apart from the village, and had to accept leftovers from the high caste people, in return for their endless toil." (Introduction xxi) They were usually asked to live with waste and filth near cremation grounds or on the margins of villages. This was a deliberate onslaught on their integrity and dignity. Caste also imposed many behavioural restrictions. Assertion of personhood and expression of will and desire was strictly prohibited and they were made to behave submissively or in a way that indicated their Dalitness and subordination. They were not allowed to wear new clothes, ornaments or footwear; rags or clothes removed from corpses were the only dresses they were allowed to wear. Dalit autobiographies such as Daya Pawar's *Baluta*, Baby Kamble's *The Prisons We Broke,* Urmila Pawar's *The Weave of My Life*, Limbale's *The Outcaste*, and Byapari's *Interrogating My Chandal Life* among others show how casteist forces colonised Dalit bodies and violated their human rights. Poor lifestyle and filthy, untidy appearance were the imperative religious sanctions for them. Caste also accounted (and still accounts) for gender oppression as it interacted with patriarchy and exposed women to certain oppressions and prohibitions. Dalit literature exposes how caste operates in Dalit lives and interacts with other repressive ideologies such as religion, class and gender. It condemns every form of exploitation that Dalits are subjected to.

Dalit literature, which began to be written systematically in the beginning of the twentieth century, had its early roots in Gautam Buddha's religious teachings and the Buddhist literature of sixth century BC. Buddha denounced chauvinistic

Varna and caste system and preached that all humans are born equal. Dalit literary historians are of the opinion that the *Theragathas*, the songs of Buddhist monks and *Therigathas*, the songs of Buddhist nuns were the first critical literary expressions on the prevalent caste system in India. According to Rajat Rani Meenu, it was because of the impact of Buddha that Ashwaghosh, one of his Brahmin disciples, produced *Vajrasuchi*, a collection of poems that criticised caste and the discrimination espoused by it. Although, Ashwaghosh was a Brahmin by birth his *Vajrasuchi* is considered the first seminal text censuring casteism. (34) Buddha inspired Dalits to enlighten themselves and also encouraged them to register their dissent against Brahmanical Hinduism and the caste system through their compositions. Krishna Dutt Paliwal and Santosh Kumar Shukla write that the literature produced by *Natha* saints in the ninth or tenth century criticised caste as a Hindu religious hypocrisy and emphasised on the purity of body, soul, actions, equanimity, renunciation and selfless love to God. (491-92) Caste system and Brahmanical hegemony were further challenged by the medieval *Bhakti* saints through their writings and preachings. According to Eleanor Zelliot and Rohini Mokashi-Punekar, though the Bhakti movement began in South India in the seventh and eighth centuries (10) it gained momentum from the twelfth century only. The *Bhakti* saints challenged the basic principles of Brahmanical socio-religious orders and defied the infallible character of the Vedas, idol worship and numerous rituals. The conception that untouchables were intrinsically impure and despicable, was condemned as hypocrisy and a Brahmanical strategy to enslave Dalits. Saint poets such as Thiruppaan Alvar,

Chokhamela, Janabai, Rami, Nirmala, Soyarabai, Namdev, Tukaram, Eknath, Ravidas, Kabir and others challenged the very concept of purity and pollution and preached that all humans are equally pure and precious, and can attain *Moksh* through their devotion to God. Prominent untouchable Bhakti saints such as Chokhamela, Janabai, Ravidas and Kabir to note a few, asserted their identity as untouchables without any camouflage, pretence or feeling of inferiority. Saint Ravidas, who was a *Chamar* by caste, worked as a shoemaker and Kabir was a weaver by profession. Their writings pioneered Dalit literature in terms of themes, tone and use of language. Some critics even went to the extent of saying that modern Dalit literature is a continuation or resurgence of the radical medieval *Bhakti* literature. Baburao Bagul argues that the saint poets were preoccupied with religion and wrote mainly to reform Hinduism not to eradicate caste. He opines that the function of saint literature was not to emancipate Dalits but to 'prop up the crumbling' Hindu State and resist the proliferation of Islam. (280-281) Sharankumar Limbale also says that the "saints did not struggle against caste discrimination and for deliverance of untouchables. They assuaged women and Shudras with mere sympathy. In most cases, the Bhakti saints, instead of revolting beseeched gods to redeem all the wretched of the earth without any consideration of caste. (26)

It is true that caste as an institution received a serious challenge from the Bhakti movement but despite that it not only survived but also strengthened. So, the Dalits still remained enslaved to the hegemonic social and religious forces. The arrival of alien rulers such as Muslims and Britishers also did not bring any hope and change for them. Bagul argues that the Muslim rulers, for whom caste had no religious relevance, were well aware that this social divide among Hindus was idyllically suited for oppressive purposes. (281) The Christian Missionaries used them to strengthen their faith by converting them to Christianity. Although, like Muslims, caste was not a consideration for British rulers, but they educated and helped only those Dalits who accepted their faith and remained heedless to the impoverished unconverted ones. As part of their policy of non-intervention, the Britishers did not offer any direct encouragement or help to the Dalits, but the spread of education, arrival of the new intellectual system, advent of new trade, commerce and scientific techniques benefitted them in numerous ways, leading them to enlightenment and rational thinking. Dalit literature began taking shape when some of the educated Dalits and Shudras such as Jyotirao Govindrao Phule in Maharashtra, Iyothee Thass and EV Ramaswamy Naicker in Tamil Nadu opposed the caste system both in theory and praxis. These intellectuals and activists organised and encouraged Dalits to educate themselves, and write about their predicament as dwellers of liminal space.

Dalits began their literary articulation in the latter half of the nineteenth century but their writings remained confined to just a few regions such as Maharashtra, Tamil Nadu, Andhra Pradesh and Punjab. Dalit literary movement, as initiated by non-Brahmin intellectuals, could not become a mass movement at an all-India level because most regions were silent on the question of caste. So, the historiography of Dalit literature is located in different periods of time in different languages. Most Dalit writers and theorists are of the opinion that the tradition of writing was initiated in Marathi in the thirteenth century when the noted untouchable saint poet, Chokhamela composed *Abhangas* (devotional songs) to express his contempt for untouchability and to call for equality and fraternity. Although, his songs were dominated by devotion to God, but he is considered the pioneer of Marathi Dalit literature. After the writings of Bhakti saints, the Dalit literary surge was again noted in the middle of the nineteenth century, when an essay by Muktabai and writings by Jyotirao and Savitribai Phule were published in Marathi. These writings by Dalit intellectuals reflected Bhakti traditions but both streams of writings were different. The corpus of writings produced by saint poets was reformist in nature, but those by Dalit intellectuals such as Phule's *Gulamgiri* (Slavery) were characterised by rebellion and transformation. Phule and his followers challenged the hegemonic castes and classes through their radical writings and laid the foundation of Dalit Literature. After Phule, the tradition of writing on caste was carried forward by the twentieth century Dalit intellectuals such as Gopalbaba Valangkar, Shivram Janaba Kamble, Kisan Fagoji Bansode and others. These intellectuals revolted against Hinduism and attacked religious texts such as *Manusmriti* for their biases against Dalits. Valangkar was in the Indian Army and wrote to organise Dalits, especially the Mahars, when the British stopped their recruitment into the Army. According to Urmila Pawar and Meenakshi Moon, Shivram Janaba Kamble also wrote on caste and gender disparities and against social evils such as the custom of *Devadasi* (religious prostitutes) in his magazine *Somvanshi Mitra.* (72-73) Daya Pawar writes that the diary of Kallappa Dhale, written in the early years of the twentieth century, also records the moving account of suffering that Dalits were coerced to endure by casteist forces. It also describes the insurmountable hurdles that Dalits had to face in pursuit of their education and better life conditions. (50) Dalit literature was being written sporadically in the opening years of the twentieth century by Dalit intellectuals and activists who aspired to bring the question of caste into the literary domain.

Dalit literature gathered momentum with the rise of Bhimrao Ramji Ambedkar as the leader of Dalits in the second decade of the twentieth century in Maharashtra. Although, Ambedkar did not produce creative writings himself but his academic writings on the origin and mechanism of caste prepared a theoretical background for Dalit literature and supplied it themes. He encouraged illiterate Dalit masses to educate themselves and published creative writings by miscellaneous Dalit writers in his newspapers and magazines such as *Mooknayak, Bahishkrit Bharat, Janta, Prabuddha Bharat* and others. Janardhan Waghmare also argues that "Ambedkar gave the Marathi Dalit writers a new mind, a new mood and this began to find expression in short stories and poetry." (320) Sharankumar Limbale writes that Ambedkar was the chief shaping force behind Dalit literature as he not only provided it vision and philosophy but also published their writings that were rejected and despised by the high caste editors and publishers. The years of his activism (1920-1956), constituted the backbone of Dalit literature. (24-25; 45) Pointing out Ambedkar's contribution to the inception and proliferation of Dalit literature, Dangle writes that the two colleges – Siddhartha (1946) and Milind College (1947) founded by Ambedkar for higher education of Dalit youth, further accelerated the proliferation of Dalit literature. Young Dalit students graduated from these colleges, produced literature on issues of caste and class differences and published them in college magazines, Dalit newspapers and periodicals. They also set up a literary body, Siddharth Sahitya Sangh for Dalit literary discussions and provided a front for many young Marathi Dalit writers. (Introduction xxv) These writings presented the problems faced by Dalits but their vision and treatment of caste lacked consciousness and revolutionary fervour.

The decade of the 1960s brought out a considerable number of literary writings on caste as in addition to Dalits, many non-Dalit writers influenced by the philosophy and liberalism of Gandhi, also wrote on the issue of untouchability. These writings were reformist and depicted the exploited and poor with a sympathetic attitude. It was with the advent of The Little Magazine Movement of angry young men in the mid nineteen sixties that Dalit literature began to take a permanent shape. Prominent Dalit writers of the sixties such as Annabhau Sathe, Shankarrao Kharat, Bandhu Madhav, Baburao Bagul and others began to publish in Dalit magazines such as *Fakta* and *Asmitadarsh*. Some of the early Dalit writers such as Sathe and Bagul were influenced by Marxism. For them, caste was a distinctive discriminatory institution that exposed Dalits to class and gender-based exploitation. Dangle says that the publication of Bagul's short story collection, *Jevha Mai Jaat Chorli Hoti* (When I Had Concealed My Caste) in 1963 took the entire Marathi literary world by storm and gave Marathi Dalit literature a permanent shape. (Introduction xxix) A literature of an awakened Dalit consciousness began making its way into the high caste, class dominated Marathi literary circle in the late 1960s as Dalit writers also began to organise literary conferences to discuss Dalit literature, its nature and role. Resultantly, Dalit literature established itself as a distinct genre in Marathi by the beginning of the 1970s.

The foundation of the Dalit Panther Movement on 9 July 1972 revolutionised Dalit literature. The founding members such as Arjun Dangle, Raja Dhale, Namdeo Dhasal and JV Pawar were writers and activists. They composed poems, plays and fiction to spread their revolutionary ideas and to mobilise Dalits. The Panthers contributed many classics to Marathi Dalit literature. After the Dalit Panthers, Marathi Dalit writers such as Daya Pawar, Waman Nimbalkar, Vaman Kardak, Hira Bansode, Asha Thorat, Jyoti Lanjewar, Mina Gajbhiye, Tryambak Sapkale, Umakant Randhir, Tarachand Khandekar, Yogiraj Waghmare, Avinash Dolas, Yogendra Meshram and many others published their poems and short stories. The publication of autobiographies of noted Dalit writers in the late seventies and in the early eighties created a stir in the caste dominated Marathi literature and established Dalit literature as a new form of writing. The closing years of the twentieth and the opening years of the twenty-first century brought out a corpus of Dalit writings in Marathi, many of which have been and are being translated into English, Hindi and other Indian and non-Indian languages.

With the spread of education and Dalit consciousness, strong Dalit writings were being registered in some Indian languages such as Tamil, Telugu, Kannada, Malayalam, Gujarati, Bengali, Hindi, Punjabi, Oriya and English. Critics opine that the Dalit writings in Tamil are as strong as in Marathi. Traditional Tamil singers/writers described aristocratic lives and culture in their literary creations. Social issues such as gender and caste disparities did not figure adequately in the early Tamil literature. Illustrating the absence of caste in ancient Tamil literature, Ravikumar argues that because of the strong influence of Buddhism and Jainism Brahmanical Hinduism could not take strong root in ancient Tamil societies. (Intoduction xv) Untouchability had its roots in the rise of Hinduism and the defeat of Buddhism. The defeated Buddhist monks, who otherwise were enlightened and knowledgeable, were categorised as untouchables by the crooked Hindu Brahmins. S Sundararajan argues that the mention of *gotra* names in *Purananuru* suggests that a kind of caste stratification existed during the Sangam period. (77) Vijaya Ramaswamy also argues that "The occupational groups are referred to in Sangam literature as *Khudi*. It is only in the texts of the late Sangam period that one comes across the word *Jati* for the first time, as a result of Brahmanical/Sanskritic influences." (42-43) Caste was resisted by Buddhism and Jainism for a long time and it operated less rigidly and oppressively in Tamil lands for many centuries. Scholars, historians and epigraphists such as Thass and Y Subbarayalu are of the opinion that caste system and untouchability were institutionalised in Tamil Nadu only after the eleventh century. Two Thanjavur inscriptions of Rajaraja dated AD 1014, supply information relating to separate quarters for landholders (*ur-irukkai*), artisans (*kammana-ceri*), and the *paraiya* (*parai-ceri*), respectively. An inscription by Virarajendra at Gangaikonda Cholapuram (GKC), also gives almost similar descriptions of settlements in Thanjavur and Tiruchirappalli districts in AD 1068. (qtd. in Ravikumar, Introduction xx)

Writings of the medieval Bhakti saints illustrated that caste became a rigid and discriminatory institution by the beginning of the twelfth century in Tamil Nadu. Women Bhakti saints revolted against the restraints of caste, gender and body and also Vedic ritualism as their religion. They subverted the conventional societal norms and asserted their autonomy and agency. For them, caste and gender were no consideration as their whole emphasis was on devotion and love to God. The songs and verses composed by these radical women contributed to the tradition of anti-caste writings initiated by the Buddhist and Jain monks in ancient Tamil Nadu. Most Tamil Bhakti saints, especially in the initial years of the Bhakti movement, remained fanatically adhered to Hinduism and turned violent and hostile to Buddhists and Jains. They conspired against them, killed them and also destroyed their powerful writings against caste and Vedic Hinduism. It was mainly because of this repression and resistance by the emerging Brahmanical forces that the lower castes such as Paraiyars, Pallars and Chakkiliyars could not produce their own literature outside the Buddhist, Jain and Bhakti traditions.

It was only in the middle of the nineteenth century that some strong Dalit voices were registered. Pandit Iyothee Thass (1845-1914), a Buddhist by conviction and Paraiah (Dalit) by birth, can be regarded as the first prominent Tamil anti-caste activist and writer. He was the first non-Brahmin voice to oppose Hinduism and demand rights and dignity for Dalits. J Bala argues that Thass initiated many Dalit organisations such as *Advaidananda Sabha* in 1870 and *Dravida Mahajana Sabha* in 1891. He was well versed in Sanskrit, Pali and English. To awaken Dalits, he started a Tamil Weekly *Oru Paisa Tamilan* 1907 (which he later called *Tamilan*) to which he contributed his scholarly writings, thus, inaugurating the tradition of Dalit writing in Tamil Nadu. (n. page) Thass wrote more than five hundred articles on politics, literature, culture, society and religion. His ideas were innovative, secular, progressive and transformative in nature that problematised dominant social, religio-cultural forces and also brought out a systematic argument against the dominant class ideology. Though his writings were instrumental in evoking Dalit consciousness but this could not sustain long after his death in 1914.

It was with the activism of EV Ramaswamy Naicker (also known as Periyar) that Dalit issues received another serious attention and also got a forum. Periyar argued that the problems and sufferings of Dalits and other non-Brahmins were located in the orthodox Brahmanism that kept them illiterate and poor for centuries. He revolted against hegemonic Brahmanism and advocated a strong non-Hindu Brahmanical culture. According to Tapan Basu, "Periyar's movement advanced a blueprint for a Ravan Rajya as against the Ram Rajya model of the ideal social and economic order posited by a number of Hindu thinkers including Gandhi. As against the celebrations of Ram Lila festivals in Northern India, Periyar advocated that in Southern India there should be the celebration of Ravan Lila festivals, as a mark of regard and respect for the non-Brahmins, non-Hinduized legacy of the Dravidians." (Introduction xxx) V Geetha and SV Rajadurai argue that Periyar and his Self-respect movement gave direction to non-Brahmin voices and also spearheaded Tamil Dalit literature. According to them, Periyar not only encouraged Dalit education but also inspired Dalits to write about themselves. He published their writings in his newspapers and magazines such as *Kudi Arasu, Puratchi, Paguthariyu, Viduthalai, Unmai* and *Modern Rationalist.* (362-70) Periyar's humanism, rationalism and revolt against Brahmanical patriarchy could not initiate a vibrant Dalit literary tradition in Tamil as Ambedkar did in Marathi. Despite his spirited exertions most Dalits remained silent as they were illiterate and unaware of the mechanism of their marginalisation in society.

In the seventies and eighties of the twentieth century, some Marxist writers attempted to write on issues of socially, economically, culturally and politically marginalised Dalits, but their writings also could not be called Dalit literature as these were mainly concerned with class conflicts. Their literary work lacked authenticity and an awakened Dalit consciousness. Mittal writes that Poomani and Daniel, a Sri Lankan Tamil, portrayed Dalits as incapable of fighting back. (174-75) The division of Tamil Dalits between Marxism and Dravidian ideologies thwarted their autonomous literary productions. It was only in the late 1980s or early 1990s that Tamil Dalit writers began to produce their own literature with a heightened Dalit consciousness. The publication of Sivakami's novel, *Pazhaiyana Kazhithalum* in 1986 and Bama's life narrative, *Karukku* in 1992, established Dalit literature as a separate genre in Tamil Nadu and espoused a staunch Dalit and feminist perspective. In recent years, Tamil Dalit writers such as Irathina Karikalan, Imayam, P Sivakami, Bama, Pratibha Jeyachandran, Cho Dharman, Indumathy, Anuradha Ramanan, Malathi Maithri, Sankya, Yazhan Aathi, S Sukirtharani, M Jeeva, V Venkatachalam, Thai Kandasamy, Abhimani, Ramani Chandran, Kabilan, A Vincent Raj, Ku

Umadevi, ND Rajkumar, Ravikumar and many others have produced and are still producing powerful literature. Some of their works have been translated into many Indian and non-Indian languages as part of syllabi in many colleges and universities in India and abroad.

Like in Marathi and Tamil, the tradition of Dalit writing has been strong in Punjabi as well. Traditional Punjabi societies have been little less casteist as compared to other regions in India. According to Harish K Puri, the liberal ethos induced by Buddhist Dhamma, Islam and Sikhism which have been dominant faiths in Punjab, left a viable space for Dalit literary expression and articulation as unlike Brahmanical Hinduism caste was not a consideration for them. So, the Dalits in Punjab did not experience the kind of indignity and repression as had been the fate of their counterparts in Maharashtra, Tamil Nadu, Andhra Pradesh, Karnataka. (Introduction 5-6) The early roots of Punjabi Dalit literature can be located in the writings and preachings of the Sikh gurus who fostered liberal ethos among the intelligentsia of Punjab and denounced all kinds of discriminations. They preached that all humans are born equal and composed verses to spread the messages of love, humanity and fraternity without consideration for caste. The humanism and egalitarianism espoused by the Sikh gurus pioneered Punjabi Dalit literature as their messages and writings were critical of caste and inclusive of the pain that Dalits endure because of their outcaste status.

Guru Nanak Dev (1469-1539), the founder of Sikhism, was the first to produce anti-caste literature in Punjabi. Although, Nanak Dev's writings were primarily religious in nature, they had great social and cultural significance. Emphasising the social significance of Nanak Dev's teachings, Anand writes, "Nanak wanted to bring an end to the conflict among various religions. That is why he vehemently rejected the caste system, authority of the Vedas and the Quran and idolatry or image-worship." (n. page) Nanak denounced caste and communal differences as just a bigotry and expression of human smugness, ego and accepted both Hindus and Muslims as his disciples. Besides Nanak Dev, other Sikh gurus who all hailed from high caste of Khatris, also condemned caste and remained durably adhered to the equalitarianism promulgated through principles such as *Sangat* and *Pangat* and *Karah Prasad.* Underscoring the contribution of Sikhism, Puri states that "The teachings of the Sikh gurus, the religious institutions of *Sangat* and *Langar*, the absence of a caste-based priesthood, and respect for manual labour – all these aimed at creating a community in which distinctions of caste, creed and status are not relevant." ("The Scheduled Castes..." 190-91) The *Guru Granth Sahib* compiled by the fifth Sikh Guru Arjan Dev (1563-1606) also condemned caste.

The radical anti-caste verses of untouchable saints such as Kabir Das and Ravi Das included in the *Guru Granth Sahib* critiqued caste as a manmade institution and located it as the biggest hurdle in human salvation. Rhymes such as *Rangrete Guru Ke Bete* (Rangretas are sons of the Guru) not only increased the popularity of Dalits in Sikhism but also gave momentum to Dalit literature. Eminent historian and literary critic Rajkumar Hans says that it was because of the influence of gurus that some Dalits such as Bhai Jaita alias Jivan Singh (1649-1705) came out with their literary compositions. Subsequently, saint-poets such as Sadhu Wazir Singh (1790-

1859) who 'attained the status of Brahmgyani,' problematised caste and religious institutions and advocated the 'non-dualistic approach to life'. Dalit intellectuals such as Giani Ditt Singh (1858-1901) and Sadhu Daya Singh Arif (1894-1945) produced verses criticising caste and Hindu ritualism. ("Rich Heritage..." 73-74) Reformist movements such as Singh Sabha Movement and Arya Samaj also played a significant role in the origin and flourishing of Punjabi Dalit literature.

Founded in 1873, Singh Sabha aimed at moral, spiritual and educational reawakening of Sikhs and opened many schools and colleges for their education. Activists of Singh Sabha condemned caste and Hinduism and declared *hum Hindu nahin* (we are not Hindus). The ideology of Singh Sabha Movement provided opportunity for Dalits to educate and express themselves in literary domains. Arya Samajis also encouraged the education of Dalits and attempted to give them dignity. Hans says that due to the influence of Arya Samaj, low caste and class writers such as Pandit Bakshi Ram and Sant Ram Diye wrote extensively on caste issues and challenged the hegemonic castes and classes. (Personal Interview) Repressive laws such as the Punjab Land Alienation Act 1900 that denied Dalits from owning land and coerced them to do minimal farming in villages, also could not suppress their creative genius. Punjabi Dalits kept on voicing their resistance against the nexus of caste and class through their poems, stories and plays. Non-Dalit writers such as Nanak Singh, Jaswant Singh Kanwal, Kartar Singh Duggal, Surinder Singh Narula, Gurdial Singh and others also wrote poems, stories and novels on Dalit issues. These writers were artistic and vociferous of Dalit issues but they were inadequate and inauthentic in their depiction of the pain that Dalits have to endure. For instance, in *Marhi Da Diva (The last Flicker)* Gurdial Singh, a Shudra (non-Dalit) presents his Dalit protagonist Jagseer as a passive recipient of humiliations and injustices. He is not aware of his rights and exhibits no sense of dignity and integrity, indicating that Dalits are submissive and incapable of fighting against injustices.

The emergence of Ad-Dharm Movement initiated and led by Mangu Ram Mugowalia in the 1920s revolutionised Punjabi Dalit literature. This movement emphasised the need for morality and attempted to create a sense of self-respect and dignity among Dalits. It also strived to construct the identity of Punjabi Dalits as Ad-Dharmis, entirely different and independent of both Hindus and Sikhs. The Ad-Dharmis attempted to evoke Dalit consciousness in the Ambedkarite way. Ronki Ram says that two weekly papers – *Adi-Danka* and *Ujala* started by Ad Dharmis not only spread Dalit consciousness but also brought into light the creative writings of Gurdas Ram Alam, Sant Ram Azad, Chanan Lal Manak, Sansar Chand, Charan Singh Safri and Bhagat Ram Mandali. Writers such as Alam and Manak set the tradition of radical Dalit poetry in Punjabi through the columns of these weeklies. In addition, newspapers such as *Hamara Jeewan*, *Bheem Patrika*, *Ravidas Patrika, Kaumi Udarian* and others also published Dalit writings and contributed profusely to Punjabi Dalit literature. (164-66)

Writer Hazara Singh Mushtaq was closely associated with the Indian National Congress. Thus, his writings were influenced by Gandhian ideology, vision and philosophy, but his caste concern was no less strong and vociferous. Some Dalits such as Sant Ram Udasi and Lal Singh Dil were influenced by

Naxalism that sauntered into Punjab in the 1960s. Their poetry offers a sharp critique of caste and class. Contemporary Punjabi Dalit poets such as Balbir Madhopuri, Siri Ram Arsh, Sulakhan Mit, Madan Vira, Sadhu Singh Sudharak, Kamal Dev Pall and many others have also written and are still writing poetry of revolt against the prevalent caste and class differences. Short story writers such as Prem Gorkhi, Bhura Singh Kaler, Lal Singh, Nachhatar, Makhan Maan, Bhagwant Rasulpuri, Ajmer Sidhu, Des Raj Kali, Jinder, Gurmit Kadialavi, Sarup Sialvi, Gulzar Mohammad Goria, Mohan Lal Philoria and others also contributed to the explosion of Punjabi Dalit literature. Apart from poems and short narratives, Punjabi Dalit writers have also produced powerful novels on caste and caste-based oppression.

According to Hans, Gurcharan Singh Rao's *Mashalchi* (1986), Karnail Singh Nijhar's *Sargi Da Tara*, Surjit Sokhi's *Aurat te Aurat* (1983), Karamjit Singh Aujhla's *Ooch Neech* (2000), Nachhatar's *Buddhi Sadi da Manukh* (1988) and *Nikke Nikke Asman* (2004), Gurmel Madahad's *Dulla* and Des Raj Kali's *Parneshwari* (2007) are significant contributions ("Rich Heritage…" 78). Pandit Bakshi Ram's *Mera Jivan Sangharsh* 1983 (My Life Struggle), Prem Gorkhi's *Gair Hazir Aadmi* (1994), Dil's *Dastan* (1998), Balbir Madhopuri's *Changiya Rukh* (2002) and Gurnam Aqida's *Kakh Kande: Nij ton Haqiqat Val* (Blades of Grass and Thistles: From Self Towards Reality) are important contributions to the Punjabi Dalit autobiographies. Punjabi Dalit writers have mediated every genre and produced magnum opuses in every form of writing. Punjabi Dalits living outside India are also writing extensively on Dalit issues. Publication of a collection of poetry, *Days Will Come Back* by Kamal Dev Pall, a Punjabi Dalit residing in America, is the finest illustration on the vibrancy and consistency of Punjabi Dalit literature.

Hindi Dalit writers have produced several significant and powerful literary works in the form of poetry, short stories, novels and plays to awaken Dalit masses and also to shoot down the hovering vultures of caste and class discriminations. Literary critics and theorists argue that early spores of Hindi Dalit literature can be traced back to the time of radical medieval Bhakti saints such as Kabir, Ravidas, Sen, Namdev, Trilochan, Garibdass, Rajab and others in North India as they composed songs and poems critiquing caste. Among these Bhakti saints, Kabir and Ravidas were the most powerful voices. They asserted their identity as untouchables and revolted against the caste divide and the notion of purity and pollution. The Bhakti saints pioneered a literary tradition that was entirely different from traditional Hindi writings or rather it was a reaction against it.

With frequent invasions from Muslims and the expansion of colonial rule in North India, most of the then Indian writers began to produce literature to awaken and mobilise Indian masses against alien rulers. Most Hindi writers wrote on the conflict between tradition and modernity, the need of Indian struggle for political freedom, nationalism and the splendour of ancient Indian civilisation. Hindi Dalit literature gained momentum in the beginning of the twentieth century in North India. Dalit thinkers, intellectuals and activists such as Achutanand Harihar, Ram Charan, Nirghin Ram and others mainly wrote to awaken Dalit masses. Dalit critics and writers agree that Achutanand was a key figure in initiating Dalit social and political movement in the Northern region and also in reviving Dalit literary conventions in modern ways in the early twentieth century. Achutanand, whose actual name was Heera Lal, was a follower of Arya Samaj and a fervent social activist. According to Virdi, he founded *Achut Mahasabha* in 1917 to organise subordinated Dalits against untouchability and the caste system. He also started two newspapers - *Achut* (1922) and *Adi Hindu* (1925) to give expression to Dalit voices. (86-87) In his newspapers, Achutanand published his songs, poems and ghazals to vocalise his dissent against the caste system and to encourage the impoverished Dalits. Being an ardent supporter of Ambedkar, his vision and ideology, Achutanand composed poems to propound that Dalits were the original inhabitants of India and they were deceitfully suppressed and enslaved by Aryan invaders. The Hindu *Varna* system is a religious fraudulent and was imposed forcibly on Dalits by the Aryans who subsequently became rulers. Chaman Lal writes that Achutanand was the pioneer of modern Hindi Dalit literature. His poems and plays such as *Shabhuk Muni*, *Ramrajya Nayay* and *Apurn* were opposed to the prevalent caste system and were an overt expression of Dalits' rights and dignity. (*Dalit Sahitya* 62-64)

Nirghin Ram, a supporter and activist of Congress, also produced literature in Hindi to awaken the poor and illiterate Dalit masses. Heera Dom's poem *Achut ke Shikayat* published in 1914 was a seminal work against the prejudice of caste. In addition, Dalit writers such as Bihari Lal Harit, Swami Shankarananda, Kaviratna Mahatma Bakshi, Ayodhya Nath Brahmachari, Pandit Moji Lal Morya, Moti Lal Sant and others also produced literature to vocalise Dalit issues and censure caste. (Meenu 37-43) Literary writing by early twentieth century Hindi Dalit writers problematised caste and amplified

Dalit literature. These early writers wrote under the influence of leaders such as Gandhi, Ambedkar and Jagjivan Ram. So, Hindi Dalit literature despite its sustained articulation, was scattered in different directions in the early twentieth century.

It was only after Independence and the adoption of the Constitution that Hindi Dalit literature began to appear regularly and acquired a permanent shape. Saroj Kumar Mahananda opines that Hindi Dalit literature, "is largely a product of awareness brought about by State efforts to educate and uplift the masses through various Constitutional provisions in post-Independence India." (89) Hindi Dalit literature composed in the early twentieth century was heterogeneous in nature and purpose. It demonstrated heightened Dalit consciousness in the Ambedkarite way and propounded an authentic Dalit perspective which began appearing in the late 1980s. During this period eminent Dalit writers such as Mohan Das Namishray, Omprakash Valmiki, Suraj Pal Chauhan, Jai Prakash Kardam, Susheela Takbhore, Lal Chand Rahi, Purushottam Satyapremi, Kusum Viyogi, Ratan Kumar Sambharia, Sheoraj Singh Bechain, Kavari, Dharamveer, Tulsi Ram, Ajay Navaria and many others began to produce literature to give voice to their pain and demand their rights, justice and equity. The contemporary Hindi Dalit writers use poetry, fiction, autobiography, plays and literary criticism to challenge the paraphernalia used by high castes to suppress and dehumanise Dalits. Their writings are sharply opposed to the sympathetic literature produced by high caste writers such as Bharatendu Harishchandra, Maithili Sharan Gupt, Siyaramsharan Gupt, Ramchandra Shukla, Subhadra Kumari Chauhan, Sohan Lal Dwivedi, Suryakant Tripathi Nirala,

Sumitrnandan Pant, Ramvilas Sharma, Nagarjuna, Narender Sharma, Shivmangal Singh Suman, Bal Krishna Sharma Naveen, Shamsher Bahadur Singh, Gorakh Pandey, Munshi Premchand, Pandey Bechan Sharma, Acharya Chatursen Shastri, Rangeya Raghav, Uday Shankar Bhatt and many others. They attempted not to eradicate caste but to improve it, that too without altering the structure of Hinduism.

The other group of non-Dalit writers influenced by Gandhi, Ram Manohar Lohia and Karl Marx were also inauthentic as they remained focused on the economic exploitation unleashed on Dalits. They could not show the mental anguish that Dalits undergo on account of their caste. They were adhered to the Marxist view that economic empowerment and equal distribution of resources will lead to an automatic alleviation of caste severity.

In Kannada, writing against caste could be located in the religious verses of Basavanna, a twelfth century social reformer, philosopher, poet and saint. He refuted the authority of Vedic scriptures and censured the differences of caste, class, gender and religion promoted by them. He treated Dalits and women as equals and condemned the Brahmanical proposition that they were born as despicable and not fit to be free. Zelliot and Punekar maintain that Basavanna, the founder of the Lingayat sect was "arguably the most radical of all Bhakti saints in terms of caste." (257) His poems subverted the Brahmanical form of writings that were focused on religion, Gods and held Dalits and women with contempt. Besides Basavanna, radical saints such as Jedara Daasimayya, Channabasavanna, Allama Prabhu, Urilinga Peddigala Punya Stri Kalavve, Akka Mahadevi and others also wrote powerful anti-Brahmanical verses in the twelfth century. Somashekara says, "Mystics like Male Mahadeshwara and Manteswamy triggered a religious revolution against caste discrimination and untouchability in the fifteenth and sixteenth centuries." (33) Subsequently, Sufi saints too continued this process of resistance against the caste system.

Christian missionaries who became active in South Indian states in the latter half of the eighteenth century, also contributed to the evolution of Kannada Dalit literature by writing about their sufferings in the local vernacular newspapers and magazines in colonial Karnataka. Most Kannada Dalit writers continued writing within the Brahmanical literary tradition that hardly left any space for expression of Dalit personhood, identity and dignity. Mahananda says, "The Raja of Mysore had banned the entry of Ambedkar into the state. So, Karnataka largely remained insulated from the Dalit movement which was spreading so successfully in the neighbouring state of Maharashtra." (108)

In Karnataka, the anti-caste literature with staunch Dalit perspective made its appearance in the latter half of the twentieth century. D Somashekara believes that the Kannada Dalit literature was inspired and piqued by many events and happenings in the 1970s, such as the murder of a Dalit at Tumkur and the massacre of Dalits in Belchi. (33) The modern Kannada Dalit literature was triggered by the historical '*Boosa* incident,' where B Basavalingappa, the Minister of town administration, while speaking in a seminar on 'New Waves' organised by Ambedkar's school of thought in Mysore on 19 November 1973, censured traditional Kannada literature for having a great deal of *Boosa* (chaff). K Satyanarayana and Susie Tharu argue that this statement by the young Ambedkarite Minister led to a terrible controversy. Many of the so-called defenders of tradition took to the streets demanding his resignation. Basavalingappa was supported by young educated Dalits who rallied enthusiastically around him. Finally, when it looked as though the Urs Government itself might fall, Basavalingappa was forced to resign from his post. (Introduction 3-5) Basavalingappa lost his Ministership but his revolutionary words had an awakening influence on Dalit masses. Underscoring the significance of the *Boosa* incident in Kannada Dalit history, Satyanarayana and Tharu write that "the *Boosa chaluvali* (agitation) not only created Dalit intellectuals and writers, it also brought them together, and the energy of that moment continued to shape and inspire the next two generations of Dalit writers and critics in Karnataka. The arrival of these new writers changed the face of Kannada literature itself." (Introduction 11)

The rational, educated young Dalits who were part of the *Boosa* agitation and supported Basavalingappa, were writers and they formed the *Dalita Lekhaka Kalavidhara* (*Daleka*) in 1974, which later in the same year expanded the scope of its work to become the historical Dalit Sangharsh Samiti (DSS) (Satyanarayana and Tharu Introduction 5). The literary journal, *Panchama* started by the members of DSS in 1974 offered a forum for Dalit writers. They published their songs, poems, fiction, plays and criticism and brought untouched social, economic and political issues to the literary domain. Prominent members of DSS such as B Krishnappa, Chennanna Walikar, Devanoora Mahadeva, H Govindaiah, Indudhara Honnapura and Siddalingaiah produced a literature of Dalit consciousness and revolted against the high castes' dominance in all spheres. The writing by high caste Kannada writers, also known as 'Navya,' was highly academic, technical and middle class in character; it had no concern for social themes such as caste and gender inequalities.

The eminent non-Dalit Kannada writer UR Ananthamurthy says, "There have been several examples of non-Dalits writing on the Dalit situation, like the famous Kannada novel *Chomana Dudi* by Shivaram Karanth. But there was a kind of arrogance when non-Dalits claimed to represent Dalits. When Dalits write about their situation, it imparts a new strength and idiom". (n. page)

Dalit writers revolted against this misrepresentation. For instance, Mahadeva's stories and Siddalingaiah's poetry, were rebellious and knocked at the very foundation of the caste institution. The early Dalit writings in Kannada presented a blend of Marxism, Gandhism, Ambedkarism, Lohiaite socialism, Naxalism and also Periyarism. In the words of Satyanarayana and Tharu, it was with the emergence and spread of Bahujan Samaj Party (BSP) in Karnataka in the 1990s that Ambedkar was fully introduced to the Kannada Dalit writers. (Introduction 29-30) It was in the writings of the second generation Kannada Dalit writers such as Aravind Malagatti, Mogalli Ganesh, MB Puttaiah, BT Jahnavi, Du Saraswathi, Devaiah Harave, MN Javaraiah, Satyananda Patrota, V Munivenkatappa, Mulluru Nagaraja and others that Ambedkar's influence was felt adequately. In recent years, Kannada Dalit writers are articulate on issues of caste, class, gender and they also write about intra-caste conflicts, and internal caste hierarchy. Literary works of Mahadeva, Malagatti and Ganesh have been translated into different Indian and foreign languages and are widely acclaimed.

The traditional Bangla literature that mainly comprised of folk tales, songs and ballads, did not refer to caste as a repressive ideology. It was mainly because Brahmanical Hinduism had a rather belated entry mostly into the tribal inhabited Bengal. The Aryan invaders started their movement towards the East and North-East regions after many centuries of their stay in India. Bengali historian Niharranjan Ray writes that the "The dominance of Brahmanical religion was contested by Buddhism under ruling dynasties such as the Palas between the eighth and twelfth centuries, the Kambojas in Northern and Eastern Bengal in the tenth century and the Chandras in the Eastern and Southern Bengal between the tenth and eleventh centuries." (qtd. in Bandyopadhyay 18) Early Bengali texts such as *Charyapadas* written by Buddhist monks refuted caste as hypocrisy of Hindu Brahmins and preached universal love and equality. Despite the thriving of Buddhism, Brahmanical Hinduism took its roots in Bengal by the thirteenth century. The new regime and religion relegated Dalits, who were mainly fisher-folk, hunters and agricultural labourers, to the socio-economic margins and subjected them to oppressive rules of caste and untouchability.

Bengali Dalits were alienated from education, learning and economic resources. They were relegated to the socio-economic and literary margins and could not write about their plight. With the advent of Bhakti movement in the fifteenth century, caste as a socio-religious practice was held with scorn and criticised by the Bengali Bhakti saints such as Sri Chaitanya. He challenged the predominance of Hindu Brahmins and the hegemonic *Varnashram Dharma*. He emphasised the need for simple devotion to Lord Krishna as a way to *Moksha* without any consideration for caste status. Chaitanya accepted lower castes as his disciples and subverted the codes of caste. He did not hold lower castes as untouchable and polluting. But after his death, the Bhakti movement lost momentum in Bengal and digressed.

Bandyopadhyaya says, "Some of Chaitanya's followers began to practice caste and refused to accept lower castes as disciples. These lower caste devotees were called *Jat Vaishnava*, a distinctive and separated group. They were treated as low and not allowed to initiate high castes as their disciples." (83) The *Jat Vaishnavas* opposed Brahmanical ritualism and condemned caste as pretence. They promoted ideas of justice, equity and compassion. They were highly critical of patriarchal concepts such as chastity and the sanctity of marriage and accepted widows as their disciples. Bandyopadhyay argues that the major allegation against the radical *Jat Vaishnavas* was that they had loose sexual morals and their cult was merely a refuge for fallen women and criminals. (86) Jogendra Nath Bhattacharya writes, "The ranks of Chaitanites, as of many other sects, swelled with bachelors and widowers unable to get brides for marriage in an orthodox form." (369)

Historians maintain that the arrival of Islam and the British colonialism also could not improve the condition of vulnerable Dalits in Bengal. They were still treated as untouchables and positioned on absolute margins in socio-economic, political and literary spheres. The reformist efforts initiated by the nineteenth century high caste intellectuals such as Raja Ram Mohan Roy, Ishwar Chander Vidyasagar also left impoverished Dalits out of the scope of their reforms. They attempted to correct the socio-cultural wrongs within the limits of Hinduism.

In the middle of the nineteenth century, caste and issues of Bengali Dalits were articulated vociferously in socio-political and literary spheres by Dalit leaders such as Harichand Biswas, popularly known as Harichand Thakur (1812-1878), and his son Guruchand Thakur (1846-1937). The Matua sect formed by Harichand Thakur, offered a social and religio-cultural alternative and prepared a way for Dalit uprising in Bengal.

Manoranjan Bypari and Meenakshi Mukherjee argue that Harichand and Guruchand Thakur revolted against the oppression and humiliation of Dalits and demanded dignity and equal rights for them. They mobilised the illiterate *Namasudras* and demanded that they should not be called *Chandalas* and the name of the community should be changed in official records. The British Government conceded and the name was changed in the 1911 census record. (4117) Guruchand Thakur's emphasis on Dalit education and intellectual growth encouraged Dalit literary expression in Bengal. Byapari and Mukherjee argue that modern Bengali Dalit literature has its roots in the 'Matua Sahitya' that flourished in the nineteenth and early twentieth centuries under the leadership of Harichand and Guruchand Thakur: "Although the initial impulse was religious, the Matua Movement soon began to emphasise education in a big way. Matua creativity expressed itself in three ways: '*Kathakata*' (story-telling), '*Jatra*' (folk plays) and '*Kobi-gaan*' (rhymed couplets) composed in traditional '*Payar*' rhythm and presented orally in public. Most of these compositions were a combination of poetry, history and popular philosophy geared towards raising people's awareness." (4118) Angana Dutta and Jaydeep Sarangi argue that the literary journal, *Namasudra Suhrid* founded by Guruchand Thakur in 1912, provided a front for Dalit articulation in Bengal. (Introduction xxv) The writings by Harichand Thakur also problematised caste and added significantly to the emergence of Dalit literature. But the death of Guruchand and the emergence of Ambedkarism in Bengal, created an ideological division among Dalits. According to Mahananda, "The second phase of Bangla Dalit literature that started in the 1940s was influenced by Jogendra Nath Mandal, an associate of Ambedkar. He encouraged Dalits to educate themselves and started journals like *Pataka* and *Jagaran* to bring out their voices and publish their writings." (100) Though Mandal had a great influence on Bangla Dalit literature but after independence and partition of the country, he became the Law Minister in Bangladesh (East Pakistan) and naturally lost influence in Bengal, India.

The socio-political upheavals such as partition of the country, communal frenzy and cataclysm obstructed Dalit literary activity in Bengal. Most Dalits were uprooted from their original homes and had no access to economic resources and education in the new land where they were coerced to flee. Most Dalits were put in refugee camps where they starved and died of malnutrition and epidemics. The surviving Dalit refugees were discriminated against in terms of distribution of food, clothes, medicines and access to health care services by high caste officials who were incharge of these camps. Dalit refugees were not allowed to build their homes and settle on government land. Byapari's *Interrogating My Chandal Life* and Manohar Mouli Biswas's *Surviving in My World* are the finest and elaborated illustrations of these facts.

The literary efforts by Dalits such as Raju Das, a Bangla poet, short fiction and play writer during the sixties and seventies spearheaded Bangla Dalit literature. Das published the writings of Dalits in journals — *Nabarun* and *Nabarup* edited by him. Other Dalit literary journals such as *Gram Bangla* (1978) edited by Nakul Mallik, who also established the *Bangiya Dalit Lekhat Parishad* in 1987, gave momentum to the proliferation of Bangla Dalit literature. Byapari and Mukherjee say that Dalit journals such as *Dalit Kontho, Neel Akash, Adal Badai, Ajker Eklavya, Chhiyanobboi, Ekhan Takhan* that began to appear in the 1990s, published literary compositions of numerous Dalit writers. (4118) The literary works of the 1990s are characterised by Dalit consciousness and perspective. Dutta and Sarangi write that "Modelled after the Ambedkar-inspired Dalit Panther literary movement of Maharashtra, the *Bangla Dalit Sahitya Sanstha* (Bengali Dalit Literature Association) made significant contributions for the empowerment of Dalits in Bengal. Since its inception in 1992, it groomed Dalit writers, published their literature, held conferences, rallies, and promoted Dalit culture and their condition in Bengal and across India." (Introduction xxv) The publication of literary magazines such as *Chaturtha Duniya* and *Aikyatan* brought into light many Dalit literary geniuses. The publication of Debayudh Chatterjee's *Bhor Rater* (2012) and *Baishnab Flirt-er Padabali* (2015), and Manoranjan Byapari's *Interrogating My Chandal Life* in 2017 shows that with the passage of time Bangla Dalits writers are maturing. They are confident, intimate and skilled in the expression of their lived experiences. They have produced almost every genre: poems, short stories, plays and novels. Dalit writers such as Anil Sarkar, Anil Ranjan Biswas, Kapil Krishna Thakur, Manoranjan Byapari, Kalyani Charal, Shyamal Pramanik, Achintya Biswas,

Manju Bala, Manohar Mouli Biswas, Mohan Tanu Mandal, Amar Biswas, Narendra Das, Shanti Biswas, Binoy Majumdar, Mohitesh Biswas, Sudhir Ranjan Haldar, Mani Mandal, Brajen Mallick, Bimalendu Haldar, Dhirendra Nath Mallik, Jatin Bala, Sunil Kumar Das, Gautam Ali, Baby Halder and many others have contributed significantly to Bangla Dalit literature.

In recent years, Dalit literary movement has become an all-India phenomenon. It is being produced in Indian languages such as Malayalam, Telugu, Gujarati, Oriya and Assamese. Some Dalits, living out of the country are also writing about their issues within the Indian context. The publication of Yashica Dutt's autobiography *Coming out as Dalit* (2019) is another example of a powerful anti-caste writing by an Indian living abroad. Besides Dutt, literary works of Meena Kandasamy and S Chandramohan, who also write in English, are equally articulate on caste, class and gender issues. The younger generation of Dalit writers use a blend of history, myths and folk-tales to defamiliarise the common theme of caste oppression. They also use post-modern techniques such as pastiches, intertextuality, flash-back, flash-forward and stream of consciousness. Their writings are wide in scope as they are inclusive of the pain of other marginalised groups such as women, peasants, labourers, nomads and tribals.

Dalit literature is transformative in nature and revolts against unjust socio-economic and political system that oppresses and discriminates against them. It demands a viable space in every sphere of life. Contemporary Dalit writers maintain that Indian literature discounted the personhood of Dalits and ignored their issues. High castes have always been biased and inauthentic in their depiction of the untouchables.

Ancient Indian texts such as *Manusmriti* and *Puranas* despised Dalits, portrayed them as despicable, religiously impure and of possessing certain negative traits. Untouchables were denied voice, agency, autonomy, will and desire.

Dalit writers problematise this 'politics of representation' in high caste writings and claim that Dalits can be represented only by Dalits. Even the twentieth century highly educated, high caste, middle class writers such as Mulk Raj Anand, Raja Rao, RK Narayanan, Rabindranath Tagore, Munshi Premchand and others were also inadequate in their portrayal of Dalits as they have no experiences of the harshness and difficulties that Dalits have to undergo. What they write is imaginary and sympathetic. In addition, Dalit women are depicted as inactive and mere mannequins or string-puppets in the hands of both non-Dalit and Dalit men.

Anand's portrayal of Dalit characters such as Lakha, Bakha and Sohini in *Untouchable* also lack a Dalit standpoint. Bakha does not retaliate when he is abused by priest Kalinath for unknowingly climbing the temple steps and neither does he revolt when he comes to know that his sister Sohini was molested by the same priest. Lakha also does not express anger when his son Bakha tells him that he was abused and slapped by the high castes. He simply tries to conciliate his flustered son. Again, there is no retaliation from Sohini when the old priest molests her. She does not even tell her father and entombs her pain and humiliation in her bosom. Dalits, especially, Dalit women writers are sharply opposed to this kind of superficial portrayal. Gogu Shymala says that Premchand and Anand's depiction of Dalit women was inauthentic and unjustifiable as they show them suffering silently. They did not bring out the inherent strength of Dalit women and their capacity to work and survive in a casteist and masculine society. They also ignored the fact that Dalit women are capable of fighting back. (Personal Interview) The high caste writers also discounted strong historical Dalit women such as Uda Devi, Mahaviri Devi and Jhalkari Bai who fought for the nation during the mutiny of 1857. They also ignored the voices of rebellious women such as Janabai, Rami, Akka Mahadevi, Muddupalani and many others and depicted them just as immoral or fallen.

The high caste writers excluded Dalit intellectuals and heroes in their writings. They produced sympathetic literature in a Gandhian way and like Gandhi did not attempt to demolish the basic structure of Hinduism by annihilating caste. They strived to reform Hinduism. Dalits reject the non-Dalit writers' point of view and their attitude and call their writings on caste *Dalitvadi Sahitya* (Dalitist literature), different from Dalit literature. (Meenu 18-24) Their chief argument is that non-Dalits cannot retain the originality of pain and anguish of Dalit lives as they did not go through the pangs of caste-based humiliation. So, they are superficial in their representation of Dalits and their issues.

To understand the difference between Dalit and Dalitist literature it is significant to understand the words 'Dalit' and 'Dalit literature'. Both have been defined, interpreted and used in different ways and contexts by scholars and writers that led to a considerable debate on who are Dalits and who can write Dalit literature. The word 'Dalit' is of Sanskrit origin which means broken, grinded, scattered, cracked, suppressed and trodden. It is generally used to refer to those ethnic groups in Indian society that were traditionally deprived and subjected to rigorous untouchability on account of their outcaste status. This word was first used by Jyotirao Phule in the nineteenth century to indicate the oppression and dehumanisation faced by the then untouchables. Dalits were excluded from the four-fold *Varna* system and formed the unnoticed and unmentioned fifth caste called *Avarnas*, *Panchamas*, *Atishudras*, *Achoot* or *Chandalas*. The word came into prominence and common usage after the foundation of the Dalit Panther Movement in 1972 in Maharashtra.

Most contemporary Dalit writers and theorists are of the opinion that Dalit is a person who is subjected to untouchability and is denied education, land, a dignified profession and life. Such a person is considered defiling and is relegated to the social, economic, political, cultural, literary and geographical margins and is coerced to undertake all kinds of unhygienic, filthy works for survival. Caste is a chief differentiator. This definition of Dalit seems to be relevant and rational but there are some Dalit writers who argue that caste is not the only essential for being a Dalit. Sharankumar Limbale, for instance, offers a more inclusive definition when he says, "The term describes all untouchable communities living outside the boundary of a village, as well as Adivasis, landless farm-labourers, workers, the suffering masses, and nomadic and criminal tribes." (*Towards* 30)

Another faction is of the opinion that the word Dalit does not signify any caste rather it accentuates the anger of the oppressed by the laws of caste. On the basis of definitions offered by different Dalit writers and critics it can be inferred that Dalits are persons who are subjected to untouchability, impoverishment, dehumanisation and exploitation in the name of caste. They might or might not be conscious of their oppression. Defining Dalit literature, Limbale says, "By Dalit literature, I mean writing about Dalits by Dalit writers with Dalit consciousness. The form is inherent in its Dalitness, and its purpose is to inform the Dalit society of its slavery, and narrate its pain and suffering to the upper caste Hindus." (*Towards* 19) According to S Srinivasan, "Dalit literature is an insider's report of experiences, memoirs, recollections and rebellions rendered in a forthright, imaginative, often predominantly colloquial style." (25)

Arguments and opinions suggest that the exhibition and evocation of Dalit consciousness is the hallmark of both Dalitness and Dalit literature. Dalit consciousness makes Dalit literature different from the writings about Dalits by non-Dalits. Dalit literature brings out the pain of Dalit masses, expresses their will and desires, and articulates their agency. Here, they are not passive recipients of humiliation, violence, oppression and injustices inflicted on them rather they are the speaking subjects, who not only report the wrong done to them but also demand their rights. They are awakened and active individuals and exhibit an acute sense of their rights and dignity. Limbale also says, "'Rejection' and 'revolt' in Dalit literature have been birthed from the womb of Dalits' pain. They are directed against an inhuman system that was imposed on them. Rejection is double-edged – rejecting the unequal order and demanding equality, liberty, fraternity and justice." (31) Dalit voices as articulated in Dalit literature are transformative in nature. Most Dalit writers subscribe to Ambedkar's view that being a religious construct, caste cannot be reformed. They want to awaken the silent and impoverished masses and mobilise them to revolt against dominant social and economic forces that kept them marginalised and poor over centuries.

Dalit writers reject the high-born heroes as they stand for exploitation and repression that Dalits underwent for centuries. Exposing the deliberate glorification of the high-born war-like characters in Indian literature, Baburao Bagul says, "The brave heroes upon whom Hinduism has bestowed sacredness and divinity, have in fact fought for power. Their wars and the stories about them have been sanctified as Holy Scriptures. Moreover, a number of Hindu festivals too have been celebrations of such wars. Violent traits of characters such as jealousy, malice, scorn, hatred, enmity and vengefulness have been cherished ideals with a cultural significance. These tendencies clearly indicate that war has been in the forefront of the Hindu value structure." (278) Dalit writers pick up their ideals and myths from their own history, culture and community and celebrate those low born heroic figures who were traditionally despised and represented as anti-heroes in hegemonic literature. Mukherjee refers to this proclivity in contemporary Dalit literature: "Dalits are no longer a people without history, much less the subalterns of society's history, its demonized Ravana or violated Angulimala, Eklavya or Shurpanaka. Here, they are the central figures of their own history, and from this history they derive the confidence and the right to assert their humanity." (15)

Dalit writers liberated literature from the religious confinements and Brahmanical traditions. They do not flummox and bamboozle the illiterate Dalit masses by writing on complex philosophical concepts such as soul, gods, salvation, and metaphysical entities like heaven and hell. The repressed and deprived masses were their characters and protagonists, and they wrote about the problems being faced by them. According to Dangle, Dalit writers wrote with social responsibility and aimed not to appease the gods but to awaken, empower and liberate the deprived and enslaved sections of the society. They do not indulge in sexually explicit narratives in the name of psychoanalysis. They produce a life-affirming literature and depict Dalit lives realistically. (Introduction xlix) In Dalit literature, the dominant theme of religion is replaced by humanism and the concept of *Moksha* by Dalit empowerment. Dalit literature depicts the vulgarities and harshness of Dalit lives in a caste dominated society. The aesthetics of Dalit literature is located in the pain and suffering of Dalit masses and in the revelation of truth.

Dalit writers hold the theory of *Varna* with contempt. They are of the opinion that their literature should not be appraised on the basis of established Indian aesthetic considerations of *Satyam* (true), *Shivam* (holy), *Sundram* (beautiful). They revolt against it and claim that the truth of their lives is different from what is generally held true, holy and beautiful. Limbale says, "*Satyam, Shivam, Sundram* – are fabrications used to divide and exploit ordinary people. There is no truth and beauty in the world comparable to that which is found in human beings. Therefore, it is essential to discuss the equality, liberty and fraternity of human beings." (21-22)

Dalit literature is also a revolt against traditional Indian literature in terms of the use of language. Dalit writers prefer to write in the language used by them in their daily lives. The rejection of standard language by Dalit writers is an assertion of their identity and also a revolt against the hegemony of high castes, especially the Brahmins. Dalit writers are unconventional and inventive in their selection and use of symbols and images. They use distinct images and symbols in their writings and peep into Dalit culture and history to search for their literary icons and heroes. There is an abundance of *Vibhatsa* (horrendous) and *Karuna* (sad) rasa in this literature.

This book seeks to examine how selected Dalit writers apprehend, approach, represent and respond to caste, class, gender as discriminatory institutions and what are their strategies to liberate and empower the hitherto impoverished and repressed Dalits. It further attempts to analyse how Dalits articulate their agency, express their will, desire, and assert their identity, dignity and culture through their writings. Most of the selected texts are English translations from regional languages. Meena Kandasamy's *When I Hit You* is the only text written in English.

This book is divided into an Introduction, six chapters and a conclusion. The 'Introduction' traces the origin and expedition of Dalit literature and gives its comprehensive history with special reference to Marathi, Tamil, Kannada, Hindi, Punjabi, Bengali and English. It further looks at the nature, purpose, scope and significance of Dalit literature and also casts a searching spotlight on its aesthetics. Chapter One: 'From Erasion to Enunciation' seeks to examine how selected Dalit autobiographies – Omprakash Valmiki's *Joothan*, Manohar Mouli Biswas' *Surviving in My World* and Manoranjan Byapari's *Interrogating My Chandal Life,* apprehend caste, class, culture and identity and their responses and strategies to counter these repressive ideologies. It further seeks to pinpoint the changes that occurred in Dalit responses and strategies with the passage of time. Chapter Two: 'Polemics of Representation' discusses Dalit women in Daya Pawar's *Baluta*, Sharankumar Limbale's *The Outcaste* and Balbir Madhopuri's *Changiya Rukh*. It studies the images of Dalit women as constructed and represented in selected Dalit male autobiographies. It further attempts to locate the adequacies and inadequacies in Dalit men's representation of Dalit women and also in their general attitude towards them, both in theory and praxis. Chapter Three: 'Paradigm of Resistance' talks about Dalit Women's Autobiographies such as Bama's *Karukku* and Baby Halder's *A Life Less Ordinary*. These highlight Dalit women's resistance against caste, class and gender discriminations and how they fight against it. The chapter also measures the changes that occurred in Dalit women over decades and underlines how they are different from Dalit men in terms of their nature, tone and manner of articulation. Chapter Four: 'Re-writing Patriarchy' analyses Meena Kandasamy's *When I Hit You Or, a Portrait of the Writer as a Young Wife* and discusses how the second generation Dalit women writers understand, respond and resist internal patriarchy. It further underlines how the modern educated Dalit women refuse to submit to men and how they express their body, assert their rights and strive for their agency, individuality and identity. Chapter Five: 'Writing Oppression' seeks to underscore how selected Dalit short story writers – Bandhu Madhav, Waman Hoval, Omprakash Valmiki, Irathina Karikalan, Abhimani and Mogalli Ganesh perceive and address oppression that Dalits have to undergo in the name of caste, class, religion and culture. It further attempts to underscore the caste and class sensibilities. Chapter Six: 'Voices of Dalit Awakening and Mobilisation' in Kamal Dev

Pall's *Days Will Come Back* and Balbir Madhopuri's *My Caste-My Shadow* examines how revolutionary poetry brings out the exploitation of Dalit masses and how it attempts to awaken and mobilise them against injustices and discriminations prevalent in contemporary Punjabi society. The 'Conclusion' summarises the foregoing discussion to note the significance, effects and relevance of Dalit literature to the Dalit movement. It also underlines the points of convergence and divergence in the selected Dalit writings to establish that these texts together form a chorus of strong voices to assert their autonomy, dignity and identity not only in Dalit writings but also in contemporary Indian literature.

Works Cited

- Abimani. "Ailment." Translated by N Kalyan Raman, *The Oxford India Anthology of Tamil Dalit Writing,* edited by Ravikumar and R Azhagarasan, Oxford UP, 2012, pp. 101-106.
- Anand. "Life and Teaching of Guru Nanak." *History Discussion*, n.page, www.historydiscussion.net/history-of-india/life-and-teaching-of-guru-nanak/3178. Accessed 20 February 2020.
- Anand, Mulk Raj. *Untouchable*. Arnold Heinemann, 1983.
- Ananthamurthy, UR "Dalit Literature an Integral Part of Indian Literary History." *Hindustan Times*, 13 September 2010, n. page. www.hindustantimes.com/india/dalit-literature-an-integral-part-of-indian-literary-history-ananthamurthy/storQ7HwJO7bBVIfchFn6dp1uI.html. Accessed 13 May 2020.

- Bagul, Baburao. "Dalit Literature is but Human Literature." Translated by Milind Malshe, *Poisoned Bread: Translations from Modern Marathi Dalit Literature*, edited by Dangle, new edition, Orient Black Swan, 2014, pp. 274-294.
- Bala, J "Pandit Iyothee Thass and the Revival of Tamil Buddhism." *Round Table India*, 2014, n.page, roundtableindia.co.in/index.php?option=com_content&view=article&id=7569:pandit-iyothee-thass-and-the-revival-of-tamil-buddhism&catid=119:feature&Itemid=132. Accessed 25 April 2020.
- Bama. *Karukku.* Translated by Lakshmi Holmstrom, Oxford UP, 2000.
- Bandhu Madhav. "The Poisoned Bread." Translated by Ramesh Dnyate, *Poisoned Bread: Translations from Modern Marathi Dalit Literature*, edited by Arjun Dangle, new edition, Orient Black Swan, 2014, pp. 167-175.
- Bandyopadhyay, Sekhar. *Caste, Culture and Hegemony: Social Dominance in Colonial Bengal*, Sage Publications, 2004.
- Basu, Tapan. Introduction. *Translating Caste: Stories, Essays, Criticism*, edited by Basu, Katha, 2002, pp. ix- xxxv.
- Bhattacharya, Jogendra Nath. *Hindu Castes and Sects: An Exposition of the Origin of the Hindu Caste System and the Bearing of the Sects Towards Each Other and Towards Other Religious Systems*, Kalpaz Publications, 2017.
- Biswas, Manohar Mouli. *Surviving in My World: Growing Up Dalit in Bengal.* Translated and edited by Angana Dutta and Jaydeep Sarangi. Samya, 2015.
- Byapari, Manoranjan. *Interrogating My Chandal Life: An Autobiography of a Dalit.* Translated by Sipra Mukherjee, Sage/ Samya, 2018.
- Meenakshi Mukherjee. "Is There Dalit Writing in Bangla?"

Economic and Political Weekly, vol. 42, no. 41, Oct. 2007 pp. 4116-4120. www.jstor.org/stable/40276544. Accessed 19 May 2020.

- Chakravarti, Uma. *Gendering Caste: Through a Feminist Lens.* Stree, 2013.
- Dangle, Arjun. Introduction. *Poisoned Bread: Translations from Modern Marathi Dalit Literature*, edited by Dangle. Translated by Daya Agarwal, new edition, Orient Black Swan, 2014, pp. xix-liv.
- Dutt, Yashica. *Coming out as Dalit: A Memoir.* Aleph Book Company, 2019.
- Dutta, Angana, and Sarangi, Jaydeep. Introduction. *Surviving in My World: Growing Up Dalit in Bengal.* Translated and edited by Angana Dutta and Jaydeep Sarangi, Samya, 2015, pp. xiv-xxx.
- Gajarawala, Toral Jatin. *Untouchable Fictions: Literary Realism and the Crisis of Caste*, Fordham University P, 2013.
- Ganesh, Mogalli. "The Paddy Harvest." Translated by Raghavendra Rao, *Translating Caste: Stories, Essays, Criticism*, edited by Tapan Basu, Katha, 2002, pp. 12-24.
- Geetha, V and SV Rajadurai. *Towards a Non-Brahmin Millennium: From Iyothee Thass to Periyar.* Samya, 1998.
- Halder, Baby. *A Life Less Ordinary*. Translated by Urvashi Butalia, Zubaan, 2006.
- Hans, Raj Kumar. "Rich Heritage of Punjabi Dalit Literature and its Exclusion from Histories." Beyond Borders, vol. 6, no. 1-2, 2010, pp. 73-81.
- Personal Interview. 25 April 2020.
- Hoval, Waman. "The Storeyed House." Translated by MD Hatkanangalekar, *Poisoned Bread: Translations from Modern Marathi Dalit Literature*, edited by Arjun Dangle, new edition,

Orient Black Swan, 2014, pp. 176-184.

- Juergensmeyer, Mark. *Religion as Social Vision: The Movement Against Untouchability in the 20th Century Punjab*. University of California P, 1982.
- Kandasamy, Meena. *When I Hit You: Or, A Portrait of the Writer as a Young Wife*. Juggernaut Books, 2017.
- Karikalan, Irathina. "Oorakali." Translated by Hephzibah Israel. *Translating Caste: Stories, Essay, Criticism*, edited by Tapan Basu, Katha, 2002, pp. 2-9.
- Lal, Chaman. "Dalit Life in Punjabi Novel." *Dalits in Regional Context*, edited by Harish K. Puri, Rawat Publications, 2004, pp. 297-306.
- Lal, Chaman. *Dalit Sahitya: Ek Mulyankan* (*Dalit Literature: An Evaluation*), Rajpal, 2008.
- Limbale, Sharankumar. *The Outcaste: Akkarmashi.* Translated by Santosh Bhoomkar, Oxford UP, 2003.
- Limbale, Sharankumar. *Towards and Aesthetics of Dalit Literature: History, Controversies and Considerations.* Translated by Alok Mukherjee, Orient Longman, 2004.
- Madhopuri, Balbir. *Changiya Rukh: Against the Night.* Translated by Tripti Jain, Oxford UP, 2010.
- Madhopuri, Balbir. *My Caste-My Shadow: Selected Poems.* Translated by TC Ghai, LG Publishers and Distributers, 2020.
- Mahananda, Saroj Kumar. *Towards Dalit Historiography: Imaging the Gandas through Various Narratives*, Archive Press, 2017.
- Meenu, Rajat Rani. *Hindi Dalit Katha Sahitya: Avdharanayen aur Vidhayen* (*Hindi Dalit Prose: Concepts and Genres*), Anamika, 2010.
- Mittal, Mukta. *Dalit Women in India: Survival and Current Dilemma.* Arise Publishers and Distributers, 2010.

- Mukherjee, Alok. "Reading Sharankumar Limbale's *Towards an Aesthetic of Dalit Literature*: From Erasure to Assertion." *Towards and Aesthetics of Dalit Literature: History, Controversies and Considerations* by Sharankumar Limbale. Translated by Mukherjee, Orient Longman, 2004, pp. 1-18.
- Muktibodh, Sharatchandra. "What is Dalit Literature?" Translated by Anil Raghunath Kulkarni, *Poisoned Bread: Translations from Modern Marathi Dalit Literature*, edited by Arjun Dangle, new edition. Orient Black Swan, 2014, pp. 270 -273.
- Premchand, Munshi. *Godan: A Novel of Peasant India*. Translated by Jai Ratan and P Lal, Jaico, 2010.
- Murugkar, Lata. *Dalit Panther Movement in Maharashtra: A Sociological Appraisal*. Popular Prakashan, 1991.
- Nimavat, BS "Chokhamela: The Pioneer of Untouchable Movement in Maharashtra." *Dalit Literature: A Critical Exploration*, edited by Amar Nath Prasad and MB Gaijan, Sarup and Sons, 2007, pp. 9-16.
- Omvedt, Gail. "Literature of Revolt: Prefatory Note." *Poisoned Bread: Translations from Modern Marathi Dalit Literature*, edited by Arjun Dangle, new edition. Orient Black Swan, 2014, pp. ix-xviii.
- Pall, Kamal Dev. *Days Will Come Back*. Translated by Rajinder Azad, Panther's Paw Publications, 2019. Personal Interview. 25 December 2019.
- Pallival, Krishan Dutt, and Santosh Kumar Shukla. *"Madhyakaleen Bharat Mai Hindi Sahitya ka Vikas: Dharmik aur Sanskritik Prishtbhoomi."* (Development of Hindi Literature in Medieval India: Religious and Cultural Background), *Madhyakaleen Bharat* 750-1540, edited by Harishchandra

Verma, Delhi University, 2007, pp. 485-496.

- Pawar, Urmila, and Meenakshi Moon. *We Also Made History: Women in the Ambedkarite Movement.* Translated by Wandana Sonalkar, Zubaan, 2008.
- Pawar, Daya. *Baluta.* Translated by Jerry Pinto, Speaking Tiger, 2015. "History of Dalit Literature." *Dalit and Women Writing in Indian Literature,* edited by Chaman Lal. Saransh, 2001, pp. 47-54.
- Puri, Harish K Introduction. *Dalits in Regional Context,* edited by Puri, Rawat Publications, 2004, pp. 1-20. "The Scheduled Castes in the Sikh Community: A Historical Perspective." *Dalits in Regional Context,* edited by Puri, Rawat Publications, 2004, pp. 190-224.
- Ram, Ronki. "Limits of Untouchability, Dalit Assertion and Caste Violence in Punjab." *Dalits in Regional Context,* edited by Harish K Puri. Rawat Publications, 2004, pp. 132-189.
- Ramaswamy, Vijaya. *Walking Naked: Women, Society, Spirituality in South India.* Indian Institute of Advanced Study, 1997.
- Ravikumar. Introduction. *The Oxford India Anthology of Tamil Dalit Writing,* edited by Ravikumar and R Azhagarasan, Oxford UP, 2012. pp. xv- xxxiii.
- Satyanarayana, K, and Susie Tharu. Introduction. *From Those Stubs, Steel Nibs are Sprouting: New Dalit Writing in South India Dossier 2: Kannada and Telugu,* edited by Satyanarayana and Tharu, Harper Collins, 2013, pp. 1-54.
- Shyamala, Gogu. Personal Interview. 15 June 2019.
- Singh, Gurdial. *The Last Flicker.* Translated by Ajmer S Rode, National Book Trust, 2010.
- Somashekara, D "Ideological Traits of Kannada Dalit Poetry." Proceedings of 142nd IIER International Conference, Florence,

Italy, 21-22 December 2017, pp. 33-36, x. Accessed 14 May 2020.

- Sreenivasan, S "Why Does Dalit Literature Matter?" *Beyond Borders*, vol. 6, no. 1-2, 2010, pp. 24-28.
- Sundararajan, S *Ancient Tamil Country: Its Social and Economic Structure.* Navrang, 1991.
- Valmiki, Omprakash. *Joothan: A Dalit's Life*. Translated by Arun Prabha Mukherjee, Samya, 2003. *Amma and Other Stories.* Translated by Naresh K Jain. Manohar, 2008.
- Virdi, SL *Casteism: The Eighth Worst Wonder*. Dalit Sahit, 2001.
- Waghmare, Janardan. "Black Literature and Dalit Literature." Translated by PS Sabnis, *Poisoned Bread: Translations from Modern Marathi Dalit Literature*, edited by Dangle, new edition, Orient Black Swan, 2014, pp. 312-321.
- Zelliot, Eleanor, and Rohini-Mokashi Punekar, editors. *Untouchable Saints: An Indian Phenomenon*. Manohar, 2005. Introduction. pp. 9-54.

CHAPTER 1

FROM ERASION TO ENUNCIATION

DALIT WRITERS use autobiography as a medium to express their pain and enunciate their 'self' that was negated and suppressed in traditional Indian literature. Dalit autobiographies bring lived experiences of scorned, browbeaten Dalits and expose the prejudice of caste that dehumanises them and further exposes them to poverty and class oppression. They give an authentic expression to the harsh realities of Dalit lives and depict how they live like sub-human beings and strive for survival in an unbendingly caste and class divided society. These are authentic accounts of Dalits' recollections of their experiences as wretched, impoverished and socio-cultural pariahs. They share the sufferings of Dalit masses collectively and give expression to their will, desire and agency. The individual 'self' that emerges from these life narratives is not isolated as it is always concerned about community and speaks for its liberation as a whole. They demonstrate Dalits' assertion of identity as equal human beings and subvert the hegemonic culture that was imposed on them by the high castes and classes in the name of tradition and gods. Dalits write to express their experiences of pain and anguish as the oppressed section of society and also to awaken the repressed Dalit masses, voice their indignation and demand a viable space for them in an inequalitarian society. Historically, Dalit autobiographical writing had its inception in Marathi in the late 1970s. Daya Pawar was the first Dalit to write his life story *Baluta* which was published in Marathi in 1978. *Baluta* was followed by the publication of many other powerful Dalit autobiographies such as Laxman Mane's, *Upara*, Vasant Moon's, *Vasti*: *Growing up Untouchables in India*, Laxman Gaikwad's, *Uchalya*, Sharankumar Limbale's, *Akkarmashi,* Baby Kamble's, *The Prisons We Broke,* Urmila Pawar's, *The Weave of My Life,* Kumud Pawde's, *Antasphot* and many others. In recent years some significant Dalit autobiographies have been published in Tamil, Malayalam, Hindi, Punjabi, Bengali, Kannada and other languages. Together, these autobiographies voice a revolt against hegemonic castes and classes, assert Dalit identity, dignity and problematise their alienation from the power structure, education, land and property. They are a significant addition to the Dalit liberation movement as they break the silence imposed on Dalits in the name of traditions, religion and gods and mobilise them against caste, class and religion based disparities. The present chapter seeks to examine how selected Dalit autobiographies: Omprakash Valmiki's *Joothan: A Dalit's Life*, Manohar Mouli Biswas's *Surviving in My World: Growing up Dalits in Bengal* and Manoranjan Byapari's *Interrogating My Chandal Life: An Autobiography of a Dalit* apprehend and represent the issues of caste, class, culture and identity and their responses and strategies to counter these repressive ideologies. It further seeks to underscore the changes that occurred in

Dalits' views and perceptions over the years and also in their strategies to mobilise and protest against them.

Joothan: A Dalit's Life

Dalit activist, writer and critic, Omprakash Valmiki was born in 1950, in a *Chuhra* (sweeper) family in Barla village of Muzafarnagar district in Uttar Pradesh. He wrote several poems, short stories, critical essays and books on Dalit issues and caste questions but his life narrative, *Joothan: A Dalit's Life* occupies a significant place in the history of Dalit literature for its overt exposition of the prejudice of caste and the critique of hypocrisies and remorselessness of the high-born Hindus. This life narrative opens with a general description of Dalit settlements and geographical surroundings at Barla. Valmiki's father Chotan Lal was an agricultural labourer and his mother Mukundi worked in the high caste Tyagi household. She did sweeping and cleaning and was given *joothan* (scraps) for discharging her duties. Valmiki had three elder brothers – Sukhbir, Jasbir and Janesar and a younger sister Maya. His siblings could not go to school because of wretched poverty and constant starvation and helped their parents in their work. Valmiki was the only child of the family to attend a local primary school. But there he was frequently discriminated against, insulted, beaten and tortured by the high caste teachers for his low caste status. He was not allowed to sit in the class with other students and was assigned a place in the corner where he could not get his lessons properly. During examinations he was not allowed to drink water from the glass. Valmiki undergoes frequent humiliation and violence but despite all that he continued his studies and took admission in DAV College, Dehradun, for higher studies.

Before the completion of his degree, he joined the Ordnance Factory at Dehradun as an apprentice and subsequently got a job in the same department. After serving in Maharashtra for some years, Valmiki got transferred to Dehradun and finally settled there with his wife Chanda.

Joothan is an authentic description of the author's life as a suppressed and impoverished Dalit. It recounts his experiences of frequent humiliation and torture and also revolutionises the demand of his personhood, rights, dignity and identity as a Dalit. This autobiography exhibits a powerful assertion of an individual self but despite that it is not merely a one-fold record of Valmiki's journey from adversity to prosperity and the celebration of his achievements or accomplishments. Like other Dalit writers, Valmiki also identifies himself with his community and so his suffering and struggle also epitomises his community's suffering and struggle. Vinod Kumar says, "On the surface this book seems to be an autobiographical account of Valmiki's journey from his birth and upbringing as an untouchable in the newly independent India of the fifties to his present as a Dalit writer. But at a deeper level it is not only a personal story of Valmiki's own life but of all those subalterns who are not in the main stream of society. So *Joothan* articulates those painful experiences which could not find a place in literary representations." (126) Valmiki shows how caste is used to suppress Dalits, alienate them from the power structure and position them on socio-political, economic, cultural and geographical margins. His description of the squalor of Dalit *basties* (settlements) in the beginning of his life narrative shows how rigidly caste operates in the lives of Dalits and how it lowers them to the level of sub-human beings: "There was muck strewn everywhere. The stench was so overpowering that one would choke within a minute. The pigs wandering in narrow lanes, naked children, dogs, daily fights, this was the environment of my childhood." (1) Through his vivid description of the geographical location of Dalits, Valmiki not only exposes the high caste strategies to dehumanise Dalits but also asserts their right to live a dignified life. Besides geographical marginalisation, the high caste Tyagis, also called Tagas, dehumanised and humiliated *Chuhras* in numerous ways for their outcaste status. They never considered them human and always called them by their caste names: "They did not call us by our names. If a person were older, he would be called 'Oe Chuhre'. If the person were younger or of the same age, then 'Abey Chuhre' was used. Untouchability was so rampant that while it was considered all right to touch dogs and cats or cows and buffaloes, if one happened to touch a *Chuhra*, one got contaminated or polluted. The *Chuhras* were not seen as humans." (2) The laws of caste were so strict that Dalits were not allowed to draw water from the well of the Tagas. They were forced to drink polluted water from the well in their basti. A Dalit wearing good clothes was considered conceited and was tortured and taunted for the alleged transgression of caste laws. Caste is so deeply rooted in the Indian social system and human psyche that even highly educated high caste people are not free from its effects. Valmiki gives the example of his educated teachers who not only humiliated and discriminated against him but also frequently attempted to obstruct his studies and intellectual growth. He gives a glaring example of untouchability in school when his teacher Narendra Kumar Tyagi, asks him to bring a glass of water from the pitchers in the Principal's room. But Narendra Tyagi stops Valmiki when he tells him about his caste. (65) This incident divulges that even the educated high caste people practiced caste and instead of censuring the caste system as a socio-cultural hypocrisy they attempted to strengthen it both in theory and praxis. For instance, Ambedkar was neither taught nor discussed in his school at Barla: "Ambedkar was an unknown entity to me then. I knew about Gandhi, Nehru, Patel, Rajendra Prasad, Radhakrishnan, Vivekananda, Tagore, Saratchandra, Bhagat Singh, Subhas Bose, Chandra Shekhar Azad, Savarkar, and so on, but was completely ignorant about Dr Ambedkar. The college library also did not have a single book on Ambedkar." (71) The exclusion of Ambedkar from popular academic circles shows how the high castes attempted to erase the history of Dalit intellectuals and conspired to stifle their voices and movements as they did not want Dalits to demand their rights and assert their place in the power structures. Valmiki shows how a high caste teacher in a school in Maharashtra asked his students to tear a lesson on Ambedkar from their books.

Valmiki argues that caste is not only a series of rules of untouchability, rather it is a complex system of inequality that operates beyond the level of purity and pollution. It harbours numerous complexities and is closely associated with class and promotes economic exploitation of Dalits. *Joothan* exposes the close congruence between caste and class and shows that the caste system leads to economic exploitation of Dalits and their subsequent impoverishment by the high castes. "Everyone in the family did some work or the other. Even then we didn't manage to get two decent meals a day. We did all sorts of work for Tagas, including cleaning, agricultural and general labour. We would often have to work without pay." (2) The unpaid work kept the Dalits poor and dependent on leftovers given to them by the high households for their ceaseless work. Valmiki shows how his mother was scolded by Sukhdev Singh Tyagi when she asked for food for her children as wage for her work on the day of his daughter's wedding: "You are taking a basketful of joothan. And on top of that you want food for your children. Don't forget your place, Chuhri. Pick up your basket and get going." (11)

The wageless labour is used as a weapon by the high castes to keep the Dalits poor, powerless and perpetually positioned on the socio-economic margins. Apart from the high castes, government officials also exploited the poor Dalits: "As always a government employee came to the Bhangi Basti. Some people were required for clean-up work, for which they would not be paid. For days on end, hungry and thirsty people would work to clean the *Kothi*. In return they would be sworn at." (37) Dalits' efforts to speak against exploitation were dealt violently; they were beaten and tortured if they refused to work without money. The high castes used police to coerce Dalits to work for them. Valmiki details how one day two policemen came to the Dalit basti and arrested ten Dalit young men when they denied unpaid work. The policemen took the arrested Dalits to the office of the *Panchayat* to punish them. The Dalit young men were beaten openly to frighten the basti people and also to trample their assertion of rights. Dalits were also looted by the high caste money lenders such as Teja Taga. These money lenders gave loan at very high rates and Dalits were cheated when they tried to pay back the loan.

Dalits' pursuit of education was considered a transgression

of tradition and a crime by the high castes as they did not want Dalits to educate themselves, get into prestigious, salaried jobs and leave their caste-based professions. Valmiki gives his own example of being beaten by his high caste teachers to discourage him, frustrate his pursuit of education and keep him away from learning and knowledge. It was because of this nefarious intention that headmaster Kaliram used to debase, beat Valmiki and keep him away from class. His caste bias comes out openly when he asks Valmiki to sweep and clean the school: "'Chuhre ka? Headmaster threw his question at me.' 'Ji.' All right...See that teak tree there? Go, climb that tree. Break some twigs, make a broom and sweep the whole school clean as a mirror. It is, after all, your family occupation." (4) Kaliram lost his temper when Valmiki joins his class after cleaning the school for two days. He scolded and dragged him out of the class and ordered him to sweep the playground. The headmaster was determined to drive Valmiki away from school and put him in his caste-based occupation.

In addition to Kaliram, there were other high caste teachers such as Yogendra Tyagi and Brajpal Singh who would humiliate Valmiki and discriminate against him and other low caste students. Whenever Valmiki made a mistake while answering a question, Yogendra Tyagi, instead of punishing him would mockingly ask him how many pieces of pork did he eat? This scorn by the teacher would give the high caste students an opportunity to insult Valmiki and jeer at him. (18) It is because of such kinds of humiliation and caste biases against Dalit children in schools that the number of dropouts is greater among Dalits as compared to non-Dalits. Valmiki suffered humiliation and discrimination from high caste teachers even in the higher classes at Tyagi Inter College. His chemistry teacher, Brajpal Singh would not allow him to sit in the laboratory and do his practicals. Despite being one of the few good students in class, Valmiki flunked in chemistry in the final examination as he was given low marks in the practical test. (65) Brajpal's attitude shows that education is still under the control of the high castes and the traditional 'Dronacharya Syndrome' still persists in the Indian education system.

Dalit intellectuals such as Phule, Periyar and Ambedkar revolted against the Brahmins' control of education. It was again because of this Dronacharya tradition that Valmiki was not allowed to take part in extracurricular activities by his teachers. Valmiki maintains that the high caste teachers were not only reluctant to teach Dalit students but they also beat those who did not behave in the caste specific way. He relates how his mama's (maternal uncle) son Surjan Singh, was beaten by Phool Singh Tyagi, the physical education teacher, simply because Surjan wore good and neat clothes and displayed unconventional mannerisms. "Moving from childhood to adolescence when my personality was being shaped, I had to live in this terror-filled environment... At times I feel like I grew up in a cruel and barbaric civilization." (57) Valmiki writes that Dalit students have to face caste based humiliation from the high caste students as well. Exposing the inherent caste biases of the high caste teachers and students, Vikas Kumar writes that "casteism was so deeply internalized in the minds of the Savarna teachers and students that they could not tolerate the presence of Dalit students in their schools." (39) Baring a few exceptions, all high caste students in schools and institutions of higher education maintain their distance from

Dalit students and never treated them as their equal. Relating his own experiences Valmiki writes that the high caste students used to tease him by calling his caste name and "sometimes beat me without any reason." (3) Valmiki narrates that he was taunted and insulted by some high caste students in DAV College, Dehradun for his rustic look, accent and untidy and unfit clothes. In response, Valmiki could only plead to the boys to let go of his already old clothes, or they would tear into rags. (69) Although, Valmiki was finally released from the grab of the hooligans by a senior teacher who happened to come there suddenly, but this incident left him feeling terribly ashamed as though he had committed some odious crime by being poor and low caste.

Valmiki writes that the Dalits' pursuits of education are also obstructed by the orthodox casteist forces outside schools and colleges. He was beaten by Surajbhan Taga's son Brajesh simply because he was educating himself despite being a *Chuhra* and was good in studies. Brajesh threw his books and school bag into a muddy ditch. (28-29) He was also dragged by Fauz Singh Tyagi to work in his field while he was preparing to appear in a math exam the following day. When Valmiki requested Fauz to leave him, Fauz simply said that he should study at night. (57) These incidents clearly reveal the high castes' attempts to thwart Dalit education and use force to alienate them from knowledge and learning. Their attitude got exposed when Valmiki went with his newly married friend Hiram Singh to do salaam in the high caste households at Morna. One of the high caste women was stunned to know that Valmiki was studying in the ninth standard. Irritated she said, "Howsoever much you study…you will still remain a *Chuhra.*" (31-32)

Valmiki also describes how Dalits themselves do not value education as a means to their progression and liberation from poverty and constraints of caste. The author maintains that the situation of Dalits was no better in cities like Dehradun: "The school-going children loitered in the streets all day. Few children took interest in their studies. Leaving home at five, the parents would return around twelve or one. They neither had time nor the desire to know what their children did all day or whether or not they went to school." (68)

Valmiki exposes the rampant superstitions among Dalits and criticises them for their hypocritical adherence to traditional Hindu fallacies. Valmiki is not only critical of the superstitions prevalent among Dalits, but also exposes the internal caste hierarchy and caste division observed by them. His description of Indresh Nagar in Dehradun exposes the internal caste divide among Dalits and criticises them for their adherence to this precept: "Although Indresh Nagar seemed well knit to outsiders, internally, it was divided into two. The relation between the Valmikis and the Jatavs was tense. They would often get into brawls and beat each other." (70-71) Valmikis and Jatavs could not unite as Dalits because they were further divided in the name of caste. Since, Jatavs were ranked higher than Valmikis, they avoided every kind of connection and socialisation with the Valmikis. The internal caste division among Dalits was so stringent that they did not establish even a professional relation among themselves. Valmiki writes how once a washer-man refused to iron his dress since he was a *Chuhra.* (17) Exposing the hypocrisy of Dalits, Valmiki says, "Even the activists harboured feelings of caste differences. Although they talked outwardly of forgetting the differences between Mahars, Mangs, Chamars and Mehtars, internally they were caught in the clutches of these beliefs." (109) The author was surprised to know that though the Mehtars had respect for Ambedkar, they remained Hindus when many other Dalits, especially Mahars, converted to Buddhism. It was because of caste biases of Mahar leaders and activists that Mehtars did not join the Ambedkarite movement in Maharashtra. The author attempts to abrogate internal caste divide among Dalits and foster unity by criticising them for being dominating and discriminatory against each other.

Valmiki brings out the pain and anguish of the distressed and other Dalit masses and highpoints how caste and class subordinates them to the high castes. Still, *Joothan* is not merely a register of Dalit suffering and haplessness, it notes several instances of both individual and collective resistance by Dalits. Although, majority of the masses in the basti were illiterate, but they were conscious and powerful enough to oppose their exploitation. Dalits' protest against the high caste is reflected in their unyielding refusal to work without wages. Valmiki describes how he and other Dalit employees of the Ordnance Factory Chandrapur, held rallies to oppose the violence being inflicted on Dalits by anti-reservation high caste protesters. (107-08) Dalits protested collectively when a Brahmin teacher asked his students to rip off the lesson on Ambedkar: "Rallies and protest meetings began all over Vidarbha as soon as the story came out. The incident had become a symbol of Dalit oppression. A huge rally was staged at Bhadravati, and thousands of people attended. I too addressed the rally." (112) The high caste people's attempts to suppress Dalit voices further awakened and organised Dalits. Undeterred Dalit activists started many new programs for Dalit empowerment such as opening schools and libraries for the education of Dalit children. (113) Valmiki also records how Dalit Panthers protested to change the name of Marathwada University to Dr Ambedkar University despite strong opposition from casteist forces. Many Dalits were beaten, arrested, tortured and killed but they continued to protest sturdily. (106) Dalit assertion and the struggle for their rights, identity and dignity in Maharashtra had a great influence on Valmiki. It widened his understanding of caste issues and heightened his Dalit consciousness.

Joothan also records several instances of strong individual resistance by Dalit characters. Valmiki's father is the most awakened and articulate as he demands his rights and dignity and fights against the high caste oppressors. He is illiterate and economically disadvantaged, but he understands the mechanisms of Dalit suffering and has the capacity to fight against injustices. He gets angry and turns rebellious when he comes to know that the headmaster does not allow his son Omprakash to study and asks him to sweep and clean the school. He not only opposes this injustice, but also threatens the headmaster: "*Pitaji* took my hand and started walking towards our home. As he walked away, he said, loudly enough for the headmaster to hear, 'You are a teacher… so I am leaving now. But remember this much, Master … This *Chuhre ka* will study right here…in this school. And not just him, there will be more coming after him." (6) With the help of Pradhan Sagwa Singh Tyagi, Valmiki's father managed to readmit his son in the same school and thus won his struggle against the casteist efforts of Kaliram. Valmiki's father was a courageous man who never submitted to the atrocious high castes passively. He goes out to punish Brajesh when he comes to know that his son was beaten by him. He took a stick to fight against Fauz Singh Tyagi also when Valmiki told him that he had dragged him to work in his field while he was preparing for examination. These details and instances show that Valmiki's father had a great Dalit consciousness as he believes that it is only through education that Dalits can improve their socio-economic condition. He advises his son to educate himself to counter caste. He also ended the custom of salaam when Valmiki criticised it as a humiliating custom imposed on Dalits to trample their confidence and dehumanise them further. He looked at his son with pride and said: "Munshiji, sending you to school has been a success... I, too, have understood your point ... We shall now break this custom." (32) Valmiki admires and reveres his father for his courage, sense of dignity, dynamism, progressive approach and acknowledges his influence on his social and psychological building.

Valmiki also shows his mother's protest and assertion of her self-esteem. She protested against Sukhdev Singh Tyagi when at the wedding feast of his daughter he offered her *joothan*, the scraps of food remaining on the leaf plates of the wedding guests. She refused to accept them as she finds it unjustified to receive just scraps when she and her family had worked hard for the wedding. She asked for fresh food and sweets that were distributed to the guests. She revolts when Sukhdev Singh Tyagi denied her rational, justified demand and scolded her: "She emptied her basket right there and said, 'Pick it up and put it inside your house. Feed it to the *baratis* tomorrow morning.' She gathered me and my sister and left like an arrow. (11) There is a clear indication of assertion of rights and dignity in mother's retaliation and revolt. Valmiki compares her to Goddess Durga, who along with her other virtues, also stands for power and destruction.

The author also exhibits an awakened Dalit consciousness from his childhood. The frequent exposure to exploitation made him understand the mechanism of Dalit suffering. His assertion of rights and resistance against caste are reflected when he questions the absence of Dalits and their issues in traditional Indian literature in his school days. He found it prejudiced that the instance of Dronacharya's feeding his famished son, Ashwatthama with flour dissolved in water, found place in the great epic *Mahabharta* but the Dalits who had been starving for centuries were ignored. According to Mohd Asaduddin, "In *Joothan*, Omprakash Valmiki deals with the issue of humiliation meted out to the Dalits by the Indian society, no matter where they lived. This humiliation stems from the fact that Dalit inferiority has gotten embedded in the psyche of the upper caste and in their literary and artistic imagination and sensibility. Even the Hindu epics, *Ramayana* and *Mahabharata*, are replete with examples of this denigration where the *Shudras* and *Chandalas* are treated as less than human." (n. page) Valmiki finds eminent Hindi poet Sumitranandan Pant artificial and exaggerative in his depiction of the Indian rustic life in one of his poems that Valmiki was taught at school: "Ah, how wonderful is this village life… each word of the poem had proved to be artificial and lie." (39) Valmiki does not find village life wonderful at all. His description of the Dalit basti, rainy seasons and the beating of poor labourers presents an inversed picture of what Pant says about village life. He writes that life may be good for those village dwellers who were not humiliated and beaten for their caste and were not forced to live on scraps. For the poor Dalits, village life is humiliating, full of deprivation, torture and is no way less hellish than any other place.

Valmiki's refusal to follow the tradition of salaam after his wedding also denotes his Dalit consciousness and his assertion of dignity and identity. Valmiki was conscious of the indignities and dehumanisation that Dalit brides and bridegrooms had to undergo while doing salaam in the high caste households. (33) He exhibits an awakened Dalit consciousness and wages open rebellion against the caste based humiliation when he refused to eat the food served with indignity by Fauz Singh Tyagi's mother: "She dropped the *rotis* into my hand from way above, lest her hand touch mine. This gesture was insulting to me. I threw those rotis in front of her and ran towards my home." (58) It was because of his exposure to the writings of Phule and Ambedkar that Valmiki's nascent Dalit consciousness subsequently transformed into a strong voice of protest both as a writer and an activist: "After reading Ambedkar, I had realized that by naming the untouchables Harijans, Gandhi had not helped them join the national mainstream, but had saved Hindus from becoming a minority. Guarded their interests, in fact." (72) Ambedkar was well aware that Gandhi's opposition to granting a separate electorate to Dalits by the Government and coining the term Harijan are part of his strategies to alienate Dalits from political power and to keep them in Hinduism. Valmiki rejects Gandhi and his views of caste but acknowledges Ambedkar's contribution to Dalit liberation. He offers Ambedkarism as an ideological alternative for Dalits. He finds religion the root of all kinds of differences practiced against Dalits. He discards his identity as a Hindu and protests vociferously against it: "If I were really a Hindu, would the Hindus hate me so much? Or discriminate against me? Or try to fill me up with caste inferiority over the smallest things?" (41) Valmiki criticises the empty ritualism of Hinduism and maintains that it not only strengthens the concept of caste purity and pollution but also promotes violence against Dalits and animals. Valmiki opines that Dalits have to abandon Hinduism and reject Hindu practices if they want to liberate and empower themselves. He also suggests that Dalits should convert to Buddhism which is egalitarian in nature and does not practice casteism.

Another significant feature of this autobiography is the author's assertion of his identity as a Dalit. Valmiki is not ashamed of his caste or being a *Chuhra* and never concealed his caste to escape untouchability and discrimination. Valmiki reiterates that his assertion of identity broke his relationship with many high caste people. For instance, a Brahmin girl, Savita, who was in love with Valmiki, went away when he revealed his caste. She also asked Valmiki not to reveal his caste identity to her father though she was never to meet him again. He describes another incident where his friend Kureishi took him to meet his high caste friend who was the Commandant of the Defence Security Corps. They were received warmly by the host but when Valmiki told him that he was a *Chuhra* he felt uneasy and stopped conversing with him as if there was nothing left to talk about. The Commandant not only broke relations with the author but also tried to create a distance between Kureishi and the author: "Kureishi Saheb, he is considered a low caste in our district. He and his likes are not allowed to cross the threshold, and here you are socializing with him, even dining with him." (115) Through these details Valmiki aspires to illustrate that caste is valued much higher than talent, education, beauty and other virtues. Valmiki aspires to maintain that education and economic progression may induce Dalit consciousness and lessen the economic exploitation of Dalits but they cannot liberate them from socio-cultural stigmatisation. Another time, Valmiki and his wife while travelling back from Rajasthan to Chandrapur in a train, befriended a high caste officer and his wife. Both families were talking enthusiastically but the atmosphere changed as soon as the officer's wife started talking about caste. They turned their faces when the author told them that they were Dalits. There was no further conversation between the two families during the rest of the journey. (132-33) Valmiki's assertion of identity affected not only his personal relationships but also professional ones. He faced wrath and opposition from casteist forces when he wrote an article on Dalit issues while training at the Institute of the Ordnance Factory in Bombay. Government employees who were supporters of Shiv Sena complained of Valmiki to the Principal of the institute. The Principal instructed him not to write such controversial articles as long as he was a trainee. (90-91) It was because of his strong Dalit consciousness that Valmiki never attempted to pass as a high caste although he was well aware of the rejection and humiliation he may have to face because of his assertion of identity.

Valmiki is highly critical of those Dalits who are ashamed of their caste and conceal their identity to pass as high caste Hindus. "Dalits who have become educated face terrible crisis – the crisis of identity – and they are trying to find an easy and instantaneous way to get out of it. They have started using their family *Gotra* as their surname after a little bit of fine-tuning." (126) They adopt the high caste culture and religious practices so they can be considered and treated as high castes. They desert every practise that marks them Dalits and even change their eating habits and behaviour according to the high castes. In this way, the precept of caste is invading Dalit culture and destroying their identity. This tendency of hiding their caste is further exemplified by eminent Hindi writer Mohandas Naimishray when the author was at his place in Delhi. Naimishray took the author to meet an editor of a magazine, who was Naimishray's friend. As they were climbing the stairs to the house, Naimishray told Valmiki that he will introduce him as Omprakash only as he does not want the editor to know about his caste. (127) Valmiki details that his niece Seema, who was studying in a college in Dehradun, also denied her relation with the author when her Hindi teacher Kusum Chaturvedi inquired about it. In the evening she told the author the whole story and tried to justify herself: "If I had acknowledged in front of everybody that you are my uncle, then my classmates would know that I am a "Valmiki". (128) Valmiki narrates another incident that took place in Dehradun. His name was not written on the wedding invitation card by his relatives when their daughter Manju was being married. Although, Valmiki was very close with these relatives but his name was left out as they did not want to disclose their caste to the neighbours. It was once again for the same reason that Valmiki's name was not written on the wedding card of his wife's niece. Valmiki's adherence to his identity as a Dalit gave rise to certain complications because his own relatives started hiding their relation with him which bothered him: "The stings this surname has made me endure are hard to describe. Why talk about others when my own have caused me unspeakable anguish." (129) Valmiki writes that Sukhvir Singh, who was a Reader in Delhi University's Shivaji College, also did not like his surname. So, he changed it from 'Valmiki' to Khairwal when Omprakash Valmiki wrote a review of his book *Suryansh*. Like other educated Dalits Sukhvir Singh was also afraid of the revelation of his identity. (130) Most Dalits portrayed in *Joothan* do not possess the courage to enunciate their identity. This escapism by Dalits in general undermined the force and intensity of the Dalit liberation movement and also kept them entrapped in a severe inferiority complex.

Finally, it can be argued that *Joothan* is an authentic account of not only the author's life but of the whole Dalit community in Uttar Pradesh. It brings out the distress of impoverished Dalits and censures harsh socio-cultural practices and customs that make Dalit lives painful. It further shows how despite numerous odds, injustices and opposition from high castes Dalits manage to survive and strive for their rights, identity and dignity. It demonstrates an awakened Dalit consciousness and suggests social, political, economic, literary, cultural and religious alternatives. Valmiki finds Ambedkar's ideology relevant and the most significant solution to the pain and suffering of Dalit masses. It appeals to Dalits to educate themselves and also forge a unity among themselves so they can annihilate caste, eradicate class and assert their identity and culture without any feeling of inferiority. He writes, "This battle can't be won in a day. We need an ongoing struggle and a consciousness of struggle, a consciousness that brings revolutionary changes both in the outside world and in our hearts, a consciousness that leads the process of social change." (132) Illustrating on the force and scope of *Joothan*, Vinod Kumar writes, "Valmiki's own struggles and success, acts as motivation for others to struggle and achieve their goals. Thus, *Joothan* symbolizes the struggle for dignity and human rights." (128)

Surviving in My World: Growing up Dalits in Bengal

One of the prominent Bangla Dalit writers and activists, Manohar Mouli Biswas was born in 1943 in a small agrarian Namasudra family at Matiargati, a remote and marginal village in Khulna district of pre-partition East Bengal. As a prolific writer, Biswas wrote extensively on themes of caste discrimination, social exclusion, economic inequalities and exploitation of Dalits by the high castes. He is one of the founding members of the Bangla Dalit Sahitya Sanstha which was founded in 1992 after the suicide of Chuni Kotal, a tribal student of Vidyasagar University. Biswas has published numerous critical essays, poems and short stories and has contributed significantly to Bengali Dalit literature in both creative and critical writings. His autobiography: *Surviving in My World: Growing up Dalits in Bengal,* one of the earliest in this genre, was originally published in Bengali as *Amar Bhubane Ami Benche Tkaki* in 2013. It was translated into English by Angana Dutta and Jaydeep Sarangi and published in 2015. Structurally, this autobiography is divided into two sections. The first section deals with the author's familial background, childhood and the struggle of his family amid severe caste and class repression in colonial Bengal. It also details how he struggles for education despite wretched poverty. Section two consists of the author's expounded interview with Jaydeep Sarangi, Mohini Gurav and Angana Dutta. In this part, Biswas relates his experiences as a refugee in Independent India, his growing up as a Dalit activist, writer and the shaping of Bangla Dalit literature, its aims and nature.

Surviving in My World opens with the description of the author's familial background and his impoverished childhood in a poor joint family of his father and his *Jetha* (father's elder brother) in colonial Bengal. Biswas writes that rampant poverty forced his family to lead a life full of hardships, scarcity and deprivation like many other Namasudra households. The author's father and Jetha slogged in the fields and weaved mattresses to run their poor household while his mother and *Jethima* (Jetha's wife) looked after domestic chores. The family was hardly able to procure food and clothes and was coerced to live in small mud huts despite incessant hard work. Biswas's father was aware of the importance of education. So, despite wretched poverty and constant starvation the author was sent to school. He had to face hardships as he was not able to buy books, clothes and shoes but despite these difficulties and handicaps, he completed his education and got a job in the Telecommunication Department. After retiring from the post of Assistant General Manager, BSNL, Biswas settled in Kolkata. He owns a small flat in Tangra and lives happily with his wife, children and grandchildren.

Surviving in My World traces the evolution of an autonomous individual in the midst of stringent caste and class repression and is well aware and informed about the collective suffering of the community. Like Valmiki's *Joothan*, Biswas's personal narrative is also the story of the whole community.

It places caste at the centre and specifies how it operates in the lives of Dalits and subjects them not only to the bylaws of untouchability but also to the economic exploitation and cultural marginalisation. Biswas brings out the miserable life conditions of the Namasudra community that was traditionally demoted to the social, economic, cultural and political margins and was deceitfully alienated from developmental and progressive works such as electricity, construction of highways and starting of railways. Most Dalits were agricultural labourers without sufficient food to eat and clothes to cover their bodies. Most Dalit children were illiterate as there were no schools in the purlieus. Dalit parents could not afford to send their children to cities for study. The author says, "About one to two years before my birth a *Pathshala* (school) was started with the initiative of a few villagers. It ran in a cowshed in the afternoon when the cows were not there. The teacher was barely literate. He taught without any remuneration and the pupils did not have to pay any fees either." (3) Thereafter, a village pathshala was set around the Date Palm on a land donated by a village widow by thrusting bamboo poles into the ground with a "covering made from the leaves of the Gol tree that were large and round." (3-4) The author had to write on the palm leaves that were prepared by soaking them in water for some days and then drying them. Since his parents were not able to provide him study material, clothes and shoes, he had to go to school half naked, barefoot and hungry: "During heavy rains when the paths got submerged in water, we went to school climbing on boats like a donga or *shalti*, made by cutting a Betel Nut tree." (24) He had no time to study and revise his lessons at home because: "I had to help Baba and Jetha on the land to such an extent that I could not concentrate on my studies. We owned a strip of agricultural land near a very watery marsh about five miles from our homes." (6)

Biswas maintains that abject poverty obstructs Dalits' pursuit of education and keeps them illiterate and illiteracy accounts for Dalits' alienation not only from the power structure but also from the basic necessities of life. Biswas writes that Dalits also have no access to healthcare and medical services. He details how his *Mejda* (second elder brother) could not be given proper medical assistance and treatment when he was wounded by the author when he threw a piece of the thorny trunk of the Date Palm at him: "Even in such grave danger, not a single doctor was found nearby. We had to do our treatment ourselves to remain alive." (30) Describing Dalits' deprivation Biswas further says, "This world of mine is the Dalit's world of illiteracy, the Dalit's world of poverty, the world of keeping the Dalits powerless, the Dalit's world of sickness, the world of spending childhood in malnutrition, the world of being unwanted, the world of jealousy-violence-hatred-abuse, the world of the multitudes staying alive, gasping." (Author's Note xix) Biswas does not prioritise himself over community as he says, "This is my autobiography, my father's autobiography, my grandfather's autobiography, my great grandfather's autobiography. This is the autobiography of remembering the bygone memories of my community." (78)

Like other Dalit autobiographies, *Surviving in My World* also brings out the distress and sufferings of the Dalit masses collectively in a heavily casteist and class-based society. It also depicts how Dalits have to live a life of deprivation, humiliation and repression but despite that the Namasudras have a rich history of struggle and uprising against their domination. Biswas locates the historiography of the struggle of Namasudras under the leadership of Harichand and Guruchand Thakur who awakened, organised the poor and disadvantaged Namasudras and mobilised them to fight for their rights. The Matua sect founded by them vocalised Dalit issues and inspired them to educate themselves and assert their dignity and identity. Bringing out the vitality and scope of Matua, Bandyopadhyay writes, "By the beginning of the twentieth century, the movement proceeded on two very distinct lines. On one hand, the educated leadership of the community chose to travel along the path of modern constitutional politics, and actively opposed the Congress-led nationalist movements, including the Gandhian mass movements. Side by side, there was also a transcendental mode of assertion of the Namasudra identity through the evolution of a religious sect called Matua, which followed the radical tradition of interrogating the notion of caste hierarchy and Brahmanical domination. This autobiography gives us a fair idea of what motivated the poor Namasudra peasants to engage in this protest movement." (Foreword xii) Matua, subsequently became the popular faith for Dalits for its opposition against caste system and its demand of a democratic and equalitarian socio-cultural and economic system. According to Praskanva Sinharay, Matua Mahasangha played a significant role in contemporary politics in West Bengal. It is the mouthpiece of Dalits and the repressed socio-economic groups there. (154) Biswas's *Surviving in My World* not only acknowledges the contribution of Harichand, Guruchand Thakur and their Matua, but also carries forward the Dalits' legacy of protest and brings out their strategies to counter caste and liberate themselves.

Biswas exposes the mechanism of caste and revolts against it. He writes sarcastically that the high castes would not enter Dalit localities as they were scared of the pollution resulting from contact. The author maintains that Dalits have to make special arrangements for a priest if they want to perform some religious rites at their homes: "If *Thakurmashai*, the priest, visited someone's home for performing religious rites then arrangements have to be made for him to cook his own food. The women of the household would neatly smear one end of the veranda with cow dung, which acted as a cleanser and a disinfectant." (10-11) All Hindu Brahmins would not perform the rituals and customary worships even for those Namasudras who are devoted Hindus. The Brahmins consider it defiling to recite *mantras* for Dalits: "There were separate Brahmin priests for conducting rituals in low caste shudra homes. Just as the lower castes were abhorred, similarly, the priest who came to worship in our homes did not get adequate respect in society because of being low status '*baun*' – Brahmin. They were known as the bauns of the charals, or priests of the outcastes." (68-69) Biswas criticises the Manuism that animal waste is more precious and purer than the lower castes. The author scorns the high castes who place themselves at the centre of power and discount Dalits and their ways of life. He describes that the Namasudras were reviled for eating pork as it was considered the food of lowly people. Biswas finds it hypocritical to link purity and pollution with food. (9) Biswas rejoices pork-eating to defy the high caste hegemony and to assert Dalithood. He announces openly that fish was the favourite dish of the Bengali Dalit families including Namasudras. He writes about his delight in fishing without paying any heed to the Hindu religious beliefs. He is proud of his community and culture which fills him with confidence and makes him rebel against the dominance of the high castes. He problematises the long preserved Hindu socio-religious assumptions and exposes the hypocrisy of the high castes who consider the flesh of sheep and goats pure and offer it to their gods, while consider pig unfit for eating by low castes. The idea of hating Dalits for their eating habits is also militantly opposed by Marathi Dalit autobiographers such as Daya Pawar, Sharankumar Limbale, Baby Kamble, Urmila Pawar and others in their respective life stories.

Biswas maintains that caste not only leads Dalits to social exclusion but also alienates them from power structures and exposes them to severe economic exploitation. Caste obstructs the economic progression of Dalits as it does not allow them access to education or run any beneficial business. Biswas writes that caste did not allow Namasudras to become boatmen: "If on the same spot there were boats of Muslims and Shudras, the high caste Hindus usually avoided the latter. They preferred to board a Muslim's boat." (56) The caste system keeps Dalits relegated to the socio-economic margins without any scope and hope for change and improvement in their lives. "Phores, middlemen appointed by the rich, bought rice and jute at cheap rates from the houses. Many times, there would not be any surplus to sell in many homes, but it was sold regardless. They were compelled to sell in order to buy necessities like oil, salt and garments. If the produce was destroyed by floods, saline water or sometimes by parali insects, the situation would turn grave. Then their agricultural lands passed into the grip of moneylenders. Farming bullocks were sold, and so were ducks or goats." (58-59) Biswas argues that: "Socially, economically, culturally and educationally, we were a massive heap of garbage at the bottom. We had failed to transform ourselves into resources. We remained a waste." (56) They were obstructed by caste in their efforts to become economically self-dependent and were coerced to survive on physical labour only.

Surviving in My World exposes and problematises Dalit sufferings and demonstrates a strong Dalit consciousness. It discusses the strategies to counter caste and liberate Dalits from social and economic slavery. Driss opines that this life story "is a powerful exposé of the life of Dalits in Bengal before and after partition. Fragments of childhood memories narrate the lot of the caste-ridden community of Namasudras, living in a marginal small village in East Bengal." (n. page) Biswas is influenced by Phule and Ambedkar as their ideologies clearly reflect in his life account. Biswas's emphasis on education and his appeal to Dalits to unite and agitate indicates that he was completely swayed by what Ambedkar suggested to liberate Dalits and annihilate caste. He does not discontinue his studies despite poverty, famine and displacement as his grandfather and father always encouraged him to educate himself. Despite wretched poverty and scarcity of food his grandfather was keen to educate his grandchildren. His father was also aware that it is only through education that Dalits can improve their socio-economic condition and create a space for themselves: "Baba believed that education would bring a new phase in our lives. Even if we could not become judges or barristers, nothing could stop us from becoming at least a lawyer's moktar or clerk. The children could reach some learned occupation and become babus. Even if they could not become a great bureaucrat in a government office, what could stop them from joining the police force as a low-level employee selected for physical strength, like a faujdar, or a guard, like peyada?" (4-5) *Surviving in My World* illustrates how education can make Dalits conscious of their subordination and how it can lessen their oppression in social and economic domains.

Like Valmiki, Biswas also believes that education and economic liberty can minimise the oppression of Dalits but they cannot abolish caste. Biswas shows that even highly educated high caste people are not free from the edicts of caste and the educated Dalits are equal victims of this system. His high caste friend Rushita's mother, who was a university Professor, also talks in a casteist way. Describing the inexorableness of caste, Biswas says, "There is caste discrimination in this country: some castes are considered high and some low. In spite of being an equal or even a little higher in educational qualifications, I failed to become equal to Rushita." (85) Biswas maintains that caste remains the prime determiner of one's social status, irrespective of a person's abilities and intelligence.

Surviving in My World exhibits an awakened Dalit consciousness and voices protest against the caste system and class based differences. Like other Dalit autobiographers, Biswas also locates the roots of Dalit suffering in religion. He opines that being a non-missionary static religion, Hinduism will not allow Dalits to surmount the steps of caste hierarchy and the high caste Hindus will never accept Dalits as their equals. Like Valmiki, Biswas also condemns the Gandhian standpoint on caste and Dalits and rejects his theory of internal reform. He argues that Dalits should abandon Hinduism as it has no respect or place for them. He writes that because of the growing influence of Matua faith and Ambedkarism most Namasudras have discontinued to observe Hindu customs and religious practices. They do not worship Hindu gods and instead they venerate Harichand Thakur as their god who was born in their community and fought for their manumission, dignity and identity. It is because of the non-Hindu religious practices that the author imbibed Dalit consciousness early in his childhood and voices his protest against Hinduism. He rejects the custom of the popular 'Durga *Puja*' in Bengal. He does not like Durga *mata* killing a dark-skinned naked person.

Biswas vociferously asserts his identity as a Namasudra Dalit: "Just as everyone is proud of their community, I am no exception." (57) Das says that Biswas's autobiography "records his deep sense of regard for his community. Their social traditions and practices are deeply rooted in him. Through his journey from childhood to maturity Biswas has experienced the cruel face of poverty, hunger, starvation, caste oppression and social exclusion. This social ostracism does not alienate him from his cultural roots, but celebrates the rituals and cultural heritage." (n. page) He maintains that Dalits are not inferior and incapable by birth; it is not the dearth of talent and intelligence that kept them poor, deprived and subordinated to the high castes, rather it is because of the prejudice of caste, illiteracy, religious deceits and lack of opportunities that they remained marginalised, poor and deprived over centuries. Biswas praises his Jetha: "What I wanted to say about my Jetha is that a kind of 'inventiveness' worked in him. No one had ever used a *patadheki* in our village before. The use of patadheki in flattening the Nal reeds lessened the strenuous labour to a great extent. Earlier, Nal reeds would be flattened by using a heavy wooden mace." (63) Biswas maintains that Dalits may be poor, disadvantaged and illiterate but they do not lack wisdom and intelligence. Organised and mobilised by Dalit intellectuals such as Harichand Thakur, Guruchand Thakur, Jogendra Nath Mandal and others, Dalits demanded social independence and equal economic and educational opportunities before political freedom from colonial rulers. They also opposed the partition of the country as in their opinion partition was being supported by self-seeking politicians. S Johny says that the author "refuses the general belief that partition was based on religion. Biswas argues that partition was the result of vested interest of a few rich people." (46) Dalits believed in communal harmony and national integrity. They did not loath Muslims for their different faith and distinct religio-cultural identity. Biswas praises Namasudras for their sense of dignity and autonomy despite acute adversities and repression. He writes that Namasudras had an indomitable spirit and even the repression of centuries could not defeat them or break their spirit.

Biswas praises Dalits for their inherent talent, abilities and wisdom and writes that social evils such as dowry system, *sati pratha* and ascetic widowhood are not prevalent among Dalits. "The widows of my community were accustomed to eating fish and meat. This practice remains among them even today. The strict restriction of widow remarriage was also not prevalent among them." (51) Biswas maintains that Dalit women have a slightly liberated and elevated status as compared to the non-Dalit women but this does not mean that Dalit women are absolutely free and have equal status within Dalit households. He shows that education of women is not taken seriously within Dalit households and communities. Dalit girls were given away in marriage at a small and tender age without caring for their physical and psychological immaturities. Biswas further argues that Dalit women were more deprived, disadvantaged and neglected as compared to Dalit men. Constant repression, humiliation, indifference and starvation sometimes forced them to commit suicide. Muron's young wife commits suicide because her life was ruined by her family by marrying her to him simply to cure his mental sickness. Muron is hardly aware that he is married to a woman who needs his support, love and compassion. His wife says: "I have not experienced what a husband is. What will I do by staying here? If I return to my father's place, no one will feed me. I will get more peace in death than in living." (47) The rampant rigid gender bias comes out when her death was not even mourned by her family members. This brings out the patriarchal insensitivities and also shows how women are dehumanised and considered nothing more than subordinate to men.

Surviving in My World is an authentic record of the pain and distress of Dalit masses and highpoints how caste joins class to exploit Dalits in every sphere of life. Awakened by education and personal exposure to the Dalit movement in Maharashtra, Biswas strikes at the very roots of the sufferings of Dalit masses. He offers powerful alternatives to replace the existing caste and class based power structures and relations. He rejects the high caste Hindu culture and detonates the myth and ideology of mainstream Bengali '*bhadralok*' that despises and looks down upon Dalit or the '*chotolok*' culture. He advocates the initiation of an egalitarian socio-economic and cultural system that allows Dalits an equal space and access to power structures. The voice that this autobiography evinces is transformative and liberatory in nature.

Interrogating My Chandal Life

Interrogating My Chandal Life is the English translation of Manoranjan Byapari's Bangla autobiography *Itibritte Chandal Jivan* published in 2014. It is an authentic description of the pain and sufferings that the author undergoes on account of his caste and class in the years of severe social, political, cultural and economic mayhem in divided India. Although, this life story offers a huge place for the author's physical, psychological, intellectual growth and also shows his struggle for justice and equity amidst severe oppression and obstruction from dominant socio-economic forces but like other Dalit autobiographies, it also offers a wider scope. The narrative is not limited solely to the description of the author's upbringing, maturing, aspirations and achievements. Like *Joothan* and *Surviving in My World*, *Interrogating My Chandal Life* also brings community to the focus.

Describing the nature and purpose of his writings in an interview with Jaydeep Sarangi, Byapari says that his writings represent all those people who are subjected to dehumanisation, discrimination and exploitation and are forced to live in inhuman circumstances. (n. page) This life narrative depicts the miserable and impoverished lives that Dalits, women, refugees and tribals were coerced to lead. It reconstructs the history of calamitous partition that made millions of Indians homeless and spread hatred among them in the name of religion and community. This also led to severe identity crisis among Dalit refugees that made their lives more miserable as compared to the Dalits of other regions. The author explores myths to describe Dalit lives and also uses literary devices such as impersonation, pun, humour and irony to scorn the institutions of caste, class and religion. The title specifies exploration and assertion of Dalit identity and the content is a realistic description of the lives of Dalits in Bengal.

A Namasudra by caste, Byapari was born in 1950 at a small place called Turuk-khali near the village of Pirichpur of Barisal district in Eastern Pakistan. He and his family moved to Bengal after the traumatic partition of the country and the outbreak of rancorous, violent communal riots on both sides. After spending several days on a platform at Sealdah Station, Byapari and his family were sent to the Shiromanipur Camp in Bankura district where thousands of refugees were already living. Unable to bear the wrenches of hunger, humiliation and dehumanisation, he fled from his home at the refugee camp in pursuit of a better life and humanity. He visited the frontiers of Calcutta, Assam, Siliguri, and Darjeeling and also went to Lucknow in search of food and employment. He had to face humiliation, exploitation and violence in callous caste and class biased society. Besides, he was subjected to scandalous sexual exploitations unleashed on him thrice - by a high caste cook Amulya Thakur, an unknown giant and a heartless police man. He was also exploited and cheated by a shopkeeper Binode Saha who lured him to work on the promise of paying him every month. He did not pay him and forced him to leave without a penny.

Byapari worked hard throughout his life but could not procure enough food to feed his family. He sold wood and worked as a supervisor at the construction work of a dam being built across the river at Palachur. Beleaguered by wretched poverty and constant starvation he also worked as a rickshaw-puller, laboratory cleaner, incharge of a crematorium and then a jungle *chowkidar* (guard). Although, Byapari suffered severe adversities, led a wretched life but he had an awakened social, economic and political conscious. Desperate and aggrieved with the existing unjust, inequalitarian socio-economic and political system, he joined the Naxalite movement after coming back to Calcutta from a futile and horrifying journey. Fascinated by the idea of a just and egalitarian society he worked enthusiastically and altruistically with activists and revolutionaries such as Ashu Majumdar, Khoka Chakraborty, Tata Dutta, Khoka Das, Nanu Das, Mohit Barman and others. It was during his activism in Naxalism that he had a narrow escape when a bomb exploded in his hands in Bardhaman. He was imprisoned for his indulgence in the naxalite activities. Byapari was beaten and tortured in jail but despite all this he learned to read and write there. After his acquittal, while living in Jadavpur, his fortuitous meeting with famous Bangla writer Mahasweta Devi encouraged and directed his literary pursuits. Being a conscious and committed Dalit, Byapari joined the political activism once again and worked enthusiastically with the popular leader Shankar Guha Niyogi and Chhattisgarh Mukti Morcha. After the assassination of Niyogi, Byapari also left Chhattisgarh and came back to Calcutta and started working as a cook in a residential school. It was here that he resumed writing seriously and began publishing.

This autobiography opens with the description of the author's familial conditions and the catastrophic socio-political and economic circumstances that made his family and many other hapless, impoverished masses leave their homes in Eastern Pakistan and migrate to Bengal. Byapari writes that Dalits were deprived and disadvantaged and coerced by wretched poverty to work for the landholding high caste Bhattacharyya families for survival. Most Dalit families were living in mud huts and there was always scarcity of food and clothes in these houses. (1) Describing his birth, Byapari writes, "The elders of our land say if you give a child a drop of honey on his entry into the world, his life will be sweetened. So, when my father arrived, she asked him to get a little bit of honey for me. This made my father break down in tears. How would he get honey when he could hardly manage rice? There had been no honey at his birth either. And he knew well the agony, the misery, the humiliation of a life bereft of sweetness. So, I got no taste of honey at my birth. My life has not been sweet. I have lived my life as an ill-fated Dalit son of an ill-fated Dalit father, condemned to a life of bitterness." (4)

Byapari maintains that the lives of impoverished caste-ridden Dalits were further embittered by the partition of the country as it not only triggered violence and spread hatred among masses but also displaced millions on the basis of religion. The religious minorities who crossed the borders in search of home had to suffer humiliation, homelessness and starvation as there were no proper arrangements nor a uniform law nor any plan for their rehabilitation on both sides. Refugees were stuffed into small canvas tents and given spoilt food to eat. Consumption of unwholesome food, constant starvation, malnutrition, poverty and outbreak of epidemics affected refugees and made them lose their lives tragically. Byapari details how his sister Manju also died of malnutrition and scarcity of food at the Ghola Doltala camp. (37) The constant foodlessness not only made Dalits eat inedible stuff such as grass and leaves but also turned them insane and inhumane:

"I saw then how hunger eats away at love and care. A mother, driven insane by her son's constant crying for food, threw him into a well. The well was dry and the child survived." (26-27)

Describing the conditions prevailing at the Shiromanipur Camp at Bankura district, Byapari writes that there was no proper water supply and not even a lavatory in or around the camp. Besides, refugees were also not given sufficient medical assistance so, naturally the ailing among them were certain to die: "It was like an epidemic of death, like an endless procession of death on every side. There was a stagnant pond about a mile down the road where the cremations were done. Throughout day and night, the pyres would burn and the sky would be clouded by smoke. It was mostly the elderly and the children who died. The adults would be cremated and the children buried." (17) The author maintains that the Indian Government was indifferent to the condition of refugees and the problems they were facing.

The Government and high ranking bureaucrats prepared a proposal to send refugees to the distant Andaman Islands. It was also proposed that they will be sent to Dandakaranya, a place filled with dense forests and haunted by wild animals. The Government used police force to repress refugees when they refused to leave Bengal. The rebellious refugees were beaten, tortured and arrested to crush their rebellion and to break their spirit. Exposing the police atrocities and treacheries against refugees, Byapari says, "The police were now following another manner of suppression. They would pick up a group of protesters in their vans, take them to a distance of twenty or twenty-five miles and set them free. The men had to walk back the entire distance to return home, exhausted and hungry.

The cunning officials realized that imprisoning these hungry refugees would only strengthen their rebellious spirit. Fed on prison meal, they would be able to stake their claims with greater vigour." (28) Byapari opines that the newly elected Indian Government was more unkind, unsympathetic and atrocious as compared to the colonial rulers.

The distant attitude of the Government is also shown when they did not take strict legal action against those zamindars who burned refugees' huts which they made on land near the Eastern Metropolitan Bypass. Government biases against refugees are further evident when they let zamindars encroach and occupy that land but did not allow refugees to live there. (45-46) Socially, politically and economically disadvantaged and displaced refugees could not account for the power of zamindars, police force and repression perpetrated by the Government. So, desperate with the prevalent situation, many of them enlisted for the Dandakaranya project and many others moved to nearby camps. Describing the attitude of the Government Bidisha Pal writes that the "Government leaders turned a clear niche from the lower caste Namo, Malo, Pod, Bagdi, Jele, Muchi and Kaoras who were reduced to nothing but sub-human species and the historical Marichjhapi Massacre that resulted from the superciliousness of the Government." (n. page)

Byapari criticises the Congress led Central Government and also problematises the attitude of Marxists towards refugees. Marxists lured despairing and desolate refugees by promises of fighting for their issues and getting them rehabilitated in Bengal itself. The author states that these assurances were nothing more than opportunism and guiles against impoverished refugees. The Communists continued to engross refugees in protest against the Central Government and thus deceitfully popularised themselves and their ideology among refugees and other disadvantaged and marginalised groups in Bengal. They used refugees to win sympathy and turn public opinion in their favour but their selfishness and avaricious drives were exposed when they came to power after winning the 1977 elections and Jyoti Basu became the Chief Minister of Bengal. Thrilled over the victory of communists, who claimed to be friends and saviours of the deprived and exploited masses, refugees sent their representatives to the Chief Minister with the demand of their rehabilitation in Bengal. But their dreams and aspirations were devastated when Chief Minster Basu showed disinclination to resolve their issue. He not only turned down refugees' demand to place them at Marichjhapi Island but also unleashed violence on those who tried to settle there. Byapari says, "Then began one of the most fearful chapters of the century's history as thousands of half-starved, unarmed people were beaten, raped and murdered. It is said that people were shot, bodies piled on boats and dumped in mid-sea and in the depths of the jungles." (240-41)

It is highly ironical that the party that was founded on the idea of justice and equality not only turned unjust and discriminatory against impoverished refugees but also ordered their ruthless killing. The communists' callousness and indifference to refugees was exposed when they insolently declared that no refugee was killed in police firing at Marichjhapi. This claim could not be disputed since there was no written record of the people who entered the island. Besides, there were no eye witnesses as the island was seized and even media representatives, political activists, sympathetic intellectuals, academics and writers could not enter. The author estimates that about two thousand people lost their lives in police firing and about two hundred women were subjected to brutal rape. (241) The Government also weaved a false narrative of illegal migrations from Bangladesh to justify the police firing at Marichjhapi and to withhold the public backlash and anger against them. Byapari criticises communists for their discriminatory and repressive attitude towards refugees and also exposes their hypocrisy and longing for power. He shows how communists swerved from their ideology and principles to lure high caste voters: "Earlier they would say that religion is like opium, it entranced the senses making rational thought impossible. Now they resolved that party members would take part in the religious festivities of Durga Puja and Kali Puja." (260) This resolution clarified that the only concern of the communists was to win elections, they were not honest to what they propagated and neither were they sincere in their efforts to eradicate discriminations and establish a just, egalitarian society.

Byapari brings out the pain and suffering that Dalits underwent in post-Independence India and also describes how caste subjected them to discrimination, humiliation, exploitation and deprivation in every sphere of life. The author offers an inclusive anthropological and mythological account of Namasudras and locates the different stages of their suffering and degradation in caste hierarchy. He writes that the Namasudras were Brahmins by birth and descended in caste hierarchy simply because their ancestor, Namas Muni, the son of great Kashyap Muni, forgot to perform the *Upanayan* ceremony for his sons as he remained lost in meditation for fourteen years in a jungle and thus, the best period for Upanayan elapsed. So, his sons could not be initiated into Brahminhood as Hindu Dharmashastras proclaim that even a Brahmin by birth remains Shudra without the Upanayan ceremony and wearing of the sacred thread ceremoniously. Consequently, the descendants of Namas Muni lost their primal place in social hierarchy and were treated as Shudras. (5)

Byapari argues that the Namasudras had a good status under the liberal regime of Buddhist Palas, but they began to lose their primal place after the fall of Palas and the rise of king Adisura. The new king subverted the Buddhist culture and belief system and endeavoured to revive the Vedic Dharma. But the Bengali Brahmins were not familiar with Vedas and Vedic rites. Adisura requested Virsingha, the king of Kanauj, to send five learned Brahmins to Bengal but Virsingha refused. He feared that any Brahmin sent to Bengal would succumb to the grave temptations and be doomed. Finally, Adisura sent seven hundred warriors wearing the sacred thread across their chests and riding on cows to Kanauj. A devoted and god-fearing Hindu, Virsingha accepted his defeat without any war and agreed to send five Brahmins to Bengal with those thread wearing warriors. Elated by this bloodless novel victory, the king granted Brahminhood to all the seven hundred warriors who helped him in securing five learned Brahmins from Kanauj and held Namasudras with more contempt.

The social downgrading of Namasudras continued in the reign of Ballal Sena of Sena dynasty who ascended the throne of Bengal after the reign of Adisura. The Namasudras opposed the king's decision of establishing his mistress's son as royal heir, and did not attend the feast that the king organised in honour of the proposed heir. This defiance angered the king and in order to punish the conceited Namasudras, he cast them out of society and ranked them with the Chandalas. (6-7) Since then, Namasudras began to be treated as lowborn, outcast and polluting in society and the Hindu religious places such as temples and shrines were closed for them. They were also dispossessed of land and property and put into servitude to the high castes. Byapari maintains that the Namasudras could not even improve their impoverished life conditions in the Muslim rule that came into Bengal after the Sena dynasty. This rule continued for seven hundred years but obstructed by prejudice of caste, the Namasudras remained disadvantaged and marginalised. They were kept poor and deprived even during the British rule. (8-9)

It was in the latter half of the nineteenth century that organised by Harichand Thakur and his son Guruchand Thakur that Namasudras fought for their socio-religious rights and dignity in Bengal. The organised Namasudras rebelled against their listing as Chandalas by the high caste colonial officers in the 1872 census: "Millions of Namasudras had arisen from their stupor of centuries under the leadership of Guruchand and strengthened by Matua faith which denounced the superiority of the Vedas and the Brahmins, began believing in their human worth and dignity. Faced with the unified strength of this large community, the British Government in 1911 changed the name of the community from Chandalas to Namasudra in the Census records." (10) Led by Harichand and Guruchand Thakur, the Namasudras struggled for their identity and dignity but this first expression of sustained resistance could not bring about any structural transformation in the institution of caste and in Dalit lives in general. Changing the name of the community from Chandalas to Namasudras could not remove the mark of untouchability. Describing the insignificance of the Namasudra movement, Byapari says, "I believe this struggle of four decades from 1872-1911 has been useless and futile. A century has passed after 1911. What has the community gained by divesting itself of its Chandal name, by ensuring entry into the Varna fold with the Namasudra name? The respect and humanity sought from the Varna elite has remained elusive. It is not a change of name but a change of heart and mind that was required. The Namasudra community has remained neglected and humiliated because that has not happened. We have no reason to believe that even an inch of dignity has been gained." (10-11)

Illustrating on the historiography of caste, rules of untouchability and their implications in the lives of Dalits, Byapari further argues that caste has kept the Dalits poor, dispossessed, illiterate and unconscious of their marginalised condition over centuries. He states that the roots of discrimination can be located in the ancient Varna system where the top three Varnas were granted all kinds of privileges and Shudras were kept poor, illiterate and unprivileged. Criticising the Hindu Varna system and its inherent biases, Byapari writes, "Belonging to the lowest strata and deserving only contempt, the Shudras can lay no claim to knowledge, wealth or dignity. Our great Hinduism directs the high-born Hindu to cut off the tongue of any Shudra who reads the Vedas, to pour hot molten lead into the ears of any Shudra who hears the Vedas being recited, to put to death any Shudra who touches a Brahmin." (8) The laws of Varna were hard and rigorous for the people of lower strata whereas, they are many privileges and relaxations for Brahmins, the chief architects of this system. For instance, it is provided that a Brahmin who kills a Shudra can unfetter himself from sin simply by reciting the Gayatri mantra for three days and bathing in River Ganga as penance. Byapari writes, "The Shastras also ordain that the habitations of Chandalas should be distant from the village. Burning of corpses and breeding of dogs or pigs would be his occupation. Not allowed to build any permanent housing, he would be required to move from place to place. He would not be allowed to acquire education or keep any name that hinted at dignity. He would need to remain alert so his polluting shadow would not fall on any Brahmin's body." (8-9) The rules of caste and class as scripted in the Hindu religious texts, turned more rigid and gruesome over the years. Byapari argues that the prejudice of caste discounts the personhood of Dalits and forces them to lead lives full of scarcity and humiliation. Relating his own experiences, the author writes that he was first exposed to the brutality of caste when he ran away from his home and started working for a high caste doctor at Ghutiari Sharif station. He shows how the high caste master and his family exploited and treated him as a despicable animal because of his impoverished condition and outcaste status. Describing his horrifying experiences at the doctor's house, Byapari says, "My entry into this house showed me for the first time the ugly side of our Hindu faith and our position within its social system. I was a Namasudra, the caste group earlier called Chandal. These people knew this and treated me as a dirty detestable animal. The plate from which I ate was an old and twisted one on which the lady of the house would let fall the rice and vegetables from a considerable height so as to evade my polluting touch. I would take that food and sit in a corner of the courtyard like a beggar.

This plate could not enter the house and so, after washing it, I would keep it in the cowshed. That was also the place where I slept, on a few sacks of ghute, the fuel made out of dried cow dung. The stench of the cow's urine and the bites of mosquitoes would not let me sleep much during the night." (42-43)

In addition, the doctor and his wife used to scold and beat him frequently even on slightest pretexts without considering his age and physical abilities. Here, like Valmiki and Biswas, Byapari also maintains that even the highly educated non-Dalits are not free from the prejudices of caste. They dehumanise the lower castes and unleash severe violence on them. He was hardly ten years old when he took his first job as a goatherd in the village that was close to his camp. (30-31) After this job, he also worked in a tea shop in Jadavpur (45) but he was exploited in every job. Byapari maintains that poverty and homelessness made him vulnerable to the external world and subjected him to violence, molestation and rape. Detailing his molestation by the head cook Amulya Thakur at Sibpur Police Mess, Byapari says, "One night, returning drunk with rum, he came up close to me, pushed his dirty lungi to one side, took out his filthy, nauseating male organ and placing it on the palm of my hand without the least hesitation, said, 'Here massage it a bit.' My mind rebelled at the deed but, shutting off my senses, I obliged, yearning to be let off. But Amulya Thakur had no qualms of imposing himself on a helpless boy and wanted to carry this further. 'That's enough,' he said. 'Now turn over and lie down.'" (55-56) Amulya got angry when Byapari refused to obey him. He used his influence and forced him to leave the job.

Again because of his poverty and homelessness Byapari

was raped by a havildar (policeman) in Lucknow. (96-97) He could not resist his rape because of his physical fragility and socio-economic vulnerability. It is both ironical and scornful that a person meant to protect people and maintain law and order victimises the poor and vulnerable in a society. The author regrets that his rape went unnoticed and unreported as he thought that there is no legal provision against the rape of a man by another man. He was also exploited by Binode Saha for whom he worked as a general help in his tea shop in Assam. (71-72) It is evident that there was no law protecting poor Dalits and they were looted, exploited and beaten by the powerful people in society. The author's brother Chitta was also beaten by the high caste political leaders Anil, Bilu and Basak, in the false case of stealing a duck. (117-19) The beating of Meghnad's father by a local *jotedar* (rich peasant) is the best illustration of how poverty and starvation led to the violation of human rights of Dalits: "Meghnad's father, unable to bear the pangs of hunger, stole half a sackful of grain from a jotedar's store one day. But the rice from the grains did not reach the empty stomachs of the family. The jotedar had spies everywhere and the sound of threshing was heard by a neighbour who carried the tale to the jotedar. Meghnad's father was brought before the jotedar who ordered the bones of his two hands to be crushed by the blacksmith's hammer. This was done so that the sight of him would drive fear into the hearts of the villagers and no villager would henceforth dare to steal grain for his hungry family." (171)

Criticising the caste based Indian capitalism, Byapari maintains: "This capitalist system was strange. The emotions of kindness, consideration, affection and love had no role. Its rationale was on the basis of give-and-take, and interactions were judged on the basis of returns made." (75-76) Byapari maintains that Dalits still have to hide their caste to secure a job and earn money. For instance, a Dalit named Megha Das, who offered work to Byapari, told him that it is mandatory for Dalits to conceal their castes if they want to earn money: "Don't tell people this name. And if people ask your caste, say it is Kayastha." (110) Describing the pangs of caste and caste based humiliation Byapari further relates how once he and his low caste friend and colleague Dukhe were insulted for coking for a feast in a non-Dalit household when they came to know their castes. (115-16) Exposing the hypocrisy of the high caste refugees in the camps Byapari writes, "The upper caste was unwilling to stay at camps with the Muchi, Nama and Jele." (20-21) The lower caste refugees were not only discriminated against but were also beaten and humiliated by the high caste officials when they raised their voice for rehabilitation in Calcutta. Exposing the prevalent biases Byapari states, "Partly as a consequence of having some education, they could negotiate with the leaders, partly through the wily network of communal brotherhood and relatives they managed, with active cooperation of political leaders and bureaucrats to secure land and means of livelihood in this new land. They were taken care of and the truth is that many among them had not been as well cared for in East Bengal. The other millions who had come over, honest workers of the land, could not find space in any of these forcibly occupied colonies because the primary condition to being given land here was education and the bhadralok identity - an identity that was unaffordable to all but the upper castes." (21)

In the interview with Sarangi, Gurav and Dutta, Manohar Mouli Biswas also talks of a similar kind of discrimination against Dalit refugees in India: "Yes, in the refugee camp people with good caste pearls in their pockets received preference in settlement in market areas, business centres, developed areas and posh localities; whereas, those having bad caste pearls in their pockets were given settlements in hilly areas, barren lands, unproductive areas, marshes." (91) Byapari exposes every aspect of caste and brings out Dalits' chauvinistic adherence to casteism and scorns them for practicing untouchability: "The laws of the village were both severe and hidebound in those days. My great uncle had lost his caste by accepting food from a Muslim. Thus, it came to pass that the youngest son of my grandfather's family became a *Khere*. One who converted from Hinduism to Islam was called a Khere." (13) Byapari further writes, "What a cursed life we had. We call ourselves Hindus and worship idols. For this reason, the Muslims look upon us as *kafirs*. Because we belong to the lower-caste Namasudra community, the upper Hindu castes treat us with contempt and spit on us." (41)

Exposing the mechanism and stringency of the caste system, Byapari argues that Dalits were (and still are) despised and humiliated by non-Dalits for their caste and untidy appearance. The sweepers and the scavengers were subjected to more severe social disparagement and exploitation. They were not allowed in public places such as hotels and common tea shops. (254) Ridiculing the caste and untouchability Bypari further writes, "In the Indian social system, and in the minds of Bengalis, especially the urban-resident Bengalis, three words are inextricably linked with each other: lowly folk, lowly caste, physical labour. All who are of low caste are lowly. They are the ones who pull carts, carry loads, wash utensils, and do many other forms of physical labour to fill their stomachs. And the ones who are gentlemen, live in nice houses, eat nice food, and work in such a manner that no sweat dirties their clothes. Within this narrow and limited orbit, lies all their vanity and conceit." (120) The prejudices of caste and class were so common that even the high caste, class children were aware of them and avoided playing with him and his siblings. (120) Bringing out the high caste people's abhorrence for low castes and poor, Byapari writes, "The children too are infected by the surroundings. Their impressionable minds are etched with this 'we' and 'they' division of class. No poor man can think of himself as a gentleman today. They are scared of doing so; they are embarrassed of doing so." (121) Dalits and poor have conditioned themselves to think and behave in the caste and class specific ways. Illustrating it further, the writer says, "I had once gone in search of a man who lived near Radha Housing near the Bypass. He had told me that he lived right behind the Housing. He was a van-rickshaw driver. On arriving behind the housing, I found three or more hutments in a row. Not able to understand which of them was this man's house, I asked a young girl standing there, 'There is a gentleman who lives here. He drives the van-rickshaw. Can you tell me which is his house?' My question put the girl in a dilemma. She said, 'the gentlemen here all live in that Housing. None of them drive van-rickshaws. My father does drive one, but he is…' The girl was about twenty-four, more or less educated, and working at Devi Shetty's Hospital. But she too had been conditioned to not think of her van-rickshaw driving father as a gentleman."

(121) It was the result of severe repression that poor Dalits have internalised oppression and surrendered to dominant forces.

Byapari problematises every institution, custom or law that discriminates against Dalits and victimises them. His voice is a collective articulation of the issues of Dalits, women, prostitutes, children, tribals and other vulnerable, silenced and marginalised groups. As a construct of caste, Indian patriarchy imposed severe restrictions and prohibitions on women and subjected them to evils such as *sati*, *purdah* and child marriages. High caste men have always been scared that they can lose their caste purity and pride if they left women's sexuality unguarded and unrestricted. Concepts such as chastity, virginity and *pativrat* were sternly imposed on women by casteist and patriarchal forces so they can repress their sexuality. Byapari scorns general patriarchal attitude towards women and shows how they are treated as objects of sex. Afflicted by poverty, hunger and homelessness many of the refugee women were hauled into prostitution. The author gives the example of his friend Naresh Thakur, whose mother, aunt and daughter became prostitutes. (111-112) Numerous impoverished and helpless refugee women were molested, raped, beaten, tortured and murdered by the ruffians or they were abducted, sold and purchased like animals by the rich men.

Byapari writes that like refugees, the tribal women were also frequent victims of exploitation, molestation and rape by non-tribal men. Describing the condition of tribal women working in the Palachur Dam construction Byapari writes, "There were many women workers at the site and the hunters would accost them as they returned from work. With the lure of money, saree, silver, or plain words, they would persuade the women onto their bikes. Some of the young girls were willing to be lured, others would be forced." (326) Although, the tribals were well aware of all this, they did not protest against it; they seemed to have accepted it as something they cannot resolve or change. It was mainly because powerful government agencies such as police, judiciary and media also had prejudices against them, so, the crimes against tribal women were not reported. In most cases of rape and violence against tribal women, the culprits were not convicted and the victims themselves were held responsible. (316) Byapari represents women as a unit and demands a just and viable space for them. The author admires and respects his mother and wife, and duly acknowledges their contribution in his life. Expressing his gratitude to his mother Byapari writes, "Ma, my debt to you remains unpaid. The debt of milk is a lifetime's debt." (147) His respect for women is further evident when he shows concern for his wife who was working hard for the family: "Anu was still working at her *Anganwadi* job. Cycling ten kilometres up and ten kilometres down. Her first baby had been born through a caesarean operation, the second was a 'forcep baby', and then there had been the *nasbandi* operation. Only she knew how painful it was cycling over hilly roads after these operations. I could hardly bear to look at her perspiring, exhausted face, burnt copper by the sun when she returned from work." (336-37) Mahadevan Dasgupta writes that Byapari's narrative is about the need for compassion and dignity in all human relationships. He does not seem to have bowdlerised his mother and his wife's behaviour and actions; he presents them as they are. Women, as depicted in this life narrative are the victims of caste, poverty and patriarchal oppression.

Interrogating My Chandal Life brings out the distress that marginalised groups undergo in different spheres of their lives. Like *Joothan* and *Surviving in My World*, this also evinces an awakened voice of protest that speaks at multiple levels. Byapari condemns all forms of oppression unleashed on marginalised groups and vocalises demand for justice and equity. He fights against injustices despite numerous handicaps such as illiteracy, poverty and homelessness. He endures humiliation, exploitation, violence and sexual assaults in the initial years of his life but as a grown-up he transforms his pain into power and fights back. With the course of time, he overcomes his pitiable, impoverished life condition and exuviates the identity of a lower caste or a chhotolok. He learns reading and writing, makes economic progression and brings stability in his life and thus challenges the bhadralok.

He strikes at the existing social, economic, political and religio-cultural systems for their unjustness and biases against Dalits. The author bursts into rage when he sees his father humiliated and beaten by a local high caste man, Anil Shah: "I swore against the All Merciful God. I denounce You as You who have never been with this man, your blind follower. I profess myself a worshiper of your rival, Satan. And I call upon Satan to give me strength. The hand which Anil has lifted against my father I would take apart from his shoulder. Give me success." (119) The author fights against the local high caste *Dadas* (goons) and chases them away when they come to beat him for scolding their siblings: "There was an axe which my father would take into the deep jungles to chop firewood. Now the axe was in my hands and I chased them. I had then forgotten that I was one and they were many, that I was weak and they were powerful, that I was poor and they were rich, and that the law of this land protected the rich and devoured the poor." (122)

In due time, he grew stronger and started to fight against local goons in Jadavpur to protect poor, helpless women and children: "Pickpockets, snatchers, kidnappers, pimps, and any colourful Romeo troubling girls from poor classes. I would thrash them all. Within days I became a terror for the goons of the locality. On the other hand, I began to be seen as saviour to many, especially the young maid servants who would come to the city to work as domestic helps." (152) He also saved a poor girl Anita, who he married later, from a local ruffian who was troubling and pestering her. (232-33) He also managed to punish Golam Gazi, who used to kidnap the poor children roaming around and sell them to rich Arab countries where the small babies were used for camel race in which they die crying. (154-56) He also fought against a high caste rich Bengali Babu when he insulted an elderly rickshaw driver, Haren Ghosh. Byapari replied defiantly when Babu asked Ghosh deprecatingly to drive him up to the station. The author not only replied back angrily but also threatened to break his hand if he tried to raise it. (153-54) The author's Dalit consciousness, strength, capacity to fight back and pursuits of empowerment, liberation and dignity are reflected in his retaliation and individual protest.

Byapari attempted to fight against rampant disparities and predispositions at every level and front. He joined naxalism to fight against the biased political system and to improve the miserable life condition of millions of deprived and underprivileged masses. Besides, he found that naxalites such as Ashu Majumdar and others were not craving for position, vote, power and luxury rather they were fighting for the poor and deprived like Byapari himself. They were fighting to establish a just and egalitarian social, political and economic system that would allow Dalits a viable space and grant them equity, dignity and rights. Describing his purpose of joining naxalism Byapari says, "What it wanted was to build a society that was classless, without exploitation, and egalitarian: a society that promised equality and equal respect to all. A society where there would be food, housing, education and medical facilities for all." (128) Inspired and invigorated by the revolutionary idealism of leaders and thinkers such as Che Guevara, Mao Zedong, Ashu Majumdar and others, Byapari struggled to transform the unjust and inequalitarian society. Byapari tried to counter caste through economic empowerment, so he remained deeply associated with far-left radical movements. He was part of many campaigns and movements for the emancipation of Dalits and economically depressed groups but he found them inadequate to annihilate caste and to abrogate the widening class disparities. So, finally he withdrew himself from leftist ideologies and movements and started working closely with Ambedkarites in Bengal.

He tried to awaken Dalits in Bengal and build an organisation on the lines of the Dalit movement in Maharashtra. (345) But soon he lost faith in Ambedkarism also. He found that both the Communists and Ambedkarites in Bengal were discriminatory and full of certain presumptions and contradictions. Expressing his disagreement Byapari writes, "I had forgotten that neither religion nor caste, nor culture, nor language could really play a role in making human beings humane and sympathetic. If some hold me in contempt as a Namasudra, others hold me in contempt as an illiterate, impoverished rickshaw-wallah.

This is why I have grown suspicious of the leaders of both communities. I have been marginalized by both groups." (346) Byapari maintains that anti-caste and class leaders were fanaticised by their respective ideologies and were self-seeking and unconcerned to the actual issues of the deprived groups. It was because of this indifference of the leaders of both groups that even after leaving naxalism, Byapari began to work with Niyogi whom he found more committed and honest. He compared him with Buddha: "Neogi could not be pigeon-holed into any single ideology. That would be difficult – no, an impossible endeavour. He was beyond all isms. He was a great humanist. The only person in history I can compare him with is Gautam Buddha who left the palace to come and stand with the poor and the suffering. Or with the great revolutionary Che Guevara." (299)

Byapari criticises the evils and superstitions widespread in the Indian society. He exposes the custom of human sacrifices prevalent among the tribals of Bengal and disparages their belief that their God, Anga will let good crops grow if they offer him human blood and also scatter it in the fields. (268; 329) He also writes how the feeling of communal violence that erupted after partition turned human beings into monsters and led to the murders of many innocent people. He gives his own example of how he also once killed one of the three rioters in self-defense. (50) He maintains that the self-seeking leaders of both communities: Hindu and Muslim spread hatred among the innocent and illiterate people and made them fight against each other. He writes how the tale of stealing the sacred lock of Hazrat Mohammad's hair in Kashmir was concocted by Muslim leaders to provoke violence against Hindus. The author knows the reality from people's discussion in the tea shop in Jadavpur where he was working. The mounting Hindu-Muslim hatred is also shown through the attitude of the doctor's wife for her husband's Muslim friends. The Doctor's wife was full of disgust and hatred for Muslims and does not like them to come to her house, sit and eat there. She considers them her enemy as she believes they compelled them to leave their homeland. (43) *Interrogating My Chandal Life* is a reflection not only of Dalit lives but also of the Indian society as a whole.

Although Byapari is full of anger against dominant and discriminatory forces, he does not spread vengeance or targets any individual. He also appreciates Dalits for their capacity to work hard and maintains that they do not leave humanity even in severe adversities. Appreciating their humanity, Byapari writes, "Our neighbours, friends and relatives from our community were as poor as us, their daily earnings going only as far as that day. Yet, there was no dearth of tenderness in their hearts, they would set aside a handful of rice from their meals for my mother." (1) Uma Mahadevan Dasgupta also writes, "*Interrogating My Chandal Life* is a powerful, affecting memoir about hunger and deprivation, but also endurance, struggle and a fierce will to live." (n. page) Most Dalit characters portrayed in this life narrative are illiterate, poor and subjected to the dominant caste and class forces but despite that they exhibit consciousness and strive to improve their miserable life conditions. The author's father, for instance, asserts his caste identity proudly and was not ashamed of being called a Namasudra. (5) He was well aware of the need of education for the empowerment of Dalits. He tried to educate his son. Although, he could not realise his dream because of poverty and homelessness but his Dalit consciousness is reflected in his thoughts and attempt. His dream was actualised only when the author learns to read and write in prison: "When eating, I drew letters on my curry-smeared plate. I wrote in my mind. I saw nothing but letters all around me. In people's faces, their smiles, their movements, the gestures of their hand. When the man dipped into his large bucket and then raised his hand to ladle out the food, I recognised a giant-sized Ta." (209)

Interrogating My Chandal Life exposes religion, gods, bourgeois morality, government, media, judiciary, police, politics and political parties as institutions that discount, dehumanise Dalits and exploit them in numerous ways. It is a vociferous assertion of Dalit rights, personhood, dignity and identity and brings out many instances of both personal and collective protest. The author suggests education, economic progression and landownership as contrivances to counter caste and empower Dalits. He wants Dalits to assert their identity, culture and desert Hinduism as the root of all ills and odds. He announces his departure from the Hindu belief system when he rejects Hindu gods and declares that the earth is not the creation of any God, rather it is created by the "Sun, an inextinguishable, eternal ball of fire." (276) *Interrogating My Chandal Life* is a powerful manifesto of Dalit liberation and enunciation of their collective rights. It adds significantly to the corpus of Bangla Dalit writings that strive to awaken and mobilise Dalits against existing disparities and discriminations.

Finally, in can be affirmed that despite different caste identities, socio-cultural, geographical locations and educational backgrounds of the writers, the selected autobiographies share certain commonalities in their understanding and representation of caste, class, culture and identity. Despite different ideological influences and political affiliations, they also exhibit almost similar visions, ideologies and alternatives. Every writer asserts his identity as a Dalit and eulogises his culture. The selected autobiographies are collective voices of pain and protest of Dalit masses, the individual portrayed in them is not separated from community. *Joothan* brings out the miserable lives of the *Chuhras* in Uttar Pradesh whereas, *Surviving in My World* and *Interrogating My Chandal Life* are authentic accounts of the miseries of impoverished Namasudras in Bengal. These autobiographies praise Dalits for their inherent capacity to work hard and survive despite severe repression. They attempt to devastate internal caste hierarchy and eradicate the superstitions prevalent among Dalits. These autobiographies are ideologically strong and protest with equal intensity for the liberation of Dalit masses and add significantly to their journey from erasion to enunciation.

Works Cited

- Arora, Namit. *Joothan: A Dalit's Life* – A Review." *Shunya*, 2010, n. page, www.shunya.net/ Text/Blog/Joothan.htm. Accessed 12 June 2020.
- Asaduddin, Mohd. "Asaduddin on Valmiki, *Joothan: An Untouchable's Life*." *H-Asia*, 2010, n.page, networks.h-net.org/node/22055/reviews/22166/asaduddin-valmiki-joothan-untouchables-life. Accessed 11 June 2020.

- Bandyopadhyay, Sekhar. Forward. *Surviving in My World: Growing Up Dalit in Bengal* by Manohar Mouli Biswas. Translated and edited by Angana Dutta and Jaydeep Sarangi. Samya, 2015, pp. xi-xiv.
- Biswas, Manohar Mouli, Author's Note. *Surviving in My World: Growing Up Dalit in Bengal* by Biswas. Translated and edited by Angana Dutta and Jaydeep Sarangi. Samya, 2015, pp. xv-xxi.
- Byapari, Manoranjan. *Interrogating My Chandal Life: An Autobiography of a Dalit*. Translated by Sipra Mukherjee, Sage/ Samya, 2018.
- Chakravarti, Uma. *Gendering Caste through a Feminist Lens*. Stree, 2003.
- Das, Suvasis. "The Subaltern can Speak: A Reading of Manohar Mouli Biswas's Autobiography *Surviving in My World: Growing up Dalit in Bengal*." *Course Hero*, n. page, www.coursehero.com/file/33958557/THE-SUBALTERN-CAN-SPEAK-A-READING-OF-MANdocx/. Accessed 12 June 2020.
- Dasgupta, Uma Mahadevan. Review. "*Interrogating My Chandal Life* Review: Everyman on the Margins." *The Hindu*, 20 Oct 2018, n. page, www.thehindu.com/books/books-reviews/interrogating-my-chandal-life-review-everyman-on-themargins/article25263122.ece. Accessed 2 April 2020.
- Driss, Hager Ben. "Book Review: Manohar Mouli Biswas, *Surviving in My World: Growing Up Dalit in Bengal*." *Research Gate*. 2016, n. page, www.researchgate.net/publication/305271777_Book_Review_Manohar_Mouli_Biswas_Surviving_in_My_World_Growing_Up_Dalit_in_Bengal. Accessed 3 June 2019.
- Johny, S. "Voices of a Subaltern Diaspora: A Reading of Manohar Mouli Biswas's *Surviving in My World*." *Research Journal of English Language and Literature*, vol. 5, no. 2, 2017, pp. 44-47,

www.rjelal.com. Accessed 17 June 2020.

- Kumar, Raj. *Dalit Personal Narratives: Reading Caste, Nation and Identity.* Orient Black Swan, 2010.
- Kumar, Vikas. *The Representation of Dalit in Dalit and Non-Dalit Literature*. Unistar Books, 2017.
- Kumar, Vinod. "Omprakash Valmiki's *Joothan: A Dalit's Life* as a Dalit Literary Text." *International Journal of Academic Research and Development,* vol. 1, no. 3, 2016, pp. 126-128, www.academicjournal.in. Accessed 12 June 2020.
- Mazumdar, Madhumita. "Investigating Narrative Voices in Biswas's *Ghatotkach and Hidimba: A Dialogue.*" *Episteme: An Online Interdisciplinary, Multidisciplinary and Multi-Cultural Journal*, vol. 7, no. 1, 2018, pp. 1-16, episteme.net.in. Accessed 17 June 2020.
- Meenu, Rajat Rani. *Hindi Dalit Katha Sahitya: Avdharanayan Aur Vidhayan* (*Hindi Dalit Prose Literature: Concepts and Genres*), Anamika, 2010.
- Mukherjee, Arun. Introduction. *Joothan: A Dalit's Life* by Omprakash Valmiki. Translated by Arun Prabha Mukherjee, Samya, 2007, pp. xi-xlii.
- Mukherjee, Sipra. Translator's Note. *Interrogating My Chandal Life: An Autobiography of a Dalit* by Manoranjan Byapari. Translated by Mukherjee, Sage/ Samya, 2018, pp. xv-xxii. Narang, Harish. "Dalits and the Indian Nation: Omprakash Valmiki's *Joothan.*" *The Politics of Literary Theory and Representation: Writings on Activism and Aesthetics*, edited by Pankaj K. Singh, Manohar, 2003, pp. 145-155.
- Pal, Bidisha. Review. "Interrogating My Chandal Life: An Autobiography of a Dalit by Manoranjan Byapari, translated by Sipra Mukherjee." *Rupkatha Journal on Interdisciplinary Studies*

in Humanities, vol. 10, no. 2, 2018, n. page, rupkatha.com/v10n227/. Accessed 11 March 2020.

- Phule, Jotirao. "Memorial Addressed to the Education Commission." 1882. *Selected Writings of Jotirao Phule*, edited and compiled by GP Deshpande, Left Word, 2002, 102-112. Sanyogita, Avinay Umesh. "A Book that Shows the Stark Difference between Knowing Caste Violence and Experiencing it." *Youth ke Awaaz*, 2016, n. page, www.youthkiawaaz.com/2016/03/omprakash-valmiki-joothan-caste-violence-against-dalits/. Accessed 12 June 2020.
- Sarangi, Jaydeep. Personal Interview. "From Wheels to Stalls: Jaydeep Sarangi in Conversation with Manoranjan Byapari." *Lapis Lazuli – An International Literary Journal*, vol. 2, no. 1, 2012, n. page, www.pintersociety.com. Accessed 2 April 2020.
- Sharma, Deeksha. "*Joothan* by Omprakash Valmiki – Book Review." *Feminism in India*, 2017, n. page, feminisminindia.com/2017/09/29/joothan-om-prakash-valmiki-review/. Accessed 12 June 2020.
- Shekhar, Hansda Sowvendra, "A Dalit Writer's Journey: of Multiple Identities and Struggles." *National Herald*, 2018, n. page, www.nationalheraldindia.com/reviews-recommendations/a-dalit-writers-journey-of-multiple-identities-and-struggles. Accessed 2 April 2020.
- Sinharay, Praskanva. "Building up the Harichand-Guruchand Movement: The Politics of the Matua Mahasangha." *The Politics of Caste in West Bengal*, edited by Uday Chandra, Geir Heierstad and Kenneth Bo Nielsen, Routledge, 2016, pp. 147-168.

CHAPTER 2

POLEMICS OF REPRESENTATION

THE PREVIOUS chapter was an attempt to examine how selected Dalit autobiographies apprehend, represent the issues of caste, class, culture and identity and what are their strategies to counter them and ultimately liberate Dalits from oppression, injustices and atrocities. The present chapter seeks to locate the images of Dalit women as they are constructed and portrayed in Daya Pawar's *Baluta*, Sharankumar Limbale's *The Outcaste* and Balbir Madhopuri's *Changiya Rukh*. It further seeks to discover how selected writers present Dalit women in their life narratives, what is their standpoint on their specific sufferings and how they respond to internal patriarchy and gender biases. Although, Dalit autobiographies speak for community, revolt collectively against caste based power structures and attempt to secure justice and equality, but modern Dalit feminist writers, theorists and critics opine that most Dalit male life narratives do not represent Dalit women's issues adequately. The severe patriarchal oppression that Dalit women undergo within their own households and community is not a concern for them. They argue that the male autobiographers present them in bits and fragments and merge their personhood and identity into the community.

With the spread of education and economic progression, Dalit men are adopting the sanskritised culture and coercing Dalit women to behave and act within the long designed Indian patriarchal laws that impose numerous restrictions and prohibitions in the name of civility, morality and *stree dharma*. Dalit women argue that they are still victims of gender politics even within their own households. The assertive and vocal Dalit women are scorned as fallen and degraded. Besides, derogatory terms such as *randi* (prostitute), *kulta* (one who goes against one's lineage) and *dayan* (demoness) are used to further humiliate, dehumanise and thwart their assertion of rights. For Dalit women, Dalit men are no way less exploitative and discriminatory as compared to the high caste men as both attempt to subjugate them and have authority over them. To bring out Dalit women's images as etched in selected autobiographics and also to find out to what extent they are true and rational in their criticism of Dalit male autobiographies, it is mandatory to examine each selected life story separately and alternately.

Baluta

Published in 1978, Daya Pawar's *Baluta* is regarded as the first full-fledged Dalit autobiography in Marathi. Its publication initiated a new trend in autobiographical writing in India as instead of individual it puts community at the centre of the narrative. It is not merely an account of the author's suffering, his struggle against caste and class and his psycho-sexual conflicts, rather it is an authentic description of Mahar life amid repressive socio-cultural, economic, and political milieu of Maharashtra in the 1950s and 1960s. *Baluta* is unconventional as it does not follow chronology. Pawar begins with the circumstances of his birth and relates how his mother lost her ten or twelve children and how finally he survived and was named Dagad or Donda. (6) The author hints that he was born in or around 1935. He writes that as a child he could not have a stable life as his family frequently kept shifting from village to city and city to village. It affected his life and he found himself split between village and city. Pawar writes that after her husband's death, his grandmother, Devki came from the village to Bombay to escape caste based atrocities and settled in Kawakhana, where her relatives were already living.

The author tells us that he and his family had a miserable life at Kawakhana as caste and poverty were not less oppressive there. Describing socio-economic and geographical locations of Mahars, Pawar writes that they were forced to live on the outer margins in small thatched huts and were exploited both economically and culturally: "The Mahars lived in squalid homes, each the size of a henhouse, each henhouse having two or three sub-tenants. Wooden boxes acted as partitions." (7) Despite wretched poverty, starvation and severe caste repression, the author got an opportunity to go to school where he was humiliated, discriminated against and not given an opportunity to learn and grow. He says that caste prevailed in class rooms, hostels and even in playgrounds and thus, discouraged many Dalit students like him. Though Pawar faced discrimination and repression but he managed to complete his education. Finally, after a long struggle and many rejections he got a job as a clerk-cum-laboratory assistant in Parel Veterinary College.

(234) After this job, Pawar had economic stability.

Baluta offers a realistic insight into the Mahar life. Pawar writes that poor Mahars were made to perform all unhygienic and filthy works without wages. Abject poverty and starvation forced them to live on carrion and leftover food given by the high castes either for the discharge of their duty or in begging. The title itself brings out the essence of exploitation as 'Baluta' refers to the share given to Mahars from the village produce in discharge of their duties ranging from disposing carcasses to announcing events and playing music in village weddings. This autobiography exposes the mechanisms of Dalit sufferings and attacks the vitriolic caste conventions that lead to their dehumanisation. Pawar casts a wide range of characters in his life narratives as he talks of labourers, government employees, *devadasis*, prostitutes and eunuchs. His treatment of women is a distinguishing feature of his autobiography as he offers an adequate place for them. He gives voice to Dalit women's issues and writes about their struggle and show their inner conflicts and sexuality: "They worked harder than men. They scavenged the scraps of papers, rags, broken glass and iron from the street, sorted them and then sold them each morning. However much their drunkard husbands beat them, they continued to serve them and indulged their addiction." (7) Pawar maintains that caste and class force Dalit women to lead the life of sub-human beings but he argues that these are not the only exploiting and aggravating factors in their lives. The internal patriarchy is also equally exploitative and hostile towards them.

Pawar presents many women characters belonging to different castes, class, communities, cultures and ages in his autobiography. His grandmother Devki, his mother, his wife Saee and his sister are main Dalit women characters in this narrative. Devki becomes a widow at a young age when her husband dies of drinking. After her husband's death she works hard to feed her two young sons. She was humiliated and tortured in numerous ways by high caste men while performing her duty as *Yeskar* in the village. The author details how once she was mocked and insulted while delivering the message of "no frying, no eating oily things" as smallpox had broken out and as per custom the chariot of Mari-Aai (the goddess of fever and pox) had to be pushed through the villages to cure the infected. Devki was delivering this message but it irritated young Kondiba so he decided to make fun of her. He blocked her way and began to say, "Catch that Mahar woman, tie her up in the village square, she's run mad. Why is she telling us *Talloo-falloo naka*?" (13) People gathered and made fun of her. Devki fell on their feet but they did not listen to her. It was her influential brother-in-law who saved her from the pranksters. (13)

This incident affected Devki deeply and she decided to leave her village. She is a poor helpless widow and has nowhere to go but she does not surrender her dignity to the conceited high caste people. She leaves her village and comes to Bombay and settles in Kawakhana. She did several menial and unhygienic jobs including that of a sweeper and cleaner in a dog clinic. (10) Her earnings were too small to even buy things of daily use but she does not follow any dishonest way to make money. She works honestly and consecrates her whole life for her family. Pawar praises her sacrificing nature, selfless support and love for her orphaned family. Devki is a victim of caste, class and gender based discrimination and atrocities but she is not a pessimist and does not surrender to circumstances.

Her strength and pursuit of empowerment are reflected in her courage and struggle against the odds in her life. Pawar acknowledges her contribution and role in the survival of his family, his upbringing, education and career.

Pawar is frank, intimate and neutral in detailing his mother. He talks about the hardships and tribulations that she undergoes. He writes that his mother was an illiterate and traditional woman who believed in the conventional roles imposed on women. She is subordinated and unheeded by her husband who shirks his familial responsibilities and wastes money on drinking and philandering. Pawar writes that although his father does not beat his wife but he was a typical patriarch as he exercises his authority and ignores what his wife and family suffer. Pawar scorns his father's womanising and his concept of masculinity. He interrogates the patriarchal conventions and laws that give authority to men to control women however beautiful, good and talented they may be. Pawar's father chooses other ordinary women, ignores his beautiful wife and remains indifferent to her emotions. She smiles sadly when the author tells her of his father's secret meeting with a woman in an Irani restaurant. (25)

Pawar shows his mother as a victim of caste, poverty and patriarchy but she is not weak and pliable. Her strength is evident in her fighting bravely against the circumstances of life. She assumes the role of both father and mother after her husband's death and slogs hard to feed and educate her children. Acknowledging her mother's role in his education, Pawar writes, "I sometimes wonder, if Dada had lived, would I have become the person I am? Who knows whether I would have studied also or not? Aai's sacrifices gave me the impetus to push myself out of the abyss." (55) Pawar's mother exhibits Dalit consciousness in the Ambedkarite sense as despite wretched poverty and starvation she decides to educate her son. She is aware that education is the only way to come out from the slime of caste and poverty.

She also exhibits an acute sense of dignity and self-respect. She refuses to marry again after her husband's death and when her parents pressurise her, she asserts her dignity: "I am no beggar at your door. I will work and bring up my little ones." (54) She does many challenging and difficult jobs to educate her children. Pawar recognises her role in shaping his life, praises her for her assiduousness, honesty and the sacrifices she made for her family. He admits that his life would have been miserable without her but he does not deify or glorify her unnecessarily by concealing facts about her. He humanises her when he writes about her longing for a male child from her daughter-in-law in almost a patriarchal way (269) and scolds her son for being friendly and supportive of his wife. His mother warns him against his blind love for his wife: "Set her on your head … and she'll shit on it." (242) Pawar follows the middle path of humanising his mother's image. He does not employ the patriarchal strategy to glorify motherhood which plays a critical role in women's subordination and subjugation. He avoids the convention of either deifying or glorifying Dalit women.

Pawar's sister is another woman who he is very affectionate and supportive of. He is furious when some boys coerce her to dance on an erotic song in the hostel: "I am coming back from school one day, hungry and tired. When I get to the hostel, I hear boys singing in a closed room. Someone is beating an accompaniment on a tin. This is not a new thing in the hostel.

I peer in, casually, through a crack in the door. What I see makes me explode. My nine-or ten-year old sister is dancing and boys are watching her, delighting in it. They are singing an erotic *laavni* number." (174) Pawar scolds the boys and brings his minor sister back. The author is not only concerned about her security but also about her dignity. Pawar acknowledges his sister's contribution in his life. As a grownup woman she has been supportive of her brother when he was distressed and homeless. He presents his sister as a courageous woman who fights bravely against poverty and caste oppression. The author appreciates his sister but like his mother he does not idealise her.

Pawar's wife, Saee is the next important female character portrayed in this autobiography. Pawar is full of love and admiration for his wife: "Saee had a very sweet nature. She followed me around like a shadow. She would get very angry at me when I went out with my friends on Saturdays or Sundays or when they come over." (240) He respects his wife's personhood, body, will and agency. He does not impose his sexuality upon her and does not force her when she refuses the carnal relation after marriage. (238) Pawar does not subordinate her in anyway. He never doubts her faithfulness and does not scold her when she complains that one of his friends pinched her palm. He does not blame her when Muslim and Jewish gamblers at a club try to woo her by waving banknotes. He also does not scold or beat his wife when she quarrels with his mother. (241) He trusts his wife and does not pay heed to the rumour of her love affair with Mehboob, a Muslim boy. Pawar shows his trust in his wife and does not question or beat his wife rather he gets angry with his mother and asks for proof.

(273) He maintains patience for a long time but he turns harsh when he sees her talking to him at a corner of the market. This incident enrages Pawar and he starts demanding the truth from her. But when she says nothing, the author mistakes it as a guilt proven and decides to desert her. (274-75) He sends her back to her parents on the pretext that he has tuberculosis and wants her to stay there for a while but he never goes to bring her back and thus, deserts both his wife and daughter. Finally, his claim that women should be treated with respect proves false and a hypocrisy. His learning and knowledge are overpowered by masculinity, patriarchal possessions and sets of beliefs, and behaviour. The author's desertion of his wife shows his lack of moral courage and also corroborates that a man's liberalism, egalitarianism has certain limitations and the inherent patriarchal whims come out while treating women. Illustrating on Pawar's attitude towards his wife and other women Jerry Pinto writes, "He marries the beautiful Saee but maddened by jealousy, he rejects her on fairly flimsy grounds. To recover from the heartbreak of a broken marriage and the loss of his daughter, he moves to another area of the city and begins a long-distance flirtation with Salma, a girl, who he loses to. But each time he lets you know that it was his lack of courage, his lack of conviction that ended each romance." (Introduction xiii-xiv)

Although, Pawar later realises the wrong he did to his wife and is pained to see her plight brought about by his patriarchal possession and jealousy but he does not apologise or bring her back. He discounts her emotions, will and desire and imposes his own decision of separation on her without caring for the mental anguish, social and economic hardships that she may have to suffer as a deserted woman. His insincerity and intrinsic patriarchal authority are further reflected when he marries another woman clandestinely and leaves his young and innocent wife to go through various tribulations and finally marry an old man. This shows that despite his love and compassion for his wife, Pawar is also given to patriarchal laws and conventions which even his education could not remove. Pinto rightly says, "It is as if he is deconstructing the entire concept of Mahar Machismo which depends on the abuse of women. Look at the models he has around him as a boy. His father, he tells us, never hit his mother but had a series of affairs with other women. His uncle beats his first wife with a stick for simply showing up in his presence. Another uncle sells his wife into a brothel. When Pawar marries the second time, this happens offstage so that his constant references to his very educated wife are almost confusing." (Introduction xiv)

Besides his paternal grandmother Devki, mother, sister and wife, Daya Pawar speaks about other women such as his aunts, maternal grandmother and other women belonging to different castes. He writes that the Hindu socio-religious conventions lead Dalit women to violation of their human rights and subjects them to evils such as devadasi and murali. (210) The author maintains that his grandmother's sister Taibai was a devadasi in a temple at Khandoba. (19) He narrates that the internal patriarchy adds to Dalit women's suffering and exposes them to violence and dehumanisation. Pawar reiterates that Dalit men objectify Dalit women, torture and beat them to compensate their marginality and powerlessness in society. Beautiful Dalit women are the most frequent victims of domestic violence as their husbands doubt their faithfulness. He details how his mother's beautiful and charming step-sister Jamuna was sold by her suspicious husband to a brothel house. Jamuna had a pathetic life after she leaves her business in the whorehouse. She loses her mind and dies untimely while roaming and begging in the streets. Pawar relates the tragedy of another beautiful Dalit woman, Venu. Her husband was also suspicious and tortured her in numerous ways. He does not allow her to sleep and locks her in a room when he goes out to avoid her contact with men. This torture makes her go back to her parental house where she was subsequently married to an old man and thus her life was ruined. (194-95) Pawar writes that Dalit patriarchy is excessively repressive for Dalit women and they are purchased and sold like animals or commodities and also shared as property. He gives the instance of a Mahar household in which a Dalit girl is married to both father and son. This shows that the position of Dalit women is in no way better than slaves or animals within their own households and communities.

Pawar shows Dalit women as frequent victims of male indifference, patriarchal authority, pride and domestic violence. He gives the example of his own uncle Tatya who abandons his wife perhaps because she has a dark complexion. He beats her when she tries to come close to him at Mahar Kund while going to the Agasti village fair: "Who knows what happened to Tatya, but suddenly he was on his feet. A cart full of sugarcane was standing there. He took a sturdy stick from it and began to beat the woman, as if she were an animal." (137) The pilgrimages freed the woman from Tatya but they approve her beating by him. It was because of Hindu social sanctions and patriarchal laws that men get power over women and treat them as they like. Tatya beats his second wife, Kaku also but she does not take the beating silently. She is a clever and capable woman and does not surrender to him. She resists against his patriarchal authority and does not let him touch her at night. (150) Although, Kaku is an assertive and defiant woman, but after her husband's death she also lives a simple and ascetic life. This shows that she was also not free from the patriarchal notions of morality and chastity. Pawar praises Kaku for leading a simple and chaste life after her husband's death but does not exaggerate these qualities and does not call her a divine woman or a goddess. He leaves it for widows to decide how they want to live.

Pawar is highly concerned about a widow's place and position in the highly casteist and masculine society. He writes that widows are not allowed a humanitarian attitude and they are tortured and humiliated both within and outside their homes. Caste rules have many conventions and codes reserved for Dalit widows. For instance, the high caste patriarchs do not allow Dalit women to own land and property. Describing the experiences of his maternal grandmother, Pawar says, "When Aai was born her father died. Hardly had her father been shoved into the earth, when the family began to torment my grandmother, for not producing a son. They starved the young mother. They made her work like an animal. They fed her *bhakri* made of chaff and husk." (54) Javji Buwa's mother Chandrav is another widow to suffer within her own household and family. She is not given her meals on time and is not helped and respected by her family members. (191-92)

Dalit patriarchal codes are highly repressive and hurl certain implications on Dalit women. For instance, sometimes, Dalit women are not allowed to wear bodice by the rules of their caste panchayat. Pawar notes the instance of a poor Dalit girl, Gaoo, who does not wear bodice even though she wants to. (187) Besides desertion, indifference and violence, Dalit women are subjected to evils such as child and enforced marriages. Gaoo is forced to marry her brother-in-law, who bribes the members of caste panchayat by serving them alcohol. Gaoo was a fatherless child and her poor mother could not oppose the match. (187) Pawar writes that Dalit women were victims of gender codes and sexual brutality, sometime they were given opium to eat to intoxicate them, to boost their libido and delay their ejaculation so that they cannot deny the frequent sexual intercourse demanded by their husbands. (237)

Baluta presents a series of Dalit women characters and portrays them realistically in their social, cultural, economic and geographical locations. His description of Dalit women indicates the noxious caste, class and patriarchal codes and conventions that operate more oppressively in their lives as compared to Dalit men. Dalit women are coerced to sacrifice their lives to their families whereas Dalit men enjoy certain privileges and liberties. Dalit women are humiliated, tortured, beaten, molested, raped and sold and purchased by both Dalit and non-Dalit men. Pawar aspires to maintain that though Dalit women are the worst victims of caste, class and gender but they are not passive and inactive sufferers. They are courageous and their strength is reflected in their capacity to survive despite unfavourable circumstances and severe repression by casteist and patriarchal forces. His paternal grandmother shows her strength when she looks after her family successfully after her husband's death. In a similar vein, his mother also proves her strength by working hard and asserting her property right.

She retains her land which was otherwise not allowed for low caste widows. (114) Although, majority of the Dalit women portrayed in this life narrative are poor and illiterate but they are vocal and assertive. They do not yield silently to the high castes. For instance, the women of Kawakhana fetch water from the well of the high castes when no one gave them water: "They had asked the administration to intervene but the government was unmoved. One day, they cracked. They got together, and lowered their buckets into the well. The women, their loins girded for action, were at the forefront of the agitation." (134)

Pawar does not deviate from his realistic approach in his portrayal of Dalit women. He writes of their victimisation, weaknesses, strengths, sexuality, their petty quarrels, jealousies, internal conflicts and their everyday life activities. The author neither conceals nor exaggerates about them. He does not deify them for the good in them and does not despise them for what is wrong about them. To some extent *Baluta* is a striking contrast to the life narratives of many middle class and high caste men where women are presented either as the embodiments of goodness and virtues or evil personified. He does not generalise Dalit women and portrays them individually with certain strengths and weaknesses. Pawar respects women, helps and supports them. He advocates women's liberation and criticises patriarchy. He criticises his father for making his mother suffer. He is concerned with Dalit women's plight under male authority. He neither passes any judgement on them nor suggests any specific behavioural patterns. He does not scorn those women who assert their personhood and desert their husbands for their indifference and neglect of familial responsibilities.

Pawar attempts to address Dalit women's issues, brings out their distress and pain compassionately and tries to humanise them. He portrays them as he sees them living and behaving in their families and society. He shows their strength and capacity to survive amid severe repression. Dalit women's images as constructed by him lack an authentic feminist vision and staunch feminist standpoint. On the surface, Pawar seems to be liberal and equalitarian in his attitude towards women but his patriarchal mindset and gender prejudices are highly visible in his attitude towards Salma and his wife. Salma was sincerely in love with him but he does not respect her emotions and feelings. He advances towards her to seek an emotional shelter to recover from the anguish of his broken marriage and flirts with her to avenge the Muslim community as one of them has destroyed his family. His hyper masculinity, male pride and degrading attitude towards women are seen in the worst form when he deserts his innocent wife without any solid reason or simply because his neighbours were talking about her love affair with Mehboob and subsequently he himself sees her talking to him in the market. He decides unilaterally and conceitedly that his wife was guilty as she has no logical explanations to her relation with Mehboob. Also, Pawar did not believe Mehboob when he told him that he was not his wife's paramour rather he shared a brotherly sort of affection towards her. Finally, he deserts her deceitfully and cowardly and marries another woman clandestinely. His decision shows not only his lack of moral courage to recognise a woman's agency, will and desire but also exposes his hypocrisy and patriarchal structure of thought deeply ingrained in his psyche. The toxic masculinity that he inherited from his father and uncle overpowers his liberalism and makes him behave in a typical patriarchal manner.

The Outcaste

Sharankumar Limbale's *The Outcaste: Akkarmashi* occupies a significant place in Marathi Dalit autobiographical writings. Published in 1984, when Limbale was twenty-five or twenty-six years old, *The Outcaste* is an authentic and forthright record of the odds and ordeals that he undergoes especially in his childhood and early youth. He begins his narrative with the description that he was born from the rape of his mother Masamai by a high caste Patil Hanmanta Limbale. Masamai and her husband Ithal Kamble were agricultural labourers and worked for Hanmanta, who was well aware of Ithal's socio-economic vulnerability and powerlessness so he frequently rapes his wife. Masamai was forced by the caste council to divorce Ithal as she has committed adultery with a high caste man and according to caste rules, she could not be allowed to live with her husband any more. The decision of the caste council separated Masamai from her suckling baby and her four-year-old son Dharma. Her sons wept and cried for their mother but she was not allowed to stay with them. After deserting Masamai, Ithal remarried but Masamai was not allowed to remarry as she was a woman who has lost her chastity and has surrendered her honour to a high caste man. Here Limbale questions the Dalit patriarchal precepts that allows men privileges and imposes restrictions and prohibitions on women.

After the rape, when Masamai was deserted by her husband, Hanmanta gave her a small rented house at Akkalkot where he kept her like his concubine and exploited her further. (36) Resultantly, Masamai became pregnant and gave birth to Sharankumar. Hanmanta refused to accept Sharankumar as his legal son firstly because he was born from a Mahar woman and secondly, he was aware that Sharankumar will legally claim his share from his property. So, in order to ward off Masamai and her son, Hanmanta weaves a narrative that her child Sharankumar resembles a nearby potter Dhondya, a noted ruffian. This false tale led to frequent quarrels between Masamai and Hanmanta and ultimately, he also cheated Masamai and deserted her after a few years. After Hanmanta, Masami lived with another Patil named Kaka as his mistress and gave birth to many more children. All children had a life of sub-human beings and endured humiliation and deprivation in every sphere of life. Masamai herself remained an object of sex for the adulterous Patils.

The Outcaste scathingly attacks the edicts of caste and patriarchy that coerced him to lead a hopeless, loveless and vulnerable life and deprived him of both father and mother's affections. (38) Through his own story, Limbale exposes the hypocrisy of caste superiority and mocks the patriarchal morality that ruined his mother's and his life. Although, *The Outcaste* describes the author's pain and experience as an illegitimate son, but the narrative is not limited to the question of identity only. The chronicle goes beyond individual and addresses the issues of the whole Dalit community. Limbale maintains that the Mahars were not only forced to lead a poor and unhygienic life but they also slogged without proper wages by the high caste landlords who controlled the economic resources and enjoyed a privileged social status. The author problematises inequalities and discriminations against Dalits and voices a strong protest against the existing caste, class and gender based power relations.

Inclusion of gender issues and articulation of Dalit women's specific suffering offer *The Outcaste* a distinctive place among Dalit autobiographies. Like Daya Pawar, Limbale also presents many Dalit women in his autobiography. There are labourers, prostitutes, widows, deserted and childless women. They are the victims of violence, sexual assaults, indifference and desertion. Limbale's maternal grandmother Shantamai, mother Masamai and step-sisters are some important female characters in this autobiography. Limbale writes that as a child, he was emotionally more attached to Shantamai who loved him more than Masamai. Shantamai was one of the seven daughters of Satubaap. She was married to a Dalit man Teerth who deserted her because she had a daughter and could not conceive again to produce him a son. Teerth marries another woman and Shantabai comes to live with her only daughter Masamai at Hanoor.

Shantamai was a sweeper by profession and also worked as a midwife in the Dalit and non-Dalit localities. Abject poverty, constant slogging and starvation make her appear older than her actual age. Limbale shares a deep emotional bond with Shantamai and she was also very affectionate to him and gave him the love of a mother. (42) When he was a little boy, she used to tie him on her back while sweeping the streets. She used to beg *bhakari* for the author whenever he felt hungry. She was very keen about her grandson's upbringing and mostly starved herself to feed him. She loved the author more than her own life and works hard for him. Once, when Limbale brings one of his friends home Shantamai serves them whatever she had. She even gives the last bhakari to the author pretending that there is more flour in her tin box. After eating, the author discovers that the box had no flour but a stone which Shantamai had put there so that he could eat comfortably without any burden on his conscience. She often ate the bhakari made from the jowar passed undigested by the cattle in the dung but she never gave it to Limbale. Shantamai ate this bhakari easily and showed no sign of being assaulted by the foul smell of the dung. It is apparent that poverty and dehumanisation made Shantamai familiar with unhygienic and unwholesome food and all sorts of filth and stinks. Karan Singh writes, "Shantamai's indifference to the smell of dung presents her as a Dalit woman who has been treated so inhumanly by the caste system throughout her life that she has now 'naturalized' to the bestial conditions." (70) Through the description of Shantamai's love and sacrifices for her grandson, the author elevates her and shows her moral strength and capacity to love other people despite continuous dehumanisation and adversities in her own life.

Shantamai loves Limbale who was the most hated figure in the caste and gender dominated society. She is proud to see Limbale when he participates in the procession with other school boys on Republic Day: "My granny looked on proudly when she saw me shouting the slogans. She must have felt her dream come true." (6) Shantamai was concerned with Limbale's education and tried hard to borrow money from people for his higher education. She was ready to pay interest on what she borrowed yet she could not arrange the money. (80-81) Finally, she stopped borrowing but somehow Limbale was able to get admission in Dayanand College in Sholapur. Shantamai helped the author in his pursuit of education. She often visited him in the hostel, however, ironically despite her love and affection, he was ashamed of her presence: "Shantamai was an old woman, she chewed tobacco all the time. Her sari and blouse were mostly in tatters. How could I take her, like this, to my room? Shantamai was quite good looking. If she had better clothes, I would have taken her to my room. I was ashamed of her. Whenever I saw my college mates approaching, I increased the distance between us by a few paces to prove that I had nothing to do with this poor woman." (88-89) Here the writer shows the Dalit women's plight who sacrifice their lives and efface their identity for the upbringing and future of their sons and grandsons but the same sons and grandsons exercise their authority, abandon them and are ashamed of them when they grow up. Although, Limbale feels ashamed of Shantamai's presence when he was in college but she does not let her love for him dwindle. She gives him meat even when he was a grown man and living in the city for his government job.

Shantamai is a poor Dalit woman constantly struggling against the adversities in her life but Limbale highlights another side of her character and another aspect of her life. Shantamai is a devoted Hindu. She also believes in witchcraft, sorcery, auspicious and inauspicious. She considers the grains and coins which Limbale picks up from the cremation ground as inauspicious and asks him to throw them away. She believes that ghosts may enter her house and harm Masamai's newly born child. (19) So, to avoid any unwanted thing to happen she asks the author to spit before he enters the house. She believes in the Hindu notion of purity and sprinkles cow urine in her house in case of defilement. She is sometimes possessed by a goddess and behaves in an abnormal way. It was Dada who used to bring her back to normal by putting a soil mark on her forehead. She goes on pilgrimage to Chivari every year. She believes in the destructive powers of goddess Ambabai. (93) Shantamai is given to Hindu socio-religious beliefs and observes untouchability. She does not like the author playing with Arjya, a local Mang boy. She scolds him when he allows Arjya to enter their house and drink water from the same cup. It is because of illiteracy and lack of Dalit consciousness that Shantamai, who herself is the worst victim of caste system, practices untouchability. Karan Singh rightly says that it is because of their lack of exposure and contact with the outside world that Dalit women are more easily ensnared in social and religious hypocrisies than Dalit men. (72) Illiteracy and less social communication kept Shantamai unaware of the mechanism of her own sufferings.

Shantamai was a vulnerable and silent Dalit woman who was in an emotional and physical relationship with a Muslim old man Mahmood Dastagir Jamadar whom the author affectionately calls Dada. Although, Shantamai shares a deep emotional bond with Mahmood but she hides this relationship. When her step-son Basumama enquires about Dada's presence in the house she simply tells him that he is a stranger who has no one in world. (58) Shantamai is a poor, simple and illiterate woman who wants to survive somehow in a dichotomous socio-economic and cultural system. Barring Dada, Shantamai never received love and respect from others but despite all hatreds and discrimination against her, she is full of love and admiration for the people around. She sacrifices her life for the author's upbringing and career and also loves Dada despite his being of another religion and community. Shantamai was forgiving by nature as she does not harbour abhorrence for her former husband who deserted her simply because she could not beget him a son. She shows sympathy and weeps for him when he dies and also attends his funeral. (57) Shantamai is depicted as loving, sacrificing, considerate and compassionate but the author does not ennoble or deify her. He humanises her when he shows her fighting with Masamai and Dada and also when she compromises her dignity by begging for survival. Her strength is reflected in her struggle for survival and economic stability. When she finds that her earnings from her professions as a sweeper and as a midwife are not sufficient for her family, she gets into the illegal business of liquor and thus attempts to add to her income.

Masamai, another important woman in this autobiography, is the worst victim of caste, class and patriarchal discrimination and repression. She is portrayed as a beautiful poor Dalit woman whose beauty becomes a curse for her as it made her prone to rape by Hanmanta who exploited her sexually and then deserted her. This rape destroyed her family life and exposed her to further exploitation and suffering. After Hanmanta, Masamai kept on shifting as an object of sex between Patils. Kaka also does not accept her as his wife. He goes to Masamai for sexual pleasure only and ignores her and her children when they try to visit him at his home. Kaka and his family also ignored and insulted Masamai when she goes to see Kaka's sick father. (54-55) It is hypocritical that the caste laws allow high caste men to establish sexual relations with low caste women but they do not allow them to make Dalit women their wives. They sleep with Dalit women but hesitate to eat the food cooked by them. Prejudiced by such caste laws, Kaka also cheated her.

Masamai always lacked food, clothes and other basic necessities as the money she received from Patil was not sufficient for survival. Constant scarcity of food, clothes, severe repression and hatred made Masamai tough and quarrelsome.

So, she exhibits a different motherhood as she is not tender, soft and sacrificing like her mother Shantamai. She scolds Limbale for eating too much. Masamai does not surrender her personhood for her son like a typical Indian mother and does not think it her dharma to feed her son at all costs. She asks him to procure food himself. Masamai is not like Shantamai who starves herself to make Limbale eat. She asserts her own body and does not yield to patriarchal notion of idealised motherhood. He writes, "I never got real love from my mother. Half of her was my mother and the other half a woman for Patil. She has to satisfy Patil. Her milk meant for me went dry even as her arms were busy embracing the Patil." (65) It is true that Masamai represents an unconventional motherhood and is slightly tough in her treatment of Limbale but it is not because she is a loveless self-absorbed adulteress. The real cause of her lack of affection for the author is that she is mostly confined with pregnancy, delivery and bringing up her little babies. Her rebuking and cursing of the author are the result of her constant severe physical and psychological repression. It is the caste system and Dalit patriarchal conventions that ruined her life and forced her to surrender her body.

Masamai is portrayed as a heavily repressed, humiliated and exploited woman but despite injustices and obstructions she shows great moral strength, humanity, dignity and capacity to fight back. She becomes vocal when the pain becomes intolerable. For instance, she strongly demands a share from Kaka's property for her son by him. She demands her right vociferously and finally makes Kaka yield and transfer two acres of land to her. She also quarrels with Jnai for her rights when she finds that it is because of her that Kaka ignores her.

(56-57) Masamai got angry and showed her power when she came to know that Nagi's husband Nandu has married some other woman secretly and cheated her daughter. She threatens to kill him when he refuses to accept his second marriage. (111)

Masamai was concerned about her children's future and fights for it. She lived a penurious and disadvantaged life but has a sense of dignity. After separation from her husband when Dadunya approaches her to work as a female singer in his performing group she refuses as she was determined to live on her own. Although, she cannot afford to feed her son adequately but she gets angry when she comes to know that Gangoobai is using her son for begging. (37) Though, Hanmanta and Kaka treated Masamai as a whore but she remains faithful to her present partner and sacrifices her body to his will and gratification. She refuses to sleep with Hanmanta when her present partner Kaka asks her to do so. She got angry and drove both Kaka and Hanmanta out of her house with a chappal in her hand. When they came back after some time, she protests against their efforts to cheapen her body and threatens to burn herself. Here Masamai not only asserts her moral strength and dignity but also shows that she was aware of her dignity, integrity and was capable of fighting back against humiliation, exploitation and dehumanisation.

Masamai's strength and her indomitable spirit are further reflected in her struggle for survival despite severe repression and deprivation. Though, she was a mistress of Patils but she does not put herself absolutely on their mercy. She starts the business of brewing liquor to feed her family. However, it was not an easy business as there was danger of police and customers were also not easy to deal with, but she runs the business skilfully. Masamai is a courageous and defiant woman. She does not surrender completely to the casteist and patriarchal forces. When the author needs his father's name for freeship in school, she asks him to tell the teacher that she was a Patil's whore. (59-60) She does not find it wrong that Nagi has a love affair with Nandu, a high caste Patil's son. She rebukes the author for beating Nagi for her inter-caste relationship and exercising masculinity upon her. Although, Masamai herself was the worst victim of male authority but her scolding of the author shows that she was in favour of women's autonomy and was opposed to male domination, patriarchal morality. Though Masamai faces humiliation and exploitation throughout her life but she does not yield passively to adversities and does not give herself to nihilism and melancholy. She shows great love for life and wants to survive and live at all costs. She reprimands the author again when he hits his sister Vani for eating banana skins thrown away by people: "Let her eat worms and live. Why do you make it a matter of prestige?" (22)

Masamai is buoyant and jovial by nature. It is the absurdities and the adversities in her life that have made her fierce but she cannot be despised and degraded. She is not delinquent and adulterous by birth. She was leading a hard but happy life with Ithal Kamble before Hanmanta raped her. She does not desert her husband for the rich and brawny Patil, she was forced by the caste and harsh patriarchal rules to go away from her husband and her sons by him. She does not sell her body just for sexual gratification and a luxurious life, rather it was for survival that she has to become the keep of Patil. Masamai forgives her former husband Ithal Kamble when he was sick and came to live with her. She not only accepts him back but also vows to save him. She does not desert or discard her identity as Ithal Kamble's wife despite the wrongs he did to her. She performed the death rites and observed the customary mourning period when he dies. She bestowed motherly love on Suryakant and Dharma, her long lost sons from Kamble, when she met them.

Limbale presents his sisters as victims of caste, poverty and patriarchal oppression. Like the author, they also struggled for food, clothes and other basic necessities. There was no privacy for them in their small house: "Masamai, Nagi and Nirmi used to bathe openly. They removed their clothes, bathed naked, and changed clothes in our presence. I was doomed to see my mother and my sister naked." (72) He further writes that his sisters were also subjected to severe socio-cultural and patriarchal oppression because they too were illegitimate. His sister Nagi was married to Kumar who was rather old for her and had already been deserted by two women. Because of the precepts of caste and patriarchal laws Nagi had to accept an unmatched marriage. (72) However, subsequently she left her husband and came back to her mother's house. It was because of her socio-economic vulnerability that she was lured and deceived by Nandu with whom she developed an emotional and physical relation despite the author's advice and opposition. Nandu marries another woman secretly and thus made Nagi his concubine. In this way, Nagi also put herself on a high caste man's (Nandu) mercy. Limbale writes that his other sisters too had pitiable lives. The marriages of his two sisters, Pami and Indira were broken just two days after the wedding as their in-laws came to know that their mother was a Mahar. (109) Like other deserted Dalit women, Pami and Indira too were subjected to social disgrace, abhorrence, exploitation and poverty. Chandamai, Shewanta, Devki, Dhanavva, Gangoobai, Kamalakka, Kondamai, Ambumai, Suman and Rangoo are some other Dalit women whom Limbale portrays in his autobiography. Chandamai is Shantamai's blood sister. She was deserted by her husband because she was barren. Chandamai did not marry again and lived separately in a hut. The author describes her as a noble and liberal woman who often gave him tea and food. She too was a victim of patriarchal oppression and had an insecure and loveless life. Shewanta was a poor Mahar girl, whom the author loves in his early youth. He describes her as strong and hard-working. She would look after her sibling and accomplish domestic chores when her mother was out for work. Her father was an idler, so, she had to work nonstop and has no rest and comforts. The author was full of admiration and passionately in love with her but he withdrew when Shantamai warns him against this proposal. Shantamai was well aware that the Mahar community will turn against this match as the author was an illegitimate child. The author has to sacrifice his love because of the rigid caste and patriarchal laws. Shewanta was finally married to some Dalit man.

Devki was a spinster who worked on Girmallya's farm. She was also a midwife and helped the village women abort their unwanted pregnancies. She made the pregnant woman lie flat on her stomach and then walked heavily all over her. She also gave them herbals to eat to help them abort but ironically, once Devki herself became pregnant and gave birth to a child. Since, she was unmarried and could not bring up her baby so, she buried it under garbage to protect her honour. Dhanavva is another miserable Dalit woman in the autobiography. She was beautiful but became a widow in her youth. After her husband's death, she was living with her father, Shankar. She was Shankar's eldest daughter so she could not remarry. Her father took advantage of her helplessness and exploited her sexually. She could not resist her father who finds it logical to rape his daughter. (67) She could not escape her plight as she has nowhere to go.

Gangoobai, is another Dalit woman who leads a life of misery and deprivation. The author portrays her as a tricky woman who used him for begging when he was a child. Limbale writes, "Close to our house lived Gangoobai, who would tie me on her back and go around the streets shouting and selling needles, charmed and coloured threads, anacardium, etc. She would exhibit me to the people in the houses she visited. Out of sympathy they gave oil, old clothes, and food." (37) It is true that Gangoobai used the author for begging but she was not inhuman and cruel. She has both sympathy and love for Limbale, so, she advises him to go to the law against his father Hanmanta. Kamalakka is a poor and vulnerable Dalit woman who is also deserted by her husband. Like Shantamai, Masamai and many other Dalit women, Kamalakka also got into the liquor business and struggles bravely for survival. (31)

Limbale is straightforward and realistic in portraying Dalit women. Like Pawar, Limbale also neither exaggerates nor hides facts about them. He shows them struggling for survival, fighting with their husbands, having love affairs with different men and eloping with them. Kondamai, Ambumai and Suman are the archetypes of some unconventional and assertive Dalit women. Kondamai was a beautiful Dalit woman married to Kerubaap. She had an affair first with Manakunna and then with Damunna. Ambumai also has an affair with Kacharuajja, though both were old and grey. Ambumai is a clever woman. She pretended to be pregnant by Kacharuajja and made him accept her as his wife. (49-50) Limbale presents Suman as a fickle and infidel woman. She was a light skinned beautiful woman whom the author considered his sister. She worked at the grocery shop and her husband was a porter. Suman had affairs with many men and repeatedly runs away with them. (87) She is not bounded by the patriarchal notion of *pativrat* and chastity. She does not feel herself bounded by her love for her children and motherhood.

Limbale shows Dalit women as victims of high caste men's lust, promiscuity and fierce masculinity. The high caste men ruin them and then leave them to lead a life full of deprivation, scorn and humiliation: "The Patils in every village have made whores of the wives of Dalit farm labourers. A poor Dalit girl on attaining puberty has invariably been a victim of their lust. There are Dalit families that survive by pleasing the Patils sexually." (38) But Limbale maintains that the lustful high caste men are not the only victimisers of Dalit women. He opines Dalit men's neglect of their wives, mothers, sisters and daughters, their idleness, drunkenness and lack of action and moral strength make Dalit women vulnerable to the external world and exposes them to exploitation and physical assaults. Practices such as child marriages keep Dalit women illiterate and poor and thwart their efforts to empower and liberate themselves from the caste and patriarchal repression. In the case of Masamai's rape, for instance, it is Masamai who is punished by the Dalit caste council not Hanmanta who raped and ruined her. Similarly, Limbale's friend Harya planned to cut his wife's nose and breasts to punish her when he caught her in a room with Jagannath Patil's son. He unfairly ignored Patil's son, the real perpetrator. (111) Dalit men use power and violence to repress and control Dalit women because they are highly conscious of their honour and masculinity. So, instead of supporting them, they deny them voice and suppress even those women who are awakened, active, courageous, responsible and capable of fighting back. Dalit women's independent moves and actions hurt Dalit men as it is opposed to their social and cultural conventions and traditions.

The Outcaste underscores Dalit women's place in society and features their responses and strategies to fight against injustices and discrimination. Though the writer has succeeded adequately in screening Dalit women's subjection to the precepts of class and gender but his portrayal of them is insufficient. Like some other Dalit male autobiographies, *The Outcaste* also lacks an authentic Dalit feminist standpoint. According to Karan Singh, "Feminism per se is absent from the autobiography. Nowhere do the women hold males responsible for their woes. The focus of the book is primarily on the experience of living as a Dalit and caste is a crucial factor." (83) The author speaks about Dalit women's issues but the expression of his agony and pain are so acute and vociferous that his concern for Dalit women's issues gets overshadowed or loses focus. It is perhaps because as a male he finds it difficult to appreciate women's assertion of self. His portrayal of Masamai shows his dilemma. On one hand he empathises with her for suffering under repressive caste and patriarchal laws but on the other, he holds her responsible for his plight as an akkarmashi and curses her for her alleged sexual debauchery. The thought that it was because of his mother's intercourse with Hanmanta that he came into the world and had a humiliating, impoverished and loveless life fills him with anger. The author's views of his mother clearly indicate the inadequacy of his standpoint and also highpoints that he was not able to support women's agency, autonomy and will. Most Dalit women portrayed in this autobiography are not conscious of their dominated position in society and are heavily subordinated to caste and patriarchal codes. It is perhaps because of lack of consciousness that despite unprecedented strength they are not able to control the course of their lives and transform themselves. They are divided and do not protest collectively against dominant forces.

Changiya Rukh

Balbir Madhopuri's autobiography, *Changiya Rukh: Against the Night* was first published in Punjabi in 2002. It was translated into Hindi in 2007 and in 2010, it became the first Punjabi Dalit autobiography to appear in English. The publication of *Changiya Rukh* opened a new phase, added many new dimensions to Punjabi Dalit literature and brought out a new perspective to describe Dalit sensibilities. Madhopuri's description of the lived experiences of Dalits is authentic, free from digression, diversion and exaggeration. *Changiya Rukh* highpoints how caste and class operate in the lives of Dalits and how they subject them to oppression, exploitation and dehumanisation in every sphere of life. Like other Dalit autobiographers, Madhopuri also places community at the centre of the narrative and collectively brings out the pain and predicament of Dalit lives. Madhopuri used the title to show that the precept of caste thwarts Dalits' efforts to grow and does not allow them to lead a self-dependent and dignified life. Explaining the title Harish K Puri writes, "*Changiya Rukh* means a tree lopped from the top, slashed and dwarfed. As the title of his autobiography, Balbir Madhopuri has used it as a metaphor for Dalit or an 'untouchable' Indian whose potential for growth has been 'robbed by the Hindu social order." (Introduction xiii)

Changiya Rukh authentically describes every aspect of Dalit lives and also addresses Dalit women's issues. The author maintains that Dalit women are the most adversely affected victims of the prejudice of caste and poverty: "The pitiable condition of the women of my community with their dirty, tattered clothes flashed through my mind. Their walk held none of the confidence and arrogance of the high-caste women. Barefoot with a hoe in one hand, supporting a bundle of grass or clothes on the head, collecting garbage, dry dung pats, or beating children with the other – that was the picture." (63) There are many women characters in this life narrative. They are depicted realistically, struggling for survival amid severe caste and class based oppression. Like Pawar and Limbale, Madhopuri also offers an adequate space for his mother and appreciates her for the support and sacrifices she has made for the family. Madhopuri writes that she used to work in Surjan Singh Jat's *Haveli*. She used to collect muck and dung with her bare hands. (122) She was as an honest woman who never took advantage of belonging to a bureaucrat's family and never thought of deserting her dominating husband. She fights bravely against poverty, hunger and starvation and supports her family. Madhopuri writes that his mother was a staunch Hindu. She was so deeply swayed by the Hindu religio-patriarchal concepts such as *pativratam*, chastity and *stree dharma* that she expunged her identity and accepted male domination in the name of religion and tradition. Her internalisation of patriarchal laws is highly evident when she hesitates to say her father-in-law's name. (76) She is a very tender, affectionate, compassionate and sacrificing mother. She never speaks against the violence and atrocities meted out to her but she becomes furious when it comes to the suffering of her children. She scolds her husband when he beats the author for eating mud. (22) This image of mother is unconventional as Dalit mothers are mostly helplessly scolding, beating their children and putting them into hard work without realising their limits and capacity.

Madhopuri's mother is simple, honest and sacrificing but despite these virtues she could not create a just and viable space for herself even within her own household. She is heavily subjected to her patriarchal husband's authority who not only scolds and jibes but also beats her frequently. (34) Madhopuri reiterates that his father imposed his authority on his wife but she never protested against his autocracy: "Bhaia often taunted Ma about her brothers. Sometimes he would abuse her, and throw things at her when his temper ran away with him. And Ma…she had steeled herself to patiently bear all the humiliations heaped on her." (120) The author says, "I was surprised that this thin, dark man of medium height and ordinary looks had so much power over my mother. Even though he beat her, she never protested against his taunts and jibes, nor was she proud of her beauty." (93) Madhopuri presents his father as an authoritative staunch patriarch who has no respect for women. He regrets the birth of his own daughter and calls it a curse. (85)

Madhopuri's grandmother, Haro is the second important female character in this autobiography. She is depicted as a wise and brave woman whose wisdom and bravery are acknowledged even by the high caste Jats. She is an autonomous woman and is not subjected to the caste rules and the authority of the land owning Jats. She is capable of action and fights against injustices. (41) She asserts her identity as a Dalit woman and claims respect from villagers irrespective of their caste status. (128) Madhopuri's grandmother was a strong and awakened woman who believes in humanism and is sharply opposed to hypocritical performances in the name of religion and gods. She had a great sense of self-respect and did not like to be dependent on others. Madhopuri writes, "The whole family wanted my mother to wash Dadi's clothes. But whenever Ma asked her, Dadi would answer abruptly, 'I don't want to be dependent on anyone; better to die.'" (131) Grandmother is assertive and exercises her power on her son, daughter, daughter-in-law and grandchildren. She scolds her son for smoking. In addition to her own family members, she scolds the daughters and daughters-in-law of other houses for not working on time. (127) Though the author's grandmother is a powerful woman, commands respect and claims agency but she is also not free from the patriarchal constraints. She behaves almost in a patriarchal way as she also subordinates her daughter-in-law and does not allow her to take decisions in domestic matters. Her behaviour and attitude towards other women confirm that in many cases the patriarchal oppression is promoted by women themselves.

Besides the women of his family, Madhopuri also represents the poor, repressed and othered women in Punjab. The poor women labourers working in the godown of the Food Corporation of India (FCI) where the author also worked, were teased and taunted and made objects of licentious jokes by the men working there. Madhopuri writes that Dalit women have a pitiable life everywhere in India. In Uttar Pradesh, the high caste Thakurs exploit Dalit women sexually. Here a Dalit bride still has to spend the first night with the Thakurs. They also call Dalit women to their homes for sexual pleasure whenever they feel like it. (72) Madhopuri takes up Dalit women's issues seriously, authentically and vociferously. He shows Dalit women as the worst victims of external patriarchy but like Limbale, he also argues that the high caste men are not the only perpetrators in their lives. He opines that Dalit patriarchy also plays an equally destructive role in Dalit women's lives. He writes that even conscious and awakened Dalits such as his father, also do not support and cooperate with their wives, daughters and beat and abuse them. (74) Although Madhopuri acknowledges his father's role in his education and shaping his career, but he does not let him overshadow his mother. He criticises his father for his gender biases and patriarchal authority and acknowledges his mother's love and support.

Madhopuri addresses Dalit women's issues and demands an equalitarian attitude towards them but like other Dalit male autobiographers, Dalit women's images as constructed and represented by him are inauthentic and fractured. Most Dalit women portrayed in this life narrative are victims of illiteracy, domestic violence, molestation and rapes. They have to suffer both within their own contexts and in the larger society. They are not aware of the mechanism of their sufferings and lead the lives of subhuman beings. Although, his grandmother is powerful and has some influence but she does not use her agency and power to liberate other women, rather she suppresses them further in a patriarchal style. She scolds her daughters, granddaughter and daughter-in-law and coerces them to behave in the conventional patriarchal way. Dalit women as portrayed by Madhopuri, are divided and not aware of the need and significance of a larger sisterhood. They either submit to the patriarchal forces or strive for individual survival. They are mostly indifferent to collective sufferings of Dalit women. Madhopuri's lack of moral courage to support women's agency and autonomy accounts for the inadequacy in his portrayal of Dalit women. Like other Dalit male writers, he also attempts to model them on the traditional roles of mothers and sisters. Despite his education, liberalism and opposition to Hinduism, Madhopuri also could not liberate Dalit women from the traditional patriarchal stereotypes. Even for the educated Dalit men their wives are nothing more than subordinates and they easily disregard their contribution and emotional support.

The selected autobiographies: *Baluta*, *The Outcaste* and *Changiya Rukh* are almost the same in their portrayal and representation of Dalit women. Though they offer an adequate space for Dalit women, bring out their distress and address their issues sensitively, but their images are inauthentic and broken. Dalit women are divided on their issues, so they strive only for individual survival. Pawar's mother, who is a victim of patriarchal oppression herself, does not cooperate with her daughter-in-law, rather she tries to turn her son against her. She also does not revolt against her husband's authority and his wasting money on women and wine. In a similar vein, Pawar's wife Saee also does not speak against her husband's authority and autocracy even when he deserts her without any reason. Instead of claiming her right as a legal wife, she uses the 'weapon of the weak' and tells Pawar that she will avenge his male pride by making his daughter a *devadasi*.

Like Pawar, Limbale also lacks authenticity as his Dalit women are physically and psychologically strong but they are not able to acquire agency and empower themselves. Shantamai is a helpless Dalit woman who compromises her hunger and effaces her personhood for the author's sake. The author glorifies her by comparing her to mother earth as she was generous and sheltered the helpless Masamai, her illegitimate son and Dada. Limbale presents Masamai as the worst victim of caste and male authority and also blames her for his birth and suffering. Apart from his grandmother and mother, Limbale presents his sisters also as helpless and suffering in numerous ways. His other Dalit women characters also endure starvation, humiliation and repression without any strategic fight against them. In *Changiya Rukh* also Dalit women are presented as vulnerable and voiceless. Like Pawar and Limbale, Madhopuri also presents his mother as a passive woman who submits herself to her husband's authority despite her beauty and her belonging to a bureaucrat's family.

Finally, it can be inferred that the majority of Dalit women portrayed in these autobiographies lack feminist consciousness as they are not aware how caste, class and patriarchy operate in their lives. Despite their physical, psychological strength and unprecedented capacity to work hard, Dalit women in these autobiographies are not able to transform their lives. They are heavily subjected to male authority and have no voice, agency and autonomy. Exposing the inadequacy in Dalit men's portrayal of Dalit women, Ruth Manorama says that the majority of Dalit male writers tend to portray Dalit women as "victims rather than victors". (165) For Dalit male autobiographers, gender issue is of secondary concern; they offer women space in the narrative but not vision and ideology. They prioritise Dalitism over feminism and Dalit women's images in the selected texts remain ambiguous and fractured. Dalit women's identity is merged into the community and they are seen as just complement to the larger Dalit society.

Works Cited

- Chodorow, Nancy J *The Reproduction of Mothering*. University of California Press, 1999.
- Devy, GN Introduction. *The Outcaste: Akkarmashi* by Sharankumar Limbale. Translated by Santosh Bhoomkar, Oxford UP, 2003, pp. xiii-xxvi.

  Hooks, Bell. "Understanding Patriarchy." *Louisville Anarchist Federation,* n. page. imaginenoborders.org/pdf/zines/UnderstandingPatriarchy.pdf. Accessed 24 April 2019.
- Kumar, Raj. *Dalit Personal Narratives: Reading Caste, Nation and Identity*. Orient Black Swan, 2010.
- Kumar, Vikas. *The Representation of Dalit in Dalit and Non-Dalit Literature*. Unistar Books, 2017.
- Limbale, Sharankumar. *The Outcaste: Akkarmashi*. Translated by Santosh Bhoomkar, Oxford UP, 2003.
- Madhopuri, Balbir. *Changiya Rukh: Against the Night*. Translated by Tripti Jain, Oxford UP, 2010.

- Author's Note. *Changiya Rukh: Against the Night* by Madhopuri. Translated by Tripti Jain, Oxford UP, 2010, pp. ix-x.
- Maitreya, Yogesh. "Daya Pawar: How an Icon of Dalit literature Fought against the Exile of Caste, and Won." *Firstpost.* 12 November 2017, www.firstpost.com/living/daya-pawar-how-an-icon-of-dalit-literature-fought-against-the-exile-of-caste-and-won-4206017.html. Accessed 19 May 2019.
- Manorama, Ruth. "Dalit Women: Downtrodden among the Downtrodden." *Indigenous People: Dalits: Dalit Issues in Today's Theological Debate*, edited by James Massey, ISPCK, 1994, pp. 152-169.
- Patil, Smita. M "Reading Caste, Gender and Sexuality in Dalit Writings." *Intersections: Gender and Sexuality in Asia and the Pacific*, no. 34, 2014, n. page, intersections.anu.edu.au/issue34/patil.htm. Accessed 25 June 2020.
- Pawar, Daya. *Baluta*. Translated by Jerry Pinto, Speaking Tiger, 2015.
- Pinto, Jerry. Introduction. *Baluta* by Daya Pawar. Translated by Pinto, Speaking Tiger, 2015, pp. ix-xvi.
- Puri, Harish K Introduction. *Changiya Rukh: Against the Night* by Balbir Madhopuri. Translated by Tripti Jain, Oxford UP, 2010, pp. xiii-xxx.
- Singh, Karan. *Dalitism and Feminism: Locating Women in Dalit Literature*. Creative Books, 2011.
- Valmiki, Omprakash. *Joothan: A Dalit's Life*. Translated by Arun Prabha Mukherjee, Samya, 2007.

CHAPTER 3

PARADIGM OF RESISTANCE

THE EARLY phase of Dalit literature (1958-1980) was dominated by Dalit men writers. Dalit women, the most silenced and dominated group, were still positioned on social, cultural, political and literary margins and naturally their writings were sparse in numbers, mild in nature and tone. Although, some liberal Dalit men attempted to articulate Dalit women's issues in their writings, but they lacked authenticity, adequacy and a radical feminist standpoint. The rigid internal patriarchal structures which add to Dalit women's sufferings and marginalisation, do not figure adequately in Dalit male writings. They portray Dalit women as subordinates to them without feminist consciousness, autonomy and agency. It was only in the late 1980s, especially in Marathi, that Dalit women began to write autonomously from their own point of view. Besides poems and short stories, some of the educated Marathi Dalit women such as Shantabai Dhanaji Dani, Mukta Sarvagod, Shantabai Krushnaji Kamble, Baby Kamble, Kumud Pawde, Urmila Pawar and others published their life histories which broke the long imposed silence of Dalit women, revolutionised their issues and also fronted their demand for justice, equity, agency, identity and dignity.

Subsequently, Dalit women became vocal in other regions as well such as Tamil Nadu, Karnataka, Andhra Pradesh, Kerala and Gujarat and produced a corpus of writings of their distinctive issues with a radical Dalit feminist perspective. These writings problematised traditional caste and patriarchal conventions and laws and constructed a discourse of resistance against discriminations and injustices that Dalit women were forced to undergo for centuries. Dalit women's literature points out that it is only through bold and assertive articulation and active resistance that they can counter prevalent differences and create a discursive space for themselves. Resistance may be individual or collective and may be active or passive. The present chapter seeks to examine how the selected texts: Bama's *Karukku* and Baby Halder's *A Life Less Ordinary* voice their resistance against caste, class, gender disparities and assert Dalit women's existence and rights. It further attempts to locate the strategies as suggested by the selected autobiographers to counter dominant ideologies and secure justice, equality, autonomy, identity and dignity for Dalit women in a casteist and heavily masculine society.

Karukku

Dalit writer, critic and activist, Bama Faustina Soosairaj (1958) was born in a Dalit Christian family, in Virudhunagar district of Southern Tamil Nadu. She was the third of six children. Her father Soosairaj was employed in the Indian Army and her mother Sebasthiamma stayed at home to look after the children and manage domestic chores. Her two grandmothers worked as labourers for the high caste Naickers. Like other Dalit children, Bama also had a poor and deprived childhood but despite wretched poverty she got an opportunity to educate herself. Despite severe humiliation and exploitation in school and college, she completed her education and started teaching mathematics in a convent school. Inspired by the teachings and messages of Jesus Christ, Bama resigned her teaching job and became a Catholic nun with the intention to serve the suppressed and impoverished. She began to work honestly and devotedly but she was distressed to see that the Church and convent were also caste, class biased and the Dalits were discriminated against. The authorities of both Church and convent were given to worldly pleasures and majority of them were leading a lavish life. Bama found that the schools were also equally affected by the prejudice of caste and it was difficult for her to help the poor and Dalit children there. So, disenchanted and disgruntled, she finally left the nunnery after seven years and joined her people. She started writing to describe her experiences of pain, hardships and humiliation. Describing the nature and purpose of her autobiography Bama says that she wrote this book to heal the inward wounds that she got on account of her caste, class and gender. (Preface ix) Though, Bama relates her experiences as a poor Dalit woman and writes her pain but *Karukku* is not a passive record of suffering aiming to evoke pathos. It evinces a heightened Dalit consciousness and voices an active resistance against discriminatory institutions, traditions and laws.

Like most Dalit autobiographers, Bama also begins her narration with the description of Dalit lives in general and their socio-geographical locations. She writes that though her village was situated in a beautiful location but the Dalits living there were not happy and prosperous; they were coerced to live the lives of sub-human beings amid poverty and severe caste oppression. They were relegated to the other side of the village and were not allowed in the high caste localities. (7) Bama's explicit portrayal of the village exposes the severe caste rules and untouchability imposed on Dalits in the name of religion and social conventions. She describes an incident where an elder of her street was carrying a packet from the bazaar by holding its string to avoid touching it. Bama conjectured that something like *vadai* or green banana *bhajji* was packed in it because the wrapping paper was stained with oil. She could understand everything clearly only when the elder went to the Naicker, bowed low and humbly extended the packet towards him. Bama tells the incident to her brother who further explains to her that the Parayas and other outcaste people are not allowed to touch the eatables of the Naickers. (15) This incident unmasks the hypocrisy of the high castes, who live on the labour of the lower castes but consider their touch polluting. This incident infuriated her and made her radically question the precept of caste. (15-16)

Bama opines that poor Dalit labourers were the worst victims of the caste based discrimination and humiliation. She notes that they were forced to work ceaselessly but were not allowed in the high caste houses; they were given scraps in an undignified way from a distance so they can avoid the pollution resulting from the touch of a low caste fellow. Bama gives the example of her own grandmother: "After she had finished all her filthy chores, Patti placed the vessel that she had brought with her, by the side of the drain. The Naicker lady came out with her leftovers, leaned from some distance and tipped them into Patti's vessel, and went away. Her vessel, it seemed, must not touch Patti's; it would be polluted." (16) The author further shows that Dalits were discriminated against and humiliated by the high castes in public places and even in buses and taxicabs: "When I went home for holidays, if there was a Naicker woman sitting next to me in the bus, she'd immediately ask me which place I was going to, what street. As soon as I said, the Cheri, she'd get up and move off to another seat. Or she'd tell me to move elsewhere." (20) Bama argues that the notion of untouchability and precept of caste dehumanises Dalits and coerces them to live a life of sub-humans without honour and dignity.

Bama opposes the hypocrisy of Hindu society and its religious beliefs which legitimise caste discrimination and thwarts the progression of Dalits in different spheres. Exposing the rigour and the inevitability of caste, Bama writes that "if you are born into a low caste, you are forced to live a life of humiliation and degradation until your death. However much you study, whatever you take up, caste discrimination stalks us at every nook and corner and because of it we are unable to study well and progress. And this is why a wretched lifestyle is all that is left to us." (26)

Bama says that Dalits were insulted and ill-treated everywhere in the name of caste. Like Dalit male autobiographers such as Valmiki and Biswas, Bama also relates many instances of caste based oppression and differentiations against Dalit students in the church-run schools. She maintains that although the concept of caste is alien to Christianity, but the schools being run by the church were equally afflicted by the prejudice of caste and poor Dalit students studying there were shamed and discriminated against in numerous ways. The author recounts a personal experience of caste based humiliation in school while she was studying in the seventh standard. She was accused of stealing a coconut which actually fell down at her touch while she was playing with her friends. She was scolded and humiliated by the Headmaster in the presence of all students at assembly the next morning and was asked to stand outside. She was insulted by the priest also when she went to him and begged him to grant her permission to go back to school. (19)

Dalit children were mistrusted and treated as disreputable and immoral. They were tortured and exploited by the high caste teachers and other employees. Criticising the attitude and caste biases of the non-Dalit staff Bama says, "Everyone seemed to think *Harijan* children were contemptible. But they didn't hesitate to use us for cheap labour. So, we carried water to the teacher's house; we watered their plants. We did all the chores that were needed about the school." (18) Bama argues that Dalit children were also insulted in the hostels by the wardens. They were taunted for their caste and rustic manners and were not served food with equal dignity: "The Warden-Sister of our hostel could not abide low caste or poor children. She'd get hold of us and scold us for no rhyme or reason." (20)

Bama writes that caste and class biases were equally prevalent in institutions of higher education where teachers were more educated and cultured. She details how she was denied permission to go home to attend the First Communion of her younger brother and sister by her college Principal and the warden. She was surprised when they said, "What celebration can there be in your caste for First Communion?" (22) Although, Bama stood against this bias and humiliation and sought permission to go home. In addition to the staff and authority, the high caste rich students were also full of contempt and prejudices against poor Dalit students. The author shows that Dalit children were also abhorred and despised for their skin colour: "As a token gesture they took four or five children into the school. These wretches lurked in corners, trembling. The rich children would say, "We don't want to sit next to them, they are dark-skinned, they are poor, they are ugly and they don't wear nice clothes. Even in a play or a dance performance the rich children don't want to put on the costume of the poor." (112) Like other Dalit autobiographers, Bama also shows how the caste system discourages Dalit students, impedes their pursuit of education, forces them to discontinue their studies and follow the caste based occupations such as sweeping, cleaning and scavenging.

Bama writes that most Dalits were poor and landless agricultural labourers working for the high caste Naickers who exploited them in numerous ways. The impoverished Dalits were coerced to work continuously and were not allowed to rest. They were also not given proper wages for their work or food to eat. They were rebuked and beaten by their employers if they slacked in work. Bama details about Dalit labourers' exploitation at the time of harvesting of groundnuts: "If we chatted in between shelling, or ate one or two of the nuts the Naicker would be furious and swear at us, using every term of abuse he knew." (51)

Bama draws an elaborated list of the works that Parayas have to do for survival such as ploughing, manuring, watering, sowing the seeds, separating the seedlings and planting them, weeding, working on the threshing floors and planting groundnuts. Besides the agricultural work, the Parayas also worked at the kilns, construction sites and gathered firewood from hills and sold them in the market. Though the Dalits work continuously without taking account of their bodies and without caring for the risks and dangers to their lives, but they are not able to improve their life condition. They are still poor and starving. Bama writes that the rainy season was the most difficult time for Dalits as they could not procure food easily. So, they mostly survived by eating and selling fish. The Dalits who slog hard and produce grains for others have to starve themselves and wrap their bodies in rags.

Bama argues that in addition to acute starvation and frequent dehumanisation, the wretched poverty also accounts for widespread illiteracy. She reiterates that poverty forces poor Dalits to send their young children to work in the matchbox and firecracker factories for survival: "Nowadays, poor things, they go to work like adults. At the crack of dawn, even before the Madurai bus makes its appearance, the van from the matchbox factory arrives. These tiny, crab-like children pour their kuuzh into their carriers half asleep, totter along to the van, climb in and go off to work. They work at sticking matchbox labels; they make firecrackers and use chemicals; and they return home exhausted at seven in the evening." (55) The illiteracy and lack of awareness obstructs the socio-economic progression of Dalits and they remain poor, unorganised and silent. The author gives her grandmother's example who did not oppose the Naicker lady when she gave her leftovers from a distance and thus insulted her. Seeing this, Bama was incensed and advised her grandmother that she should not lay herself open to such contemptible behaviour and humiliation but grandmother instead of opposing the act of the Naicker lady called them Maharajas and accepted their sovereignty. (17)

The high castes use gods, religion and several metaphysical theories as tools to make Dalits comply with caste laws and codes designed to subordinate them. "Because Dalits have been enslaved for generations, and been told again and again of their degradation, they have come to believe that they are degraded, lack honour and self-worth, untouchable; they have reached a stage where they, voluntarily, hold themselves apart. This is the worst injustice. This is what even little babies are told, how they are instructed. The consequence of all this is that there is no way for Dalits to find freedom or redemption." (28) Bama presents her grandmother as the prototype of Dalits who have conditioned themselves to live in subordination to the high castes and have lost hope of liberation.

Karukku also exposes the rampant gender biases. Bama argues that the personhood and identity of Dalit women was discounted by the dominant casteist and patriarchal forces that discriminated against them and subjected them to severe exploitation. She shows how Dalit women were paid less as compared to men for the same work. (54-55) Bama maintains that Dalit women are the commonest victims of molestation and rapes by the high caste rich men. "If a woman so much as stands alone and by herself somewhere, all sorts of men gather around her. However angry you get, however, repelled by their expressions and their grimaces, even to the point of retching, what can you do on your own? We think so many thoughts. We hope so much. We study so many things. But in real life everything turns out differently." (119) Bama also exposes the gender biases prevalent among Dalits themselves. For instance,

Dalit girls are not given the opportunity to educate themselves and most of them are forced to do household chores and look after their siblings. Though, boys and girls were allowed to play together but even in games, the boys always played the dominant roles and girls were assigned subordinate roles only.

Bama shows that Dalit patriarchal codes and conventions operate distinctively in the lives of Dalit women and impose numerous restrictions and prohibitions on them. Only little girls are allowed to play, grown-up Dalit girls were strictly prohibited to play, entertain themselves and behave, act independently: "When girls grew up, there was no more play. We went to work during the day, came home and saw to the household chores; that was it." (58) They were also not allowed to watch cinema. Dalit men find Dalit women's sexuality a problem so they hurl implications to control and hegemonise it. Bama further argues that even singing and dancing of Dalit women is considered indecent and deprecating; they are considered cheap display of their bodies and also a demonstration of their sexuality. Bama not only condemns Dalit patriarchy but also questions those Dalit males who argue that Dalit women are more liberated and autonomous than their high caste counterparts who were subjected to numerous restrictions, prohibitions and had to practice *purdah* even within their own households. Bama maintains that although Dalit women were not coerced to practice *purdah* conventionally, but denial to public exposure and expression of personhood is no way less patriarchal and dehumanising than the purdah itself.

Besides the social-cultural and behavioural restrictions, Dalit women were also the worst victims of domestic violence. The author shows a Dalit man, Uudan, beating his wife like an animal to avenge himself as he was forced by her father and uncle to marry her. All the villagers knew it but nobody ever came forward to save her: "Every day he'd drag his wife by the hair to the community hall and beat her with his belt as if she were an animal. Everyone came to watch. But nobody could go near and separate them." (61)

Bama challenges caste, class and patriarchal forces and exposes the religious order and argues that even the Church, which most Dalits join to escape the slurs and tyrannies of caste, was affected by it: "Even amongst the priests and nuns, it is the upper castes who hold all the high positions, show off their authority and throw their weight about. If Dalits become priests and nuns, they are pushed aside and marginalized." (80) The Dalit Christians were assigned unhygienic and degrading work such as sweeping, cleaning, lifting dirt and were humiliated and exploited. Even the priests and nuns who claimed that their hearts were set upon service to God, loathed the lower castes. Criticising the general attitude of the Church towards Dalits, Bama says, "They have made use of Dalits who are immersed in ignorance as their capital, set up a big business, and profited their own castes. In the Churches, Dalits are most in numbers. In everything else, they are the least. It is only the upper-caste Christians who enjoy the benefits and comforts of the Church." (80) Bama voices her protest against these inequalities and maintains, "In the name of God they actually rob from the poor who struggle for their very livelihood. They make themselves into gods so they can exploit others. So where has God gone, I wonder?" (108)

Bama writes that the Church was given to several hypocrisies and superstitions. She says that they were not allowed to touch the host while they received Communion. It was because of the assumption that Jesus was inside that host so they should not touch it with their sinful hands. They were also frequently warned that even if it stuck to their plates, they should only move it gently with their tongues and swallow it without biting. (85) Even though students found it both difficult and embarrassing but they could not oppose it.

Bama writes that children studying in convent schools were also subjected to numerous religious pretentions and hypocrisies. She says, "There was usually a catechism class on Sunday evenings. When that was over, there was Blessing in the Church. This Blessing would seemingly go on for hours and hours. The priest would come, give his sermon, and ask a number of questions. We small children would be sleepy and could scarcely keep our eyes open. If our eyes dropped even slightly, the Sister sitting nearby would land a stinging blow on your back." (86) Apart from catechism classes, it was mandatory for all children to go to morning Pusai: "If you don't go, the next day at assembly you were beaten by the priest or by a teacher. Nor were these ordinary blows. The cane fell on us with the sharpness of a whip. It left great weals." (82) The students were also beaten if they ever made any mistake while reciting the prayers. The author opposes all such tyrannies, criticises religious performances in the Church and defies the authority of priests and nuns. With the course of time, she comprehends the truth that it is not through the priests and nuns that one can connect with God and have His mercy.

Bama maintains that Churches have deviated from the messages and teachings of Jesus and have no place for Christian virtues such as love, devotion, simplicity and renunciation. She exposes the corruption and chauvinism of the Church and revolts against its authority. Although Bama was a devoted Christian, but she rejects Christianity as a religious alternative for Dalits. She opines that the Indian Churches are casteist and oppress Dalits and discriminate against them. In addition, she is well aware that the converted Dalits were not granted the reservation benefits according to the constitutional provisions in India. Although, Bama does not mention in *Karukku*, but like most Dalit writers, she also believes that Dalits should follow atheism to counter caste.

Bama subverts the constraints of genres and established hegemonic literary traditions. She experiments in textual strategies and also uses an unconventional narrative form. She does not detail adequately about her birth, parentage, upbringing and familial background in the beginning and opens her life story with the description of her village, and the Dalit lives there. Instead of describing individual pain and suffering, Bama writes about the plight of her Paraya community and thus, transgresses the traditions of autobiographical narrative. This deliberate deviation from traditional form of autobiography makes *Karukku* the biography of her community. Bama is inclusive, collective in her approach and aspires to establish a socio-political, economic system where all disadvantaged, deprived, marginalised groups such as Dalits and women can live with dignity. Like other Dalit women's autobiographies, Bama's *Karukku* is also a 'Testimonio'. It exhibits several distinctive and unconventional narrative strategies and techniques. For instance, Bama does not mention the name of her village, parents, siblings and also the high castes who exploited her people. It is perhaps because

Bama does not want to particularise the pain and experiences of suffering and deprivation. Raj Kumar writes, "The concept of anonymity in narration has a special function. By refusing to give names, Bama is perhaps trying to make a universal statement about oppression even though it exists at the local level" (233). MSS Pandian writes, "To name is to exercise power. But a deliberate refusal to name can enable a politics of collectivity. The shroud of anonymity frees events, persons and institutions from the possibility of individuation and renders them general. Anonymity thus becomes a mode of invoking larger solidarities." (132)

Bama is unconventional, innovative, resistant and revolutionary in her use of language as well. She rejected standard Tamil, which has been the monopoly of the upper castes in Tamil Nadu and wrote *Karukku* in the Tamil spoken by Dalit masses. In an interview with Amrita Dutta, Bama says she uses the language of her own people to assert Dalit identity and also to challenge the prevalent hegemonic literary and linguistic dominance. (6) Her selection of language also indicates her desperate longing to join her community and describe the anguish of her people more realistically. She does not write to amuse her readers, rather her writings aim to awaken and mobilise impoverished Dalit masses. The aesthetic that *Karukku* offers results from the revelation of truth and exposition and criticism of injustices. *Karukku* is characterised by the spirit of rejection, innovation and revolt. Even the title of Bama's autobiography indicates the pain that she undergoes and also symbolises Dalit consciousness, protest and change.

In Tamil, the word '*Karukku*' means the saw-like double-edged stem of the Palmyra leaf. Another Tamil word *karu* means embryo or seed, which also means freshness or newness. Kumar argues that "the embryo refers to the Dalit consciousness and the symbol is the new revolution, which aims at bringing a new social order into Indian society." (231-32) In addition, the title also encourages Dalits to regain their lost identity and revolt against the hegemonic powers that treat them as outcastes and contemptible. Bama writes, "There are other Dalit hearts like mine, with a passionate desire to create a new society made up of justice, equality, and love. They, who have been oppressed, are like the double-edged karukku, challenging their oppressors." (xxiii)

Bama attempts to awaken Dalit masses and mobilise them against the authority of the high castes. She appeals, "We should not accept the injustice of our enslavement by telling ourselves it is our fate; we must dare to stand up for change. We must crush all these institutions that use caste to bully us into submission, and demonstrate that among human beings there are none who are high or low." (28) Bama resists the assumption that Dalits are inferior, worthless, low and sinful by birth. She maintains that although Dalits were traditionally alienated from education and knowledge, they were not without talent, wisdom and abilities. She appreciates Dalits for their indomitable will, courage, capacity to work hard, control their lives and support their families despite numerous odds and adversities. Bama gives the example of her own mother who supported her family when her husband was not able to send money during the wars with Pakistan, China and Bangladesh. MS Wankhede writes, "Bama's writing celebrates Dalit women's lives, their wit, their humour, their resilience and their creativity." (144) *Karukku* suggests that the untouchables should not be ashamed of their identity rather they should celebrate and assert it vociferously.

The author herself suffers severe identity crisis but she refuses to hide her caste even when her mother advised her to do so. (20-21) Bama's assertion of identity is a clear reflection of her overt resistance against the precept of caste and the notion of caste superiority and inferiority.

Bama exposes and resists the whole mechanism of Dalits' suffering and demands a viable space for them in society, but at the same time she also criticises them for the internal caste divisions and conflicts. The author is pained to see that instead of fighting against the high castes, who are the real perpetrators, Dalits are exhausting their strength in fighting against each other. Through an account of the terrible conflict between Chaaliyars and Parayas and then Pallars and Parayas, Bama maintains that the internal caste divide undermined the strength of their movement and gave the high castes an opportunity to strengthen their hold. She unequivocally condemns Dalits for the intra-caste conflicts and shows the horrible fallouts of such scuffles and skirmishes. (47) Bama also highpoints that Dalit women, the worst victims of discriminations, are also divided in the name of caste and community and practice untouchability. It is evident that this internal divide keeps Dalit women weak and scattered. Bama explains that Indian women are not adequately aware of the gender issues and are opposed to each other. She aspires to awaken such unconscious Dalit women and attempts to spread caste and gender consciousness among them. The author appeals to Dalits in general to organise themselves and fight collectively against the high castes who claim ritual purity, control economic resources, deny Dalits' humanity, dignity and access to education and resources. She is optimistic and reiterates that Dalits can win equality and create a space for themselves if they protest together. (122) Bama exhibits an indomitable and buoyant spirit as despite numerous odds and injustices, she finds happiness in life. (122)

Though, most Dalits depicted in *Karukku* are poor, illiterate, unconscious of the cause of their plight and do not protest collectively against the dominant forces, this autobiography is not an ineffectual writing of pain, distress and haplessness. *Karukku* successfully locates the mechanism of Dalit suffering and resists every form of oppression unleashed on the impoverished Dalit masses. Bama strives to initiate an egalitarian system without any consideration for caste, class, gender, racial and religious differences. Lakshmi Holmstrom rightly says that *Karukku* has "a universality at its core which questions all oppressions, disturbs all complacencies, and reaching out, empowers all those who have suffered different oppressions." (Translator's Note xiv)

Bama suggests education as an effective tool to counter caste, class and empower Dalits. She offers the example of her father who elevated their status in the caste dominated society by educating themselves. She maintains that Dalits should not surrender their autonomy and rights to religious forces and should revolt against their oppression in the name of faith and gods. Bama wants Dalits to assert their identity, celebrate their rich cultural heritage and devise their own literary traditions. Finally, it can be inferred that *Karukku* is a revolutionary text as it problematises every institution and law that discriminates against Dalits and vocalises the demand for Dalit liberation. It offers powerful alternatives and discusses effective strategies to manoeuvre their resistance and demolish the existing biased social, economic, political, literary, cultural, religious institutions and power structures. Describing the nature and scope of Bama's life narrative, Kumar says that "apart from being a literary masterpiece it is a rare social document prepared by a Dalit woman activist. The new insights that come from her life's experiences will certainly give new direction to Dalit movements which otherwise are lacking in women leadership." (237)

A Life Less Ordinary

A writer and a domestic worker, Baby Halder is one of the significant Dalit feminist voices in contemporary India. The publication of her life narrative *A Life Less Ordinary* brought her to literary prominence and created a stir in traditional casteist and masculine Indian academia as it not only brings out the saga of a destitute woman but also problematises the traditional power relations between the dominant and the dominated. Originally written in Bangla, *A Life Less Ordinary* was first published in Hindi after it was edited and translated by Prabodh Kumar, one of her employers. Being a powerful critique of rampant caste, class and patriarchal oppression, *A Life Less Ordinary* was widely acclaimed in popular circles and translated into different Indian and foreign languages. The English rendering of the text was done by Urvashi Butalia in 2006. In addition to her life story, Baby Halder has also written two other books: *Eshast Rupantar,* which is a sequel to *A Life Less Ordinary* and *Ghare Ferar Path* which details how her writings have been successful in changing social perceptions and attitude towards her. *A Life Less Ordinary* is an authentic record of the lived experiences of the author as an occupant of a liminal space in hegemonic Indian society.

A Life Less Ordinary opens with the description of Baby

Halder's early childhood in Jammu and Kashmir where she lived happily with her parents and siblings for a few years. From Jammu and Kashmir, her family moved to Dalhousie and had a good stay there also. The problem started only after her father took his family back to Murshidabad, West Bengal where Baby's uncle, whom she called Jetha, was also living. Her father rented a house for his family, admitted his children in school, and after a few days, joined back his Army service. Baby's mother had to face severe hardships as her husband did not send her money regularly and also did not come home to see her. Though, the mother worked hard, managed to feed her children and continue their education somehow, but infuriated by her husband's continuous neglect of familial responsibilities, one day she picked up her youngest son and walked away from home without saying anything to anyone. Baby's father searched for her but he could not track her down. Finally, he married a woman who was adamant, conceited and cantankerous. He deserted her and married another woman who was no better. Baby was mistreated by both her step-mothers as they used to scold and insult her repeatedly.

To get rid of his daughter and also to escape the frequent squabbles at home, Baby's father married her off at the tender age of twelve to a man fourteen years her senior. This unmatched marriage further exposed Baby to violence and exploitation as her husband was also an authoritative and staunch patriarch. He never cared for his wife, starved, berated and beat her frequently at the slightest provocation. Finally, unable to bear the indifference and frequent violence by her husband, Baby fled Durgapur for Delhi with her three children and thus, joined the cohort of almost five million housemaids working in the Indian metropolis. Although, there were more job opportunities in Delhi as compared to Durgapur, but her life was not easy or comfortable. She was humiliated and exploited by her employers while working as a domestic help in Delhi. Finally, it was Prabodh Kumar (the grandson of Premchand) who not only employed her as a domestic worker but also gave her emotional support and love which she was longing for after her mother left home. Discovering Baby's interest in books, Kumar encouraged her to read and also inspired her to write her life story.

Like other marginal autobiographies, *A Life Less Ordinary* also begins with the description of pain and suffering that the author undergoes on account of her sex, poverty and caste. It shows how she was repressed, dehumanised and subjected to brutal living conditions first by her alcoholic, heedless father and then by her patriarchal husband. Though the author places herself at the centre of the narration and writes adequately about her pain, distress, struggle and bourgeoning as a writer amid severe repression, this autobiography is not an account of what she suffered and achieved in life. It locates Dalit women's place in society, highpoints how the institutions of caste, class and gender operate in their lives and how these institutions subject them to starvation, impoverishment, exploitation, repression, violence, and even ruthless murders. Underscoring the subtle collective engraved in this text, Swapna Banerjee writes, "*A Life Less Ordinary* is not just 'a book of her own,' but speaks for the millions of 'ordinary' women like her." (245)

Although, the author does not offer a history of untouchability, gender oppression and the origin, evolution of Dalit women's movements in Bengal, but her life story refers to the historical reality that the so called process of modernisation, economic progression, education and technological innovation, which started in the nineteenth century colonial Bengal, brought an uneven development in the lives of women. This process benefitted the women of upper castes and class only. The impoverished lower caste women were pushed into servitude and coerced to do the most menial and squalled works such as sweeping and cleaning for survival. Banerjee writes, "By the first decade of the twentieth century, a selected group of 'new women,' called *Bhadramahila* (respectable ladies), built women's organizations, opened schools, wrote in magazines, and participated in national politics. But the lives of the working class women deteriorated as they were subsequently pushed into domestic services, which allowed very little scope for upward mobility." (240)

The author exposes every institution that discriminates against Dalit women, obstructs their progression in social, economic, political spheres and maintains that the roots of Dalit women's suffering are located in Dalit patriarchal traditions. Baby writes that her father was an authoritarian patriarch who not only ignored and tamed his wives but also suppressed his daughters and imposed several restrictions on them. She argues that it was her father's indifference and patriarchal authority that forced her mother to leave house, children and lead a miserable life. Baby maintains that her father was jealous of his third wife and also doubted her faithfulness. It was because of her father's sexual jealousy, patriarchal possession, authority and desire to own a female body that her stepmother was caged like a bird and not given space even within her own household. She was coerced to behave according to patriarchal traditions and her husband's will.

Baby argues that her father also suppressed his daughters. He subjected them to his authority and did not let them grow and behave independently. Baby writes: "I wasn't allowed to talk to anyone, to play with anyone, and often not even allowed out of the house." (12) To control both her behaviour and sexuality, he did not allow her to interact and play with boys. (97) Critiquing her father's authority and rigid internal patriarchal structures, Baby writes that her father was not serious about his daughter's education and their physical and psychological growth. It was because of her father's gender predispositions that her elder sister was married off at a young age without even asking her. Baby was also married off at the age of twelve and not given any choice. Baby further writes that she was not even aware of the meaning and purpose of marriage when she was given away. She was happily playing outside with her friends while her relatives were making arrangements for her wedding. Baby maintains that her father used marriage as an apparatus to get rid of his daughters, to control their autonomy and also to tame their sexuality. (22-23)

Baby writes that marriage did not bring her any happiness, stability and peace, rather it subjected her to poverty, starvation, fear, violence, marital rape and unwanted motherhood. Her husband stifled her voice and repressed her personhood and identity. He did not cooperate with her and did not give her money even to buy things of domestic use. (50) Her husband was indifferent to her and did not give her emotional support and medical assistance even when she was pregnant. He was not even around when she gave birth to her second son. He ignored motherhood and also his newly born child. (95-96)

Baby argues that her husband not only ignored his familial responsibilities but also imposed his authority and numerous restrictions on her. He prohibited her public exposure and coerced her to practice purdah in the traditional Indian way. He turned her into a work machine without any desire or will: "I told him I wanted to go and watch a film. He said, there is no need. So, I asked him why. After all, everyone in the neighbourhood was going and I could go and come back early if he wished. I couldn't see anything wrong with this, but he still refused." (83) Underscoring Baby's subjection to austere internal patriarchal oppression Binjal Shah writes, "Baby's fate changed hands from one abusive male to another ever since she was born. Within a year, when she was a mere child herself, all of thirteen, she bore a child of her own. Consent and agency were not a part of the equation, and she went on to have two more children". (n. page)

Baby's husband did not allow her to even meet and talk to her friends. He did not like her going to see Shashti and her sisters living in their neighbourhood because they were considered immoral and fallen women. Baby was beaten by her husband when she continued to visit Shashti's house despite his frequent caveats: "Then, one day, Shashti's mother called me to their house. When I arrived, I realized my husband had followed me. He did not say anything but picked up a stone from the ground and hit me on the head with it. My forehead split, and blood gushed out." (84) Baby shares the brutalities that she endured and details how once a severe beating from her husband caused her to abort her child. (85-86) She argues that the traditional forms of marriage deny women personhood and agency and promote violence against them. It grants men the right to treat their wives as they like. In most cases of domestic violence as noted in *A Life Less Ordinary,* the chief perpetrators are husbands.

Baby details the plight of her elder sister and shows how her husband used to torture and beat her frequently. She was not strong enough to resist violence and fight against her husband so ultimately, he murdered her. (66-67) She was cremated without waiting for her father and other relatives so that her husband could conceal the murder. Baby details that her father could not even report the murder to the police because her sister's husband threatened to kill his children also if he was sent to prison. This incident exposes the rigid Dalit patriarchy and also reveals how women are considered property by men so they do not hesitate to scold, beat or even murder them. Baby shows how Panna, a drunkard in her neighbourhood, set fire to his wife and burnt her to death just because he saw her watching television at a neighbour's house. (103) Baby argues that most Indian women are subjected to such kind of violence and brutalities but they do not report the crimes against them. It is evident that women's silence and the internalisation of pain promotes violence and crimes against them both within their own households and the larger society. Baby opines that it was because of her father's indifference and lack of support that his elder daughter Sushila, was murdered by her husband. In addition, Baby herself was also beaten and starved frequently by her husband as he was also aware that her father and brothers were unconcerned about her.

Baby writes about her pain and helplessness and shows numerous odds, hardships and handicaps in her life but despite that she does not yield silently to dominant forces. She puts up a fight against all adversities and strives for survival, stability, dignity and autonomy in life. Describing the nature and scope of this life narrative, Urvashi Butalia writes, "Baby's story is not unique. It is the story of thousands of women caught in similar situations across the world. What makes it different is Baby's strength and resolve, her determination to not stay in an abusive situation, to escape, to make a life for herself and her children, and in the end, her absolute commitment to the one thing she had always held close to her heart, education and learning and the desire to read and write." (vii)

Baby had to face her husband's wrath and severe violence by him but she exhibits courage and challenges his authority, criticises his carelessness and neglect of familial responsibilities. (51) Baby also questions her subjection to her husband and asserts her autonomy: "I had no independence. I used to wonder at the injustice of this. It was my life not his. Did I have to behave as he wanted simply because I was with him? He treated me as if I were an animal. If I had no happiness and peace in his house, was it necessary that I should stay on in that living hell?" (68) She does not care for her husband when he expressed his objection against Dulal, her childhood friend coming to their house. She does not even listen to Dulal when he says that perhaps her husband does not like him coming to his house. (97-98) Baby is strong, buoyant and optimistic and does not surrender to the evil circumstances and oppression silently. She comes out even stronger after every repressive incident and fights back against the perpetrators. She exercises her agency and takes control of her body when she decides to go for salpingectomy without seeking her husband's permission and consent. (102) In due course of time, Baby began to take her decisions independently and liberate herself from her husband's authority. Describing the significance of Baby's decision Sonakshi Srivastava writes, "Her decision to get a tubectomy and her retort to the doctor that she is educated enough to not need 'permission' from her husband is definitely commendable. She realises early that if she cared and worried about what people say, she will forever be shackled and weighed down by patriarchy." (n. page)

Baby argues that a woman living alone is considered debauched or fallen. She gives the example of Shashti and her sisters and her own experiences while she was living in Gurgaon away from her husband. She was denied jobs when people came to know that her husband was not with her. (129) Like Bama, Baby also maintains that it is not possible for a woman to live alone in a male dominated society as she is then considered an opportunity or an object of sex by men. Baby states, "Some men would make excuse that they wanted water and push their way into my home. Or, if I went somewhere with the children, they'd follow me and try to force me to talk to them." (153) Criticising male lust and the objectification of a woman's body, Baby further details how the elder son of her landlord once tried to force her to acquiesce her body to him. (154) Baby also cites the example of a young Bengali girl named Suniti. She was teased and all sorts of remarks were made by young boys when she went for a walk to the park with a small child. (162) These incidents expose the Indian patriarchy and shows how women are seen as objects and denied free will by men.

Baby questions male authority, problematises patriarchal concepts and asserts women's autonomy. She underscores how patriarchal institutions impose restrictions on women and grant privileges to men. She illustrates this through the relationship between Shashti, her sisters and Pratap, a community leader: "A community leader called Pratap, often visited them, but that didn't make any difference to the respect people had for him! It was always the women who were judged differently." (80) Baby argues that concepts such as chastity, purity and morality are reserved for women only and have nothing to do with men. The author writes that her husband beat her for talking to his friend Ajit, but did not say anything to Ajit who was actually harassing and chasing her everywhere. (80-81) It was because of the inherent patriarchal structure that Baby's husband finds fault with her and ignored the man who was trying to force himself on her.

Baby refuses to be bound by socio-religious notions such as *patidev* and eventually deserts her husband who had no love and respect for her. She was not concerned about public opinion as she was well aware that survival was much more important than the so called social status. (2) Baby justifies her decision to leave home and desert her husband: "It is not enough to give birth, for birth brings responsibility; the responsibility to enable a person to grow into a human being. My husband could not or did not want to understand this. For if he had, it would have also meant sharing that responsibility and he was not interested in that. It also meant providing a good atmosphere and surroundings, but he did not want to change our situation and we used to fight about this in front of the children. That made me realize that things would not work out and that I had to be strong and find a way out of this mess." (130)

Baby deserts her husband to escape violence, impoverishment and also to educate her children. (235) She is confident and firm about her decision and refuses to go back to her husband even when her father asks her to do so. Baby is not scared of separation from her husband and does not think that it may affect the future of her children. She says, "I'll see to it that they study. I thought to myself that it is only because of me that my elder son has studied the little that he has; and I've managed along with looking after two small children, working, running the home…The worst thing that could happen would be my workload will increase. Nothing more." (120) Banerjee also writes, "Instead of yielding to an unfavourable situation, Baby pressed hard, displayed courage and questioned her state. Her feminism manifests through her sense of self-worth and optimism, in her ability to take charge, and in determining the course of her own life." (248) The author argues that women are not mere servants or assistants to men without any desire and will of their own. Baby resists the sexual division of labour, the feminisation of poverty and domestic services in India. She argues that to look after and run a household is the common responsibility of a man and a woman. (48)

Baby exhibits an awakened consciousness and also asserts her identity and dignity. Her pursuit of empowerment and self-esteem manifest in her struggle for economic self-dependence and a better life. She does not like to be dependent on her husband who was hardly concerned about her needs and emotions. She started teaching small children, worked in a hospital and also as a domestic help in Durgapur before she left for Delhi. She did not compromise her dignity even when she was alone in a city like Gurgaon. She refused to live on the mercy of her brothers and sisters-in-law and stopped going to them when she realised that they did not like her coming to their houses. (129) Baby does not let her dignity dwindle and did not let herself be exploited by any man even when she was penniless. She protected her body and integrity bravely. She changed her room when the elder son of her landlord tried to force her. (154)

Baby Halder is overt and authentic in her narration of pain that she underwent. In addition to patriarchal domination, she was also subjected to severe caste based oppression and humiliation. She maintains that she was humiliated, exploited and discriminated against by her Brahmin employer's family members while working as a domestic help for them in Durgapur. Exposing rigid caste discrimination by the Brahmin family, Baby further writes that the wife of her employer Ashish, considered it polluting, below a Brahmin's dignity to touch Baby and her little daughter. (109)

The author maintains that the caste system persists with equal rigidity even after many years of independence, adoption of the Indian constitution and despite numerous constitutional and legal provisions against it. Baby writes that low caste people cannot change their position and cannot win the hearts of high castes however loving and sacrificing they may be. She gives the example of an inter caste love affair between a low caste man, Vibhuda and a high caste girl, Nisha. Vibhuda lost his young and beautiful wife, who committed suicide by consuming poison because of his relation with Nisha but despite knowing this, Nisha refused to marry him. She did not care for Vibhuda's true love and sacrifice simply because she did not want to lose her caste status. (100) It can be inferred from this instance that the precept of caste and the concept of purity and pollution are so firmly ingrained in the high caste people's consciousness that they cannot even think of transgressing the caste codes and conventions. It is mainly because of caste that in most cases of inter-caste relations it is always a Dalit who is deceived and punished. Like other Dalit feminists, Baby also indicates that social practices such as *purdah*, *sati*, child marriage and ascetic widowhood were induced and imposed on women forcefully by the casteist, patriarchal forces so they can maintain the caste system and repress their sexuality.

Baby Halder is overt and authentic in her critique of caste, class and patriarchal institutions that dehumanise, exploit and marginalise women. She locates and criticises every law and convention that ghettoises and brutalises women and exposes them to dehumanisation. During the course of her narrative, she frequently indicates that Indian women themselves are responsible for their plight and wretchedness. The lack of cooperation subjects Indian women to male authority and vulnerable to the external world. In most cases, Dalit women are discriminated against and exploited by their high caste sisters who have internalised patriarchy and patriarchal oppression without even realising it. Giving her own example, Baby writes that she was exploited by her high caste employer's wife in Gurgaon. She was assigned task after task and not given even a few minutes off. Sometimes, she was not given time to even cook and eat her food and see her children. Besides, she was not allowed to go out of the house, talk to anyone and was also scolded and humiliated for being late for work. Baby ironically writes, "The family I worked with had a dog called Kesfo. He gave me much more love and attention than that family ever did." (139) Like some other eminent Dalit women autobiographers such as Baby Kamble, Urmila Pawar, Kumud

Pawde, Bama and others, Baby also maintains that Indian women are not aware of the mechanisms of their suffering and their position in a caste and gender afflicted society and because of this lack of consciousness most of them are subjected heavily to male authority. A woman who attempts to speak against patriarchal conventions is criticised and considered fallen and degraded by other women. The deprecating words and terms such as *kulta* (prostitute), *dayan* (witch) and *papin* (sinful woman) are particularly used to denote such a revolutionary woman.

Baby argues that Dalit women are not conscious of the cause of their sufferings and are opposed to each other. The author details how her second step-mother made her suffer, forced her to discontinue her studies and often provoked violence against her. She finally created a permanent gap between father and daughter when she accused them of having an illicit relation. Apart from her step-mother, Baby also did not get any support from her sisters-in-law. One of Baby's primary reasons for moving away from her brother's house in Delhi was to avoid conflict with her sister-in-law. Baby writes, "I longed for my mother. I used to think that if only I could have her love and support, my fear of Baba would be manageable. Had she been around, I would not have had to abandon my studies. In fact, had it not been for her support and constant encouragement, I would not have studied even as much as I had." (12) She also misses her mother and wishes her to be alive when she comes out successful towards the end and her life story gets published. (172)

In conclusion, it can be affirmed that both autobiographies: Bama's *Karukku* and Baby Halder's *A Life Less Ordinary* are authentic accounts of Dalit women's distress, the strong expressions of their will, desire, and also the articulation of their agency, dignity and identity. They expose every law and tradition that discriminates against Dalit women, imposes restrictions on them, suppresses their personhood and denies their rights. Both life narratives expose the internal caste divide, patriarchy and superstitions prevalent among Dalits. The Dalit women's voices in these autobiographies are expository, resistant, and reformist in nature and in tone they are aggressive, optimistic and retaliatory. They scorn repressive institutions such as gods and religion and suggest that Dalits should not surrender their rights and autonomy to them. They suggest education and economic self-dependence as alternatives to overcome all kinds of differences and liberate Dalits in general and women in particular from the precepts of caste, class, gender and religion.

Though the selected autobiographies share similarities yet there are also certain discernible differences. For instance, *Karukku* is written collectively in the name of Paraya community and exhibits an awakened socio-political vision. It launches a sensible attack on caste, class and gender based differences but *A Life Less Ordinary* is an apolitical text, essentially directed against patriarchal oppression. According to Swapna Banerjee, "Perhaps because of its non-political nature *A Life Less Ordinary* does not emphasise caste and class over gender as is usually done in the writings of politically committed and partly afflicted women." (204) Bama locates the roots of Dalit women's suffering in caste and religion but Baby opines that Dalit patriarchy is the root cause of Dalit women's vulnerability and their sufferings in society. Apart from this, both autobiographies show changes in the socio-economic position of Dalits.

Bama's Dalits are impoverished and work for the high caste Naickers as bonded labourers but some of the Dalits depicted by Baby show economic improvements. Unlike Bama, Baby maintains that Dalits were granted the right to property which was strictly prohibited earlier not only in Bengal but also in other states of India. Baby's father-in-law had a huge house with an open courtyard and also owned fields which produced enough rice to feed the family all the year. Apart from this, Dalits also got the right to run business. Baby's uncle living in Karimpur owned a restaurant and also a sweet shop. His elder son had a shop for tape recorders and radios.

Finally, it can be argued that there may be some similarities and dissimilarities between the selected autobiographies but both are significant additions to the chorus of Dalit women's voices as they strive to destroy the inequalitarian institutions, secure equal rights and dignity for women and ultimately liberate them in every sphere of life.

Works Cited

- Agnihotri, Ritika. "Attaining Selfhood: An Analysis of Baby Halder's *A Life Less Ordinary.*" *Quest Journals: Journal of Research in Humanities and Social Science,* vol. 6, no. 1, 2018, pp. 48-50. www.questjournals.org/jrhss/papers/vol6-issue1/I614850.pdf. Accessed 31 July 2019.
- Bama. *Karukku.* Translated by Holmstrom. Oxford UP, 2000.
- Preface. *Karukku* by Bama. Translated by Holmstrom. Oxford

UP, 2000, pp. ix-xii.

- Preface to the First Edition. *Karukku* by Bama. Translated by Holmstrom. Oxford UP, 2000, pp. xxiii-xiv.
- "Tamil Dalit Writer Bama Faustina Soosairaj on 25 Years of *Karukku,* Writing in the Language of People and Being a Mentor-Teacher to First-Generation Dalit Students." *The Tribune*, 21 January 2018, p. 6.
- Bande, Usha. *Writing Resistance: A Comparative Study of the Selected Novels by Women Writers.* IIAS, 2015.
- Banerjee, Swapna. "Baby Halder's *A Life Less Ordinary*: A Transition from India's Colonial Past." *Colonization and Domestic Service: Historical and Contemporary Perspectives*, edited by Victoria K Haskins and Claire Lowrie, Routledge, 2015, pp. 239-255.
- "Risking Life, Writing Selves: From the Trailblazer P Wadder to Rebellious Baby Halder." *They Dared: Essays in Honour of Pritilata Wadder*, edited by Simonti Sen, 2011, pp. 198-220.
- Butalia, Urvashi. Forward. *A Life Less Ordinary* by Baby Halder. Translated by Butalia, Zubaan, 2013, pp. vii-xi.
- Gentleman, Amelia. "In India, a Maid Becomes an Unlikely Literary Star." *New York Times.* 2 August 2006. n. page. www.nytimes.com/2006/08/02/books/02maid.html. Accessed 2 August 2019.
- Haynes, Douglas, and Gyan Prakash. *Contesting Power: Resistance and Everyday Social Relations in South Asia*. Oxford UP, 1991.
- Holmstrom, Lakshmi. Introduction. *Karukku* by Bama. Translated by Holmstrom. Oxford UP, 2000, pp. xv-xxi.
- Translator's Note to the Second Edition. *Karukku* by Bama. Translated by Holmstrom. Oxford UP, 2000, pp. xiii-xiv.
- John, E Mary. "The Problem of Women's Labour: Some

Autobiographical Perspectives." *Indian Journal of Gender Studies*. 2013, vol. 20, no. 2, pp. 177-212. citeseerx.ist.psu.edu/viewdoc/download?doi=10.1.1.1011.3138&rep=rep1...Accessed 2 August 2019.

- Kumar, Raj. Dalit Personal Narratives: Reading Caste, Nation and Identity. Orient Black Swan, 2010.
- Latha, K "Double Oppression in Bama's *Karukku* and *Sangati*." *Language in India,* vol. 17, no.1,2017, pp.119-137. www.languageinindia.com/jan2017/lathakarukkusangati.pdf. Accessed 6 July 2019.
- Ojha, Rekha. *Dalit Women in India*. Akansha Publishing House, 2012.
- Pandian, MSS "On a Dalit Woman's Testimonio." *Gender and Caste*, edited by Anupama Rao, Kali for Women, 2003, pp. 129-135.
- Ramaswamy, EV *Why were Women Enslaved*? Translated by Meena Kandasamy, The Periyar Self-Respect Propaganda Institution, 2007.
- Rege, Sharmila. *Writing Caste/ Writing Gender: Reading Dalit Women's Testimonios*. Zubaan, 2006.
- Sailpar, Anshu. "Matrix of Dalit Feminism in Bama Faustina's *Karukku* and *Sangati: Events*."*International Journal of Applied Research*, vol. 1, no. 9, 2015, pp. 476-481. www.allresearchjournal.com/archives/2015/vol1issue9/PartH/1-9-129.pdf. Accessed 27 June 2019.
- Shah, Binjal. "Child Bride at 12 and Mother at 13, how Baby Halder Went from Being a Domestic Servant to a Bestselling Author in 21 Languages." *Your story*. 3 March 2018, n. page. yourstory.com/2018/03/child-bride-12-mother-13-baby-halder-went-domestic-servant-bestselling-author-21-languages. Accessed 2 August 2019.

- Slemon, Stephen. "Unsettling the Empire: Resistance Theory for the Second World." *The Post-Colonial Studies Reader*, edited by Bill Ashcroft, Gareth Griffith and Helen Tiffin, Routledge, 1995, pp. 104-110.
- Srivastava, Sonakshi. "Book Review: *A Life Less Ordinary*." *Feminism in India*. 25 March 2019, n. page. feminisminindia.com/2019/03/25/a-life-less-ordinary-baby-halder-review/. Accessed 1 August 2019.
- Wankhede, MS "A Study of Bama's *Karukku* in the Light of Subalternity." *Literary Herald*, vol. 2, no. 4 March 2017, pp. 141-155.

  tlhjournal.com/uploads/products/18.dr-m-s-wankhede-article.pdf. Accessed 7 July 2019.
- Woerkens, Martine van. "*A Life Less Ordinary*: The Female Subaltern and Dalit Literature in Contemporary India." *Dalit Literatures in India*, edited by Abraham K Joshi and Judith Misrahi-Barak, Routledge, 2016, pp. 224-237.

CHAPTER 4

RE-WRITING PATRIARCHY

WRITER, CRITIC, translator and activist, Meena Kandasamy is one of the most powerful Indian women writing in English. As a prolific writer, she has written two collections of poetry: *Touch* (2006), *MS Militancy* (2010) and two critically acclaimed novels: *The Gypsy Goddess* (2014), and *When I Hit You Or, A Portrait of the Writer as a Young Wife* (2017). Kandasamy has also written several critical essays and articles on prevalent caste, class and gender biases in contemporary India. Her writings locate the causes of social, economic, political, cultural, and gender disparities and injustices, and revolt against institutions that promote, legitimise, and normalise them. *When I Hit You* is Kandasamy's second novel. It is a powerful piece of feminist writing and shows explicit changes, innovations and experiments in the treatment of theme, plot-construction and narrative strategy. Like her debut novel, *The Gypsy Goddess*, *When I Hit You* encompasses different voices or points-of-view that interact and intersect at multiple levels. In addition to the author's voice, the novel also records her mother retelling her daughter's failed marriage to her friends and relatives, the fragments of her telephone conversation with her parents and her meaningless interactions with locals who like to talk about the weather only. Then there are the letters that the author writes clandestinely to her imaginary lovers in the afternoons when her husband was away in his college.

Besides 'polyphony,' Kandasamy also makes use of other postmodernist fictional techniques. She uses flash-back, flash-forward and stream of consciousness techniques to cover significant events in the protagonist's life and to show the working of her mind amidst severe physical and psychological torture. She adopts an eclectic approach and makes extensive use of pastiche and intertextuality. She refers to several great writers, theorists, philosophers, politicians, their work, and mentions the classical Indian texts such as *Ramayana* and *Kamasutra*. She also uses chapter epigraphs from the works of eminent feminists such as Anne Sexton, Kamala Das, Elfriede Jelinek and others. The use of the famous dialogue *kitne aadmi thay* (How many men were there?) from the Hindi feature film *Sholay* provides comic relief to the serious plot and theme of the novel. Like other postmodernist novelists, Kandasamy also presents an artistic blend of comic and tragic elements in this novel. Instances such as killing of revolutionaries by police, the murder of his innocent wife by Althusser, mentions of the Suryanelli scandal and her own moaning and crying after beatings from her husband add adequately to the tragic mood of the novel. Humorous situations such as Althusser's learning to masturbate only in twenties and her female friends' hiding their husbands from her after her separation from her husband definitely add to the comic texture of the novel. Kandasamy is unconventional and experimental in her use of language and symbols. She uses aggressive language and so called obscene words to register her resistance against her husband's authority and also to defy hegemonic literary traditions. Kandasamy's chief emphasis is on the role of the characters and relation with the central event.

The title of the novel, which came from one of her poems, "When I Hit You, Comrade Lenin Weeps" makes a deliberate allusion to its illustrious and widely acclaimed predecessor, James Joyce's debut novel, *A Portrait of the Artist as a Young Man*. The title of Kandasamy's *When I Hit You* also indicates the texture and refers to the narrator's anguish, her fighting back against her perpetrator, and her portrait as a young wife.

When I Hit You is a semi-autobiographical novel as it presents a staggering account of the author's pain, suffering under her patriarchal misogynist husband's authority who assaults her body, mind, academic career, writings, connection to the community, and the world around. The unnamed protagonist, who is also the narrator, met her lover, a Maoist-Marxist, and also a young university professor, on Facebook when she was running an online campaign against death penalty. Enraptured by his idealism, liberal social views, commitment and equalitarian attitude towards women, the protagonist falls in love and marries him. After her marriage, she moves to Mangalore with her husband where he teaches. She expects that her highly educated and liberal husband will offer her an adequate space and let her live the way she likes. But after a few days of her wedding, she notices frequent assaults on her tongue, body and mind. He denies her personhood, strips her of humanity and imposes numerous restrictions on her. He denies her privacy and asks her to surrender her email accounts and suspend her Facebook page. He also polices her mobile phone and sets about reducing her to an idealised version of a kept woman. He abuses and scolds her frequently, calls her a whore, rapes and beats her mercilessly. This unexpected behaviour from a man who claims to be educated, liberal, progressive, and an equalitarian perplexes the protagonist.

The author endures frequent humiliation and violence. She is well aware that her voice will be suppressed by her husband and he will use his reputation as a revolutionary or an anti-establishment fighter to protect himself, cover his sadism and blame her for what happened between them. She decides to live with him and face him bravely. But he turns more brutal and violent and threatens to kill her. Finally, unable to bear the constant humiliation and violence, she deserts him and comes back to her parents in Chennai. She files a case against him in the police station and thus, initiates her rebellion not only against her atrocious, patriarchal husband but also against male dominance and women's subordination in general.

Kandasamy voices her distress and reports severe assaults on her body, mind and autonomy. She details how her husband tries to confine her to the narrow sphere of domesticity and uses violence to trample her autonomy and make her an ideal Indian wife without any will, desire, and aspiration. He expects her to surrender her personhood and identity and to perform homely duties and serve him. He gets angry if he finds things of domestic use scattered and out of their places; he thinks that it is his wife's duty to keep the house in order. (15) He does not even allow her to wear kohl around her eyes as he believes that it is worn only by women who want to seduce men: "I wear a dull T-shirt and pyjama-bottoms because he approves of dowdiness." (15)

Describing the colonisation of her body, Kandasamy further writes that her husband does not allow her to be out of the house as he doubts that she may come in contact with a man and develop a relation with him. (18) She argues that he has no respect for her individuality, space, work and career. He forced her off social media, controlled her communication, social interaction and expression. (66) He also forced her to share her email password and started replying to all email messages addressed to her. He curtailed her surfing the internet so he could control her activities and mutilate her dream to proliferate as a writer. (59-60) He monitored her mobile phone and asked her not to share her phone number with anyone. Kandasamy writes, "The daily news is what he tells me. Communication is restricted to the calls he allows me to answer, only in his presence. Emails are those I hear only through him." (204) Her husband also uses violence to impose silence and establish his authority over her and enslave her perpetually. She says, "Reconstruction of an event does not help. It always begins with a silly accusation, my denial, an argument, and along the road, the verbal clash cascades into a torrent of blows. The accusations stand out because of how trivial they are - Why does this man call you 'dearest'? Why have you cleared your Trash in your email? Why are there only nine telephone calls on the call log of your phone, whose number have you deleted? Why haven't you washed the sink? Why are you trying to kill me by trying to over-salt my food? Why can't you write as 'anonymous'? Why did you not immediately reject the conference invitation when you bloody know that I'm not going to let you travel alone? – sometimes his bone of contention is so thin that they make me wonder if any accusation is only a ruse and excuse to hit me." (69)

Kandasamy writes that her husband tried to thwart her efforts of writings and expressing herself: "Being a writer invites constant ridicule from my husband. He objected to my writing on love and sex. He opines that she is asked to write on sex because she has 'a range of experience' of men of different age groups. 'You are a slave of this corporate media. You are selling your body. This is elite prostitution, where men do not get to touch you, but they masturbate to the image of the woman you represent. This is sexual anarchy. This is not revolutionary. This is pandering to vulgar imperialist culture." (75-76) Kandasamy's husband feels offended as he thinks that his wife is infringing the laws of patriarchy by writing shamelessly on such a cheap subject as sex. He accuses her of sleeping with the editorial team of *Outlook* magazine for whom she was writing an article on sex surveys. (76) The author argues that her husband attempts to suppress her voice and intends to destroy her writing career; he calls her a writer in depression or mad and accuses her of breaking the silence and spoiling the relation.

Kandasamy maintains that education, traditionally one of the significant tools to empower and emancipate women, is also inadequate to liberate them from male authority and oppression. She argues that even the highly educated, intellectual and wise women are subjected to male authority, and are censored heavily. She mentions two famous writers, Sylvia Plath and Kamala Das who were subjugated by their husbands and had terrible lives. (150-51) Observing this feature of Indian patriarchy, Tanu Kashyap rightly says that *When I Hit You* is a "piece of work which illustrates how gender-oppressive ideology and behaviour can be perpetuated, irrespective of your education, class, political leanings. It warns us how a seemingly 'successful' marriage could be violent, oppressive and abusive without anyone around being aware of its brutality." (69) Describing the inadequacy of education in liberating and empowering women, in an interview with Sunetra Senior, Kandasamy says that it was not education and 'incredible' mind that helped her escape abuse and fight back against her husband rather "it was an innate strength that came from people who influenced and touched my life . . . the courage to keep fighting comes from those around me." (n. page)

Kandasamy maintains that despite her higher education and intellectual growth she could not create a space and respect for herself. She was not allowed to even weep when he beat her: "Now keep your mouth shut and don't wake the neighbours. You are a whore. *Thevidiya.* Stop crying, there is nothing to cry about. I should be crying for marrying a whore. You are a whore. This is what whores do. This is why I don't treat you as a wife. Stay still." (163-64) He blames her ultra-feminism as the cause of frequent squabbling and all problems between them. (233) He insults and even beats her for sexual moaning in bed as like other Indian men he also thinks that sexual pleasure is meant only for men and women should not subscribe to it. Indian women are not allowed sexual pleasure, they are forced to do sex mechanically without any expression of gratification. (68)

Kandasamy's husband rapes her not only to punish her for her alleged nymphomania but also to thwart her efforts to assert her body and agency. Underscoring the imports of marital rape, Sampriti Singha Roy writes that "marital rape is used as a weapon by a husband to punish his petit-bourgeois, whore, writer wife, as he frequently calls her, to legitimise his ownership of his wife's body, and also to normalise the violence against her." (n. page) Elaborating on the social aspect and consequence of rape, Sonia Faleiro states that "rape is used as the sharpest weapon to eliminate a woman from the socio-cultural scene as according to general cultural conventions, the defilement caused by rape victimises a woman perpetually and she will no longer be able to find a man to marry her." (n. page)

Kandasamy writes that her husband was jealous of her intellect, beauty and sexuality. He repeatedly calls her a fallen woman as he feels that she has slept with many men before marriage and she may betray him as well. (164) Kandasamy exposes the villainy of her husband and flippantly, ironically refers to the famous Bollywood film *Sholay* and compares her husband with the villain who frequently asks his goons: '*Kitne aadmi thay*?' (How men were there?). She finds her husband as angry, sadist and demanding as the villain of *Sholay.* (175) Kandasamy writes that her husband, who was already married before marrying her, finds it criminal and immoral that his second wife has male friends. It is painful for him to even imagine that his wife might have lost her virginity before marriage whereas he does not find it wrong to have had a wife and then deserted her. She maintains that to torment and test a woman for her sexual purity is a long cherished, hailed and socially sanctioned practice in India. She refers to the famous *Agni pariksha* (ordeal of fire) that Sita was forced to go through in *Ramayana* to prove her purity and chastity after she was brought back from Lanka. (49)

Her husband began to force her to produce a child as he thinks that the birth of a child will discourage her pursuit of autonomy and coerce her to surrender her personhood, identity, will and agency to motherhood. He not only pressurised her to conceive but also took her to a gynaecologist to find out why she could not conceive. He slaps her in the presence of everyone in the waiting room of a medical centre when she could not drink the required quantity of water before her pelvic exam. Infuriated he also called her father and weeps to him. (199) He got angry when he came to know his wife is deliberately avoiding pregnancy. He threatens to kill her if she did not beget a child for him. (202-03) Kandasamy argues that denial to become a mother and beget a child became a very serious crime, much more contemptible and heinous than all her previous felonies. So, he turns more violent, calls her a whore and beats her frequently as he thought that she was trying to end his lineage. Although, he used masculine power and authority to silence her but she does not surrender her personhood and rights to him. She is well aware that producing a child will encumber her and expose her further to exploitation and dehumanisation. She firmly refused to become the mother of a man's child who does not respect, love or even consider her a human being. (200) Kandasamy's denial to pregnancy is part of her fight against her husband's patriarchal authority and a feminist assertion of her body. In order to avoid pregnancy, she started taking a diet which is normally prohibited for a woman planning pregnancy. Kandasamy writes, "My skills in the kitchen are summoned in my secret plan of foiling Baby Project. I turned my kitchen into a combat zone, making sure that my cooking secured me and my womb's liberty." (201)

Kandasamy refuses to merge her identity with her husband: "I feel nauseous. I feel robbed of my identity. I'm no longer myself if another person can easily claim to be me, pretend to be me, and assume my life while we live under the same roof." (55) The narrator suffered for almost six months of her marriage. She endured humiliation and frequent violent attacks by her husband but she did not go to the police station to file a case of domestic violence against him. She was well aware that he will use his reputation as leader of proletariats to escape punishment: "He would probably want his revenge on me as well, so he would denounce me as a political courier, implicating me as a terrorist." (182-83) She opens her rebellion against her husband in her own way. Her resistance is enmeshed in her writing as she used it not only to protect herself but also to offend her husband. Kandasamy writes that her husband hurt himself when she continued to write about love or lover despite his strong objection. (88) Jonathan McAloon rightly says that Kandasamy's writing about love despite her husband's objection and dislike is an act of 'supreme defiance' as it not only indicates her assertion of agency but also makes him hurt himself. (n. page)

Describing her strategy to fight against her husband, Kandasamy says, "I remember that my defiance over the trip to the gynaecologist was enough to make him inflict burns on his own body with a glowing ladle. I began to realize, for the first time, that his violence, which is forever directed against me, can sometimes be twisted to turn upon himself." (207-8) She also teased him by keeping silent and not talking to him. (162-63) She also challenges his pseudo masculinity and makes him realise that he is not so committed and brave as he pretends to be: "Revolutionary? They shot your friend dead, and you abandoned his body to the enemy. Don't pretend you are a revolutionary. Don't tell me how brave you are. A brave man doesn't run. A brave man doesn't rape and hit his wife."

(212) She also criticises her husband for his pretentions and opportunism and makes him ashamed. In this way, Kandasamy manages to manoeuvre her retaliation and defiance against her husband and finally deserted him, left Mangalore and came back to her parents in Tamil Nadu. (213) She went to the police station against her husband, and also wrote to the St Alfonso College Mangalore where he was teaching. (230-31)

Although, *When I Hit You* recorded numerous instances of violence and the narrator's individual suffering but it is not a plain tale of a husband's tyrannies, a wife's suffering and resistance. This novel is a pointed critique of patriarchy and manifesto of women's liberation as it not only shows women's marginalisation and suffering in domestic spheres but also locates and problematises the very roots of their suffering. Her fiction is extremely hard-hitting and exposes the double standards of the society we live and operate in. As a radical feminist, she refused to yield silently and defied the traditional Indian wifehood. She did not sacrifice her life to the Hindu concept of sanctity of marriage and refused to perform the wifely duties imposed on women. She also denies the long preserved patriarchal notion of motherhood as she knows that this is used to strip women of humanity. (208) She reiterates that a woman is a living being with a body, hopes, dreams, will, desires and aspirations. She makes reference to inhuman systems such as *Sati* where widows were forced to immolate themselves on their husband's pyre. (187) She also exposes the dowry system, which came into practice after sati was abolished and maintains that women are killed for not bringing enough dowry with them, for not sexually satisfying their husbands and also for not producing sons. She refers to the bad reality that in India, "a bride is burnt every ninety minutes." (187)

Kandasamy argues that in addition to physical violence, Indian women have been the worst victims of sexual exploitation and brutalities. The religio-cultural conventions such as devadasi or jogini exposed the women of lower strata to sexual exploitation. Historians maintain that temples in ancient India had troupes of dancing girls attached to them. These girls were made to sing, perform 'Nautch' dances and to prostitute themselves to the chief priest and to others. Kandasamy writes that the poor and vulnerable women were victims of sexual exploitation by British colonialists' armies as well: "Regiments of British Army had their retinue of native sex workers who stayed close to the cantonments." (73) Jeremy Paxman writes that the poor, deprived and dehumanised Indian women such as *devadasis* and other religious prostitutes, were hired by British soldiers on meagre payments and forced to amuse them sexually. Some of them were kept as mistresses and paid regularly. The bodies of these women were commercialised. (n. page)

Kandasamy maintains that politics also excludes women and discriminates against them. According to her, like right wing political ideologies, Marxism and Leninism also do not account for women's issues. Kandasamy underscores the inadequacy of Communism, exposes the hypocrisy of its followers and condemns their attitude towards women: "A Communist woman is treated equally and respectfully by comrades in public but can be slapped and called a whore behind closed doors." (34) She scorns Communism and questions how a patriarch and an oppressor like her husband be accepted as a leader by those who call themselves equalitarian or revolutionaries. She finds it unjust that a perpetrator like him has acquired the status of a leader in a party that is based on the premise of justice and equality. (89) She exposes the hollowness of the Marxist ideology and makes reference to French Marxist philosopher and theorist Louis Althusser who killed his wife. Althusser used the 'power of knowledge' and his reputation as a scholar to escape the murder charge and also to obviate defamation in public: "He would rationalize it with his theory as suicide-by-proxy. A kind of non-consensual consent. A *no* meaning a *yes*. She *wanted* it. Because he was an intellectual, he had the guile to legitimize the murder. Because he was an influential professor, he could make others stand in his support. Because he had an anti-establishment reputation, even the state absolved him." (189-90)

Kandasamy finds her life in danger like that of Althusser's wife, Helen, as her husband is also an aggressive Marxist who can also murder her and use his reputation to legitimise the murder. Describing her own experiences of communism Kandasamy shows how her husband's comrades were trying to intimidate and pressurise her to withdraw the case against him as he was their leader. They were anxious that a case against him will damage his image and also of the party as a whole. They also offered her money to remain silent. (233) These details and descriptions show the Communists' attitude towards women and even a man beating, torturing and threatening his wife to murder can be respected as a revolutionary.

Kandasamy also criticises certain Indian politicians and problematises their attitude towards women. She shows ironically how male politicians who ignored, tortured and deserted their wives and beloveds shone luminously on the political horizon: "A man free of a visible woman would be free of visible progeny who would lay claim to his legacy. Maybe it was meant to signal that having no heir these men would have no impulse to be corrupt, to amass wealth, to build dynasties." (123) She gives the example of Mohan Das Karamchand Gandhi who denied sexual pleasure to his wife, 'made his celibacy public' and thus attained 'sainthood' in India. She also mentions the former Indian Prime Minister Atal Bihari Vajpayee who with an 'adopted daughter, and a live-in-partner' also managed to maintain his bachelordom to show that his only motive in politics is to selflessly serve the masses. Similarly, the current Prime Minister has also deserted his wife for the same purpose and rose up to his present position. (124)

Kandasamy launches a personal attack on a popular anonymous politician who was once her lover while studying in Kerala. He was the grandson of a great revolutionary and considered the most dynamic and charismatic leader in the state, but his attitude towards women was no different from other men. He pretended he had a great emotional and physical bond with her and exploited her sexually on this pretence. The narrator recounts an experience in a hospital when she goes to see him: "In the presence of others, my politician-lover treats me like a perfect stranger. He makes polite enquiries, not for a moment showing any sign that he had spent the last afternoon in bed with me." (128) He refuses to marry the narrator. His hypocrisy, affectations and degrading attitude towards women is evident in his arguments and logics against marriage. He says that marriage is not the only goal of love. (120) It is evident that the politician wants to retain her as a sex object and is not concerned about her will, integrity and dignity.

Kandasamy writes that a single woman is always seen as an opportunity for sexual pleasure by men and the intellectuals and academics are no exceptions. She details how one of her college teachers also tries to woo her when she was his student. He used the story of separation from his wife to win Kandasamy as his sexual partner. But he gets angry when she rejects his advancements; in desperation and frustration, he tells the entire college that she tried to seduce him. (42) His story was taken as true by everyone in the college except a few girls whom he had already tried to woo. Through this, the author once again exposes patriarchy and shows how a man can use his power and position against a woman, and how everything he speaks is believed to be the truth.

Kandasamy criticises the general social attitude towards women and argues that a woman who leaves her husband under any circumstance or whose marriage breaks, is considered fallen or bad. She offers her own example and details how after separation from her husband, she was considered an immoral and inauspicious woman. Kandasamy writes that even her female friends doubted her to be a seductress or a sex monger who can seduce any man. So, they always hid their husbands. (218)

Kandasamy problematises the traditional gender norms by sharing an experience in her life when a seventy-five-years old family friend, , complains to her father that his daughter has uploaded a picture on Facebook in which her bra strap was visible. (235-36) Kandasamy maintains that decorousness, decency in clothes, eating habits and behaviour are other patriarchal concepts that are frequently used to curtail women's agency, repress their desires and colonise their bodies and minds. Describing her own anguish, she writes that it was because of patriarchal codes and conventions that stepping out from an abusive relationship became a serious offence. She became a subject of public disgrace and criticism. Her parents were scared that separation from her husband will ruin her life and bring them social disgrace. Her father expresses his anxiety in a telephone conversation, "If you break off your marriage, everyone in town will mock me. They will say his daughter ran away in less than six months. It will reflect on your upbringing. Please. Think about us this once." (158-59) In addition to her father, the narrator's mother also advised her to behave within the patriarchal framework and asked her not to desert her husband as she also believes that it will disparage her and her parents.

Kandasamy shows that the concept of honour is so powerful that it overshadows the traditional Indian motherhood. For instance, the narrator's mother is well aware that her daughter's life is in danger but she still advises her not to walk out from the marriage. She believes that humiliation and violence are a part of a woman's life. She is also aware that all men are almost same in their attitude towards women: "Finding the perfect man is a myth. Do not believe in it, work with what you have." (160) Mother blames the narrator's friends and the silly feminist writers. (159) Her attitude towards Kandasamy's situation clearly reveals that even educated Indian women are conditioned to live in patriarchy and they cannot even imagine the life of women without connubial relation or a husband.

Kandasamy defies patriarchal structures, asserts women's autonomy, resists patriarchy and scorns every institution and law that discriminates against women. She condemns government agencies such as police, law and media for their gender bias and indifference to women's pain and issues.

Critiquing the gender biases of the police, she writes that the Additional Public Prosecutor, who was appointed to defend her and argue her case against her husband, was not convinced that her case was genuine. He, like many other people, also believed that she is making false charges against her husband because she is jealous either of his fame or his new girlfriend. (233) Through this event, Kandasamy highpoints the reason why most Indian women do not go to court, why most crimes go unnoticed and why their victimisers are easily acquitted. She gives the example of a girl from Suryanelli in Idukki district of Kerala who was abducted and then raped by forty-two men on 16 January 1996. Kandasamy writes, "It is the story of a girl we call after the place of her birth, lacking the integrity to even utter her name - The Suryanelli Girl. Forty-two men raped this girl over a period of forty days. She is sixteen years old. The police do not investigate her case. The high court questions her character. The highest court in the land asks the inevitable. Why did she not run away? Why did she not use the opportunities that she had for escape? Why did she stay if indeed the conditions were as bad as she claims? How much of this wasn't really consensual?" (218-19)

Kandasamy maintains that even highly educated women are not free from the precepts of gender and influences of patriarchy. Even the women who are in the system, hold power are also indifferent to the suffering of other women and do not cooperate with them. Kandasamy illustrates it through an instance when she goes to the police station to register a case against her husband. The female inspector on duty shows no interest in her pain and instead of helping her in securing justice she mocks and blames her. In addition, she also berates the narrator's mother for not giving enough dowry to her son-in-law as she believes that a woman who brings dowry is treated nicely by her husband. (230-31) She narrates another incident in the hospital when she was there to find out why she cannot conceive. She writes that the lady doctor, who examined her, did not ask her whether she wants a child or not. Surprisingly, it was enough for her that her husband wants a child. (197) Through this incident, Kandasamy shows how even the highly educated Indian women have internalised patriarchy and how they are distant and indifferent to their sisters. They do not even try to initiate a sisterhood.

Kandasamy is overt in her critique of patriarchy, police, law, judiciary, media and the internal divide among women that subject them to male oppression and debilitates their position as a marginalised section of the society. She voices her revolts against every institution that accounts for injustice and discrimination against women. Though the author places herself at the centre of the narrative, but the text is not a simple tale of her distress and struggle to escape an oppressive marriage. The novel as a whole propounds a strong feminist standpoint and resists women's exploitation in different spheres of life. It revisions, revisits patriarchy, underscores how it operates, exposes the basic structures of society and problematises women's place in them. The author discards patriarchal notions such as wifehood, motherhood, sisterhood and daughterhood and revolts against the concepts of celibacy, chastity, and virginity. She exercises her agency, claims her individuality, identity and deserts her schizophrenic husband without any consideration for the patriarchal concept such as *pativrat*. She claims that women are individuals and have a life without their husbands.

Sampriti Singha Roy says, "Fleeing from her husband, from the fear of death in ignominy, the narrator in *When I Hit You Or, A Portrait of the Writer as a Young Wife* towers as a resilient woman who managed to carve a self for herself and her art despite the violent male infiltration that disguised itself in the form of marriage. Kandasamy as an awakened, rebellious woman problematises the traditional concept of 'power' and 'knowledge' and criticises the so-called educated intelligentsia for its distant or oppressive attitude towards women. Finally, it can be inferred that Kandasamy's, *When I Hit You* dissects patriarchy and powerfully asserts women's body, rights, agency, autonomy and identity."

Works Cited

- Bande, Usha. *Writing Resistance: A Comparative Study of the Selected Novels by Women Writers.* Indian Institute of Advanced Study, 2015.
- Brownmiller, Susan. *Against Our Will.* Simon and Schuster, 1969.
- Chakraborty, Proshant. "On Reading and Writing Violence in Meena Kandasamy's '*When I Hit You.*" *Medieum.com*, 2017, n. page, medium.com/@MrPositiveCynic/reading-writing-violence-meena-kandasamy-when-i-hit-you-1349ab518a06. Accessed 8 Oct 2019.
- Choudhary, Sonal Singhvi. "Twentieth Century Women Poets: Voicing the Silence." *World Journal of Gender and Literature*, vol.

1, no. 1, 2014, pp. 100-12.

- Faleiro, Sonia. "*When I Hit You* by Meena Kandasamy – Murder on the Mind: A Female Narrator Writes of Her Violent Marriage in this Memoiristic Novel Set in Southern India." *Financial Times*, 2017, n. page, www.ft.com/ content/d34732ee-3654-11e7-99bd-13beb 0903fa3. Accessed 22 Sep 2019.
- Kandasamy, Meena. *When I Hit Or, a Portrait of the Writer as a young Wife.* Juggernaut Books, 2017.
- *The Gypsy Goddess*. Fourth Estate, 2014.
- Kashyap, Tanu. "Feminist Study in Meena Kandasamy's Novels *When I Hit You: Or, A Portrait of the Writer as a Young Wife* and *The Gypsy Goddess.*" *Research Journal of English Language and Literature*, vol. 6, no, 3. 2018, pp. 66-77, www.rjelal.com/6.3.18/66-77%20Dr.%20TANU%20%20KASHYAP.pdf. Accessed 6 October 2019.
- McAloon, Jonathan. "*When I Hit You* by Meena Kandasamy: A Complex Tale of Abuse." *The Irish Times*, 2018, n. page. www.irishtimes.com/culture/books/when-i-hit-you-by-meena-kandasamy-a-complex-tale-of-abuse-1.3511330. Accessed 30 Sep 2019.
- Paxman, Jeremy. "Jeremy Paxman on the British Empire: Where Men Went to Run Wild." *The Telegraph*, 2011, n. page, www.telegraph.co.uk/culture/books/8796258/Jeremy-Paxman-on-the-British-Empire-where-men-went-to-run-wild.html. Accessed 29 September 2019.
- Riley's, Gwendoline. *First Love.* Melville House Publishing, 2017.
- Roy, Singha Sampriti. "Review: Meena Kandasamy Pens A Scorching Critique of Hypocritical 'Communist' Men." *Youth ki Awaaz*, 2017, n. page, www. youthkiawaaz.com/2017/07/

sleeping-with-the-enemy-reading-meena-kandasamys-new-novel-when-i-hit-you/. Accessed 9 Oct 2019.

- Senior, Sunetra. "Meena Kandasamy: When She Hit Back." *Asian Voice*, 2018, n. page, www.asian-voice.com/Lifestyle/Spotlight/Meena-Kandasamy-When-She-Hit-Back. Accessed 7 October 2019.

CHAPTER 5

WRITING OPPRESSION

THE TRADITION of storytelling has always been popular in India. It is evident that classical Indian texts such as the Upanishads, Puranas, epics and other religious treatises had certain elements of a story. GD Khosla writes that early roots of Indian short stories can be located in ancient texts such as the Jataka, Panchatantra, Katha Sarit Sagara, the Puranas and the epics. (Preface 5) Thus, it can be affirmed with certainty that the spores of short narratives had always been present in conventional Indian literature. Ka Na Subramanyam opines that short story as a literary genre is of non-Indian origin and came to India through contact with the Western literary traditions. (7) Viewing the opinions expressed by Indian literary critics, it can be argued that short story as a genre was probably introduced to Indian readers through translation from English and other European languages. Short story writing was attempted by Indian writers in different regions in different languages at different times but it became popular only in the second decade of the twentieth century, when educated high caste writers such as Rabindranath Tagore, Sarat

Chandra Chattopadhyay, Bankim Chandra Chattopadhyay, Mulk Raj Anand, RK Narayan, Premchand and many others commenced writing short narratives on varied themes such as colonial repression, social evils, social awakening, national unity and caste and class differences.

Although some writers such as Tagore, Anand and Premchand focused on caste and class as evils and wrote stories on how these ideologies victimised untouchables. But according to many Dalit scholars and critics, the stories written by these writers cannot be categorised as Dalit stories mainly because they were written by non-Dalits with a sympathetic attitude and they lacked Dalit consciousness, a significant element or a benchmark of Dalit literature. Further, the Dalit characters emerging from these stories are helpless, incapable of action or fighting back against the perpetrators and in most cases they surrender to the victimisers. Dalit short story, as a distinctive genre, had its inception in the middle of the twentieth century only when Dalit literature began appearing as a peculiar form of writing.

Dalit critics and theorists maintain that the tradition of short story writing was initiated in Maharashtra when some of the eminent Marathi Dalit writers such as Annabhau Sathe, Shankarrao Kharat, Bandhu Madhav and Baburao Bagul published their stories on caste and class oppression. These early Dalit writers used their stories to awaken illiterate and depressed Dalit masses and spread caste and class consciousness among them. Their stories exhibit the influences of Dalit intellectuals such as Chokhamela, Phule and Ambedkar. Some Dalit writers such as Annabhau Sathe presented a blend of Ambedkarism and Marxism in their writings. Dalit characters etched by these writers show caste and class consciousness, strive for justice and courageously fight against injustices. Short story as a literary genre became popular among Dalits as it was capable of bringing out their pain and suffering. The decade of 1980s witnessed the publication of many short fiction by Dalit writers in Marathi. In recent years, many anthologies of short stories are published in Marathi and a number of them are being translated into many Indian and non-Indian languages.

In addition to Marathi, Dalit stories are also being written in Hindi, Tamil, Malayalam, Telugu, Kannada, Gujarati, Bengali, Punjabi and others. In Hindi, Dalit short story writing was inaugurated in the late 1960s or early 1970s. Rajat Rani Meenu writes that Hindi Dalit short stories began to appear in the 1970s with the publication of many small magazines. She opines that published in 1975, Satish's 'Vachanbadh' can be called the first Dalit short story in Hindi. (58) In recent years, many Dalit writers such as Omprakash Valmiki, Mohandas Namisray, Suraj Pal Chauhan, Ratan Kumar Sambharia, Arun Prakash, Ram Asry Diwakar, Shatrughan Kumar, BC Bharti, Dayanand Bathoi, Ajay Navaria, Kusum Viyogi, Sushila Takbhore, Kavari, Suman Prabha, Rajni and many others have published numerous powerful stories on caste and class oppression of poor Dalits in India.

Like in Hindi, in Tamil also, Dalit story as a genre came into practice in the second half of the twentieth century. Subramanyam, however, claims that some Tamil writers composed short fiction in the nineteenth century but caste as a repressive ideology and institution does not figure in the traditional Tamil literature. (8) It was only in the twentieth century that the question of caste was brought into literary sphere mostly by Dalit writers themselves. In context of the origin of Tamil Dalit short story, Ravikumar and R Azhagarasan write that "short story received significant attention in Tamil literary history in the 1960s with magazines like *Kanaiyazhi, Gnanaratham, Deepam, Ka Sa Da Tha Pa Ra* and *Nadai*. For writers of this period, who followed their predecessors like Pudhumai Pithan, short story became a preferred form of literary expression as it provided the freedom to experiment and flexibility to accommodate a whole spectrum of styles and themes." (55) Short story writing became very common among Tamil Dalit writers in the closing years of the twentieth century. Contemporary Tamil Dalit literature abounds in short fiction writings of Imayam, Azhagiya Periyavan, JB Sankya, Abhimani, S Thenmozhi, Cho Dharman, V Venkatachalam, Ravikumar, Sudhakar Kathak, Bama, P Sivakami and many others who published their short stories on the lived experiences of Tamil Dalits.

In Kannada, the tradition of Dalit short story writing was initiated in the late 1960s when Devanur Mahadeva, a student at that time, wrote his first story 'Kathalu Thiru' in 1967. The story was immature in terms of artistic techniques but was effective in the treatment of theme and articulation of the realities of Dalit lives. K Satyanarayana and Susie Tharu write that the publication of Mahadeva's short story collection, Dyavanuru in 1973, inaugurated not only the tradition of Kannada Dalit story writing but also Kannada Dalit literature. (Introduction 7) Dalit short story as a literary genre stabilised itself in the 1980s when some prominent Kannada Dalit writers such as Channanna Walikar, Indudhara Honnapura, Aravind Malagatti, Mogalli Ganesh, BT Jahnavi and others began to publish their stories on themes of caste and class oppression.

This chapter seeks to examine how selected Dalit short story writers – Bandhu Madhav, Waman Hoval, Omprakash Valmiki, Irathina Karikalan, Abhimani and Mogalli Ganesh depict Dalit lives, perceive and address oppression unleashed on them in the name of caste, class, religion and culture. The chapter further highpoints the Dalits' standpoint and shows their perspective and responses to their exploitation in different spheres. It also underscores the Dalits' striving for identity, their efforts to achieve social justice, equity and power. The stories – 'The Poisoned Bread,' 'The Storeyed House,' 'Salaam,' 'The Hide of an Ox,' 'The Killing of a Cow,' 'Shavayatra,' 'Oorakali,' 'Ailment' and 'The Paddy Harvest' are taken from different anthologies of Dalit writings published in different periods of time in different languages. So, naturally they represent diverse cultural contexts, variety of experiences and techniques but despite all these differences the selected stories share certain commonalities in terms of themes, articulation of Dalit voices and the aim of their writings.

Bandhu Madhav's 'The Poisoned Bread' is one of the best stories ever written on caste and class conflicts in India as it not only shows the exploitation that Dalits have to undergo but also depicts the outburst of their anger and smouldering indignation against injustices inflicted on them. The story is narrated by a Dalit boy, Mahadeva, who goes to meet his grandfather at Kupad. The grandfather, Yetalya, takes him to Bapu Patil's house where he goes to find a job of winnowing and treading out corn at the threshing floor. Yetalya hopes that he will get a slightly larger share of the corn and also a few ears of jowar if the narrator assists him. But his hopes are shattered when Patil turns insolent and sardonic on seeing him. He insults the grandfather and chastises Dalits for not performing their caste based duties, defying caste rules and also for profaning religion. Patil gets angry when the narrator replies back and questions the precept of caste and the long conserved notion of purity and pollution. Patil denies work to grandfather and humiliates him further saying that why did he come searching for work when his grandson is so 'well-off'. Grandfather falls at Patil's feet and persuades him to give them work. The narrator and his grandfather commence work but the situation worsens when grandfather leaves the narrator alone at Bapu Patil's threshing floor and goes to Gyanba Patil's threshing floor to fetch a tripod and a few measures of corn. Bapu Patil loses his temper when he finds Yetalya missing from work and he not only scolds him but also refuses to give him grain for the work that he and his grandson had done since morning. Grandfather implores Patil but he remains unconcerned. Finally, grandfather helplessly picks-up the foetid pieces of bread thrown on the ground for the oxen to eat. The whole family happily eats the reeking scraps mixed with dulli at supper, but their happiness and satisfaction were short lived as grandfather dies of severe food-poisoning in the morning.

Waman Hoval's 'The Storeyed House' is a powerful short narrative that exposes the caste and class based oppression of Dalits by the rich high castes. This story minutely and poignantly points out how ruthlessly the Dalits' efforts of development and progression are obstructed and repressed by the high castes. In this story, a Dalit named Bayaji works as a lifter of heavy load in the dockyard. He was given promotion and an extension for two years after his honest services of thirty-five years. Finally, he retires as a supervisor. After retirement he comes back to the village and plans to build a storeyed house with the money he saved, as the usual three portioned house was not adequate for his large family. Bayaji's family was happy with his proposal but the problem starts when news of Bayaji's proposed storeyed house spreads in the village. The envious upper caste scoundrels such as Kondiba Patil, Bhujaba and others find it discourteous that Bayaji, a low caste Mahar, is planning to build a storeyed house which is traditionally denied to him and his caste. They warn Bayaji and also threaten him. Bayaji was scared of the high caste goons so he abandons the plan of the storeyed house. Finally, the conventional three portioned house was built but the high caste people were not satisfied with the way the house was constructed as "the middle portion was a little elevated and a small first story fixed with a wooden flooring." (180) This was clear infringement of caste convention and an insult to the high castes. So, in order to punish Bayaji for his audacity, disgruntled and infuriated nefarious high caste men set aflame to his newly constructed house on the very night of the house warming ceremony. Bayaji chokes in his attempt to extinguish the fire and dies the same night. His body and dream of owning a storeyed house are thus reduced to ashes.

'Salaam' is the first story in Valmiki's critically acclaimed collection *Amma and Other Stories*. It is an overt exposition of the hypocrisy of caste and its rigidity in India. It also shows how Dalits are still subjected to caste based evils such as salaam, a custom where the newly wedded Dalit boys and girls are coerced to go for customary salutation to the high caste households, especially where their parents work. In this story, a Brahmin boy named Kamal Upadhyaya, comes from

Dehradun to attend his low caste friend, Harish's wedding in the village. After the marriage ceremony, the guests go to sleep but Kamal and Harish could not find a place to lie down, so, they lean against the wall in the school *verandah* to straighten their backs and stretch their legs. During their conversation, Kamal tells Harish that he is in the habit of getting up early in the morning and drinking tea. Harish says that he cannot find tea so early in the morning. A village elder suggests that Kamal can drink his early morning tea in the local tea shop. In the morning, Kamal goes to the village teashop and asks for a cup of tea but the shopkeeper refuses to serve Kamal when he comes to know that Kamal has come to attend the wedding of the village sweeper. The shopkeeper repeatedly asks Kamal his caste and does not believe him when Kamal tells him that he is a Brahmin. The shopkeeper finds it impossible that a Brahmin attends a sweepers' party. So, he insults Kamal and accuses him of concealing his caste just for a cup of tea. Kamal is rebuked and insulted by the people who gather around the shop because of the mess created by the shopkeeper. Rampal, the village wrestler threatens to beat Kamal. Somehow, Kamal escapes and flees to join back the wedding party.

'The Hide of an Ox' also by Valmiki, is another powerful illustration of the caste and class based exploitation frequently unleashed on Dalits. This story elucidates vividly how Dalits are coerced to perform all kinds of filthy and unhygienic work by the high castes but are not paid for them. In this story, Pandit Brij Mohan's Ox dies near the village well as it was old and weak. The Pandit searches for two Dalits – Kale and Bhoore to immediately remove the carcass from near the well but he could not find them in the village. Pandit is worried and tensed and loses his temper when he sees them coming. He abuses them for being away from their homes for so long and thus, keeping the carcass lying near the well. Kale and Bhoore peel off the skin of the dead ox and head towards the market to sell it. They could not reach the market because they were not able to find any transportation. There was no one willing to take them to the city with the bundle of stinking skin. So, they kept walking towards the market. But their journey comes to a permanent halt when they see a she-calf on the road, hit by a speeding truck. Kale and Bhoore stop their journey and return to the village without selling the hide to inform the villagers about the tragic killing of the calf.

In 'The Killing of a Cow' Valmiki shows the plight of Dalit masses and also exposes the atrocities inflicted on them by the high castes. In this story, Mukhiyaji's cow is unknowingly killed by someone in the jungle where it was taken for grazing by Kallu, a village low caste. Actually, someone hunting wild boars had thrown 'explosive material coated with flour' in the jungle. The grazing cow ate it by mistake and as soon as she pressed it in her mouth, the bomb exploded and the cow dies on the spot. Although, this killing of the cow was absolutely unintentional but Mukhiyaji plans to use this occasion to manoeuvre his vengeance against Sukka, a Dalit young man who refuses to send his newly wedded beautiful wife to him. A village panchayat was called and the Dalit young men—Balesar, Jokhu, Ragghu, Chimra and Sukka were suspected of killing the cow. A complication arises when none of the accused accept the crime. Since there was no eyewitness, the names of all five accused were written on five chits and the person whose chit gets drawn will be pronounced the criminal. Finally, it was Sukka whose name was drawn. So, he was asked to clutch the heated ploughshare with both hands while saying 'mother cow', 'mother cow' and go ten steps as punishment.

'Shavayatra' is Valmiki's another vehement exposition of the caste based oppression of poor and impoverished Dalits in India. In this story, Valmiki shows how economic progression and self-reliance are not allowed to Dalits and how their attempts to improve their life conditions are violently obstructed and thwarted by the high castes. Valmiki also exposes the internal caste divide among Dalits and shows how it affects them and their mobilisation against caste and class based oppression. The author places a Balhar family at the centre of this story. Surja, an old man of Balhar caste lives in the village of Chamars. The Chamars are very jealous of him as his son Kallu is a government employee and works as a fitter in railways. In addition to Chamars, the high caste people such as Ramjilal and Pradhan Balram Singh intimidate and insult Surja when he plans to construct a *pucca* house in the village. They threaten to drive the family out of the village if they tried to build a *pucca* house and insult their superior caste fellows. Finally, Surja has to abandon the plan of building a house and yield to the pressure from the high castes simply because Dalits are not united and organised. The Chamars, who are larger in number, stood distant to the injustice done to Kallu and his family. Not only this, they also refused to help Kallu when his daughter Saloni dies of fever.

Originally written in Tamil, Irathina Karikalan's, 'Oorakali' is a powerful exposition and critique of the domination and exploitation of Dalit masses in terms of economic control and the edict of purity and pollution. Literally meaning cowherd,

'Oorakali' vividly shows how the hegemonic castes exploit the labour of both Dalit men and women of Oorakali caste and violate their human rights. The narrator is a young Dalit boy whose father, Mandayan works as Oorakali and grazes cattle of the whole village. He was given only leftover food as wages by the high castes. The narrator and his sister Pavunamma also accompany their father to the jungle. The poor family was somehow surviving but the hardships multiplied when the narrator's father lost his job of Oorakali because of the use of tractors for farming. Now it was the narrator's turn to shoulder the responsibility of his family. So, he starts working in Nattar's house as bonded labourer for a thousand rupee advance and ten sacks of rice a year. Since the womenfolk of the bonded labourers' family were supposed to look after the threshing floor, the narrator's sister also starts working there. Unfortunately, she was seduced by someone from the high caste and was impregnated. She loses her life very much like her mother during the course of abortion by a village untrained midwife. The narrator's father also dies heartbroken with his daughter and thus the narrator was left alone to fight against the adversities of life.

Abhimani's story 'Ailment' is a pathetic account of the exploitation, suffering and dehumanisation of a Tamil Dalit woman named Karuthayi. She works as a manual scavenger in the high caste households and like other Dalit labourers is given scraps as wages. The story opens with a description of the chaotic situation in the house of a high caste woman, Manohari, created by continuous rain. Manohari is desperately waiting for Karuthayi as her toilets were not cleaned since the day rain erupted. She is anxious and exasperated because the waste from different households was overflowing into her two latrines. The tenant women were complaining but Manohari could not get her toilets cleaned as Karuthayi was absent from work. Karuthayi, who was actually unwell, comes to work despite severe stomach pain because the inspector threatens to tear up her card if she remains absent from work for four days. Manohari also scolds her severely when she enters her courtyard. She insults Karuthayi and drives her out of her lavatory when she sees her using it. Karuthayi has to come out from the toilet without relieving herself and runs to clean it with her soiled sari.

Mogalli Ganesh's 'Paddy Harvest' is also focused on the exploitation of Dalits on account of their caste and class. The narrative is constructed around a single day and a single event in which the Dalits of the village are allowed by a low caste Tehsildar to harvest the illegally grown paddy by the high caste rich landlords on land belonging to the village. The story opens with a description of the preparations being made by Dalit masses for the harvest on the encroached land. They sharpen their scythes in Muttanna's forge and rush to the paddy fields early in the morning. They begin to cut the crop at an incredible speed when the Tehsildar asks them to cut the crop without making a noise and also without being afraid of illegal owners. Dalit men, women and children, who were mostly landless labourers, were lost in their work when the Deputy Commissioner with some other officers visits the place. The Commissioner scolds the Tehsildar for letting his low caste brethren cut the crop illegally and also for destroying peace in the village. As incited by the high caste landlord, the Commissioner threatens the Tehsildar with legal action as he did not seek permission before allowing Dalits to cut the crop from the encroached land. The high caste landlords who had the support of many politicians, Deputy Commissioner and other officers placed a proposal before the officers that the untouchables should be asked to bring back the paddy they harvested and if they did not want to return the grain it could officially be counted as tax. They also proposed that the paddy stolen by the Dalits could be adjusted against the landlords' irrigation debts to the government. The officials accepted the proposal. Finally, ordered by the Deputy Commissioner, other higher officers and authorities, the police attacked Dalits to recover the paddy. The Dalits were beaten, tortured and arrested by the police. Some of the Dalits surrendered the bundles of paddy they had stored in their houses whereas, some tried to hide the grain. Dalits faced violence and humiliation simply for harvesting paddy from the land forcefully grabbed by the powerful landlords but they could not oppose the police and administration. It was only Thopamma, a Dalit widow, who resists the police atrocities by thrusting bits of stinking beef on the noses of the policemen. She also spoils the white clothes of the Deputy Commissioner to register her resistance and runs away.

The selected stories are explicit exposition and critiques of caste and class based exploitation and oppression which Dalits are subjected to over the centuries. Every selected writer maintains that Dalits are poor mainly because of their outcaste status. The selected stories refer to the established historical fact that the Indian feudal system was stringently based on caste and the high caste feudal lords controlled huge parts of land and other economic resources. They used religion, gods and culture to reserve numerous socio-economic privileges for themselves and deprived Dalits even of the basic necessities of life. Religion not only grants them access to all materialistic pleasures as agents of God on earth but also gives them the right to treat lower castes as they wish. The Dalits were forced to perform all unhygienic tasks such as scavenging and skinning in the name of traditional caste based duties which they could not deny. They were not paid for their work and were given scraps or small measures of grain as wages. Valmiki's 'The Hide of an Ox' articulates this fact and refers to the exploitation of Dalits in the name of traditions: "Whenever anyone lost his cattle, it was their responsibility to carry it outside. For this they neither received any money nor grains. Their ancestors had been doing this work for generations without desire for any gain." (55) In addition, they also have to endure scolding and beating in case they do not perform their caste based duties properly. In this story, Pandit Brij Mohan reprimands Kale and Bhoore for being away from home when his Ox dies near the village well: "Where were you, you bastards? We've worn our knees out looking for you. . . You're coming now like a maharaja . . . who will remove the Ox. . . your father?" (56) Kale and Bhoore could not oppose the Pandit as they are poor; they continue working with the hope of earning some money by selling the hide in the market and thus procure some food for their families.

Besides caste based laws and traditions, illiteracy also accounts for the exploitation of Dalits. It makes them work in the unorganised sectors and hazardous work sites without any indemnity, fixity of wages, working hours or dignity. Most Dalits are forced by abject poverty to do manual scavenging in the high caste households although this vile and inhumane practice is strictly prohibited in India under certain Acts and laws such as the 1993 Act against the 'Practice of Manual Scavenging and Construction of Dry Latrines', and the 2013 Act for 'The Prohibition of Employment as Manual Scavengers and Their Rehabilitation.' It is highly ironic and unfortunate that despite all these measures and prohibitions, manual scavenging is still in practice in several parts of the country. According to a survey conducted by The International Dalit Solidarity Network, around 1.3 million people in India (mostly women) are involved in manual scavenging. (n. page) According to Aditi Yadav, "Reports suggest that 99 per cent of those involved in manual scavenging are Dalits and among them, 95 per cent are women." (n. page)

Abhimani's 'Ailment' is an authentic illustration of the pitiable life condition of Dalit scavengers. In this story, Karuthayi, the central character, works beyond her physical capacity and endures humiliation, scolding and dehumanisation but as wages, she is given only leftovers and a few coins on special occasions or festivals. (102-3) She is denied basic humanity, a humanitarian attitude and is scolded by her high caste employer Manohari for being absent from work and keeping her lavatories unclean during the rainy days. (103) Manohari is not moved even when Karuthayi explains her condition and tells her that she is suffering from severe stomach ache for the last many days and she just came to work to avoid her dismissal. Manohari shows no sympathy with her. She rebukes her when she sits in one of her commodes to relieve herself. She finds it disgraceful and polluting that a low caste Chakkiliyar woman is defecating in her latrine. (106)

Through the description and depiction of Manohari's attitude towards Karuthayi, Abhimani shows the inadequacy of Indian feminism, scorns the attitude of high caste women towards their Dalit sisters and also underscores the reason why Indian women could not initiate a larger sisterhood to fight against patriarchy. Uma Chakravarti writes that the high caste women, who themselves are subjected to male authority and severe gender-based discrimination, not only share but endorse the ideology of their caste men and thus promote Dalit women's suffering and victimisation. ("Through Another..." 207)

Caste is an ideology or an institution through which class operates in a very peculiar manner. Karikalan's 'Oorakali' exposes the interaction of caste and class and shows how Dalits have to live under these twin oppressions. The narrator's father, who is the village Oorakali, is not paid, so naturally his family has to live on scraps given by the high caste masters. Karikalan writes, "At sunset, Appa would drive the cattle back, leave each of them in its master's cowshed, and bring us home. He would go to the village street once again, with a brass vessel this time, and at every house call out, "Oorakali has come. Give some food, thai." Unwilling to serve the first helping to the Oorakali, people would say, "food has been delayed a little today. Come tomorrow Mandayan." (5) It is both ironical and scornful that Dalits who slog hard throughout their lives cannot even procure enough food to fill their stomachs.

Constant exploitation and wretched poverty lead Dalits to dehumanisation and violation of their human rights. The relentless hunger sometimes coerces them to eat food which even animals would not eat. In 'The Poisoned Bread,' for instance, Yetalya and his family have to eat the venomous crumbs from the pen which were not eaten even by the oxen: "The flies were swarming over the mouldering crumbs which had turned green and foul. Grandpa begged Bapu Patil for those crumbs. The oxen seemed to have refused to eat them. They were smeared with dung and urine. Grandpa collected them all with happy excitement and neatly put them into his sackcloth." (172) The impact of constant starvation and scarcity of food can further be seen when grandpa threw a few crumbs for the dogs to eat and grandma brings them back. (173) The family happily eat the crumbs, satisfy their hunger but lose one member, Yetalya, who dies of severe food poisoning. His death is the result of Bapu Patil's refusal to pay him wages and grain. Alimpa Bhuyan Boruah also maintains that consumption of the poisonous bread by the family indicates their helplessness, hopelessness, passive acceptance and yielding to the existing circumstances. (336) Grandpa is aware of the mechanism of suffering but he is unable to fight back as he is supressed and impoverished. He internalises opression and ultimately loses his life. In a similar vein, Mandayan also never attempts to fight back against the perpetrators. Showing his helplessness the narrator says, "The abuses had hardened us. Of what use were feelings of self-respect to our bodies? If ever the fire of resentment raged in my father, he would douse it with liquor." (4) This shows the helplessness of the Dalits who are denied access to basic humanity and have no voice and power to resist.

In 'The Storeyed House' Bayaji has to face the wrath of high caste men when he proposes to build a storeyed house in the village. Kondiba Patil attempts to frustrate Bayaji's plan by using the traditional theories of caste: "Baiju, you shouldn't lose your head simply because you've set aside some money. Do you aspire to an equal status with us by building this house? The poor should remain content with their cottage, understand?" (180) Exposing the high caste strategies to suppress Dalits and their attempts to thwart Dalits' economic progression, Meritta Joy says, "The elites do not want the downtrodden community to be uplifted and be at par with them." (n. page) V Shivkumar and NK Jhota also write, "Even now in many villages of India, people of the upper castes believe that men of the lower castes are worthless and must not have any facility in their house or lives." (926) The use of repressive power and violence is common to frustrate Dalits' attempts to live with dignity.

Valmiki's 'Shavayatra' is also an illustration of this fact. In this story, Surja and his son Kallu also have to face the rage of the high castes when they plan to build a *pucca* house in their village. Surja is insulted and threatened by the high caste Pradhan Balram Singh when he goes to seek his permission for the construction of a house: "Now that you have made a little money, you have forgotten your limits! We didn't let the Balhars settle here so they would build a haveli on our chest... The land on which you live belongs to our ancestors. Live as you have been living, no one will have any objection. If you try and raise your head, we'll shunt you out." (217) In this story, Hoval attempts to show that the economic progression of Dalits is perceived as a threat to their caste pride and challenge to their autocracy (Upper Caste's). So, they attempt to forcibly impose the hegemonic Hindu culture on Dalits which despised, discounted, dehumanised them and coerce them to accept they are inferior by birth. The high castes reiterates that the Dalits should not strive to come out from their present life condition as it is against *Dharma* and also the will of God. Raj

Gauthaman says that there are certain regulations of language imposed on Dalits to indicate their subordination and if they ignore or defy these restrictions the dominant one brands them as conceited, scold and even beat them. (268) In Hoval's 'The Storeyed House' Bayaji is rebuked by the high caste Bhujaba when he does not greet him in the conventional way: "Bayaji was a Mahar by caste and should have greeted Bhujaba with 'My humble salutation to you, Sir, who are my father and mother.' So, when Bayaji merely said 'Greetings', Bhujaba became furious and said, "Do you think you can become a Brahmin merely by saying 'Greetings'? Can you forget your position simply because you've turned Buddhist?" (177)

In 'The poisoned Bread' Bapu Patil also taunts and swears at Yetalya because he finds that the Mahars and Mangs are not behaving in the caste specific ways. For him, it is blasphemous that the Dalits have started to sit and eat with the high castes in hotels, restaurants and shops. So, in order to discourage Dalits' attempts to equality he uses the theory of *Dharma.* (168) The concepts and theories of sin and *Dharma* are used to insult, punish and repress Dalits, their personhood, identity and dignity.

In Valmiki's 'The Killing of a Cow' the high castes used the concept of sin to punish Sukka who actually refused to send his beautiful wife to Mukhiyaji. The high caste people exaggerated the accidental killing of Mukhiyaji's cow as an unpardonable sin committed by the Dalits in the village. It was Sukka only who was finally accused of killing the cow; he was tried and punished unfairly in the village panchayat. The high castes used *Dharmashastras* and the theory of sin to penalise Sukka and also to suppress his assertion of dignity. Dalit writers are of the opinion that the high castes have reserved certain privileges for themselves and have imposed several restrictions and prohibitions on Dalits in the name of culture and religion. To silence them and legitimise their slavery they composed texts prohibiting rights and freedom for untouchables. Texts such as Puranas and Samrities predict that there will be utter chaos and diminution of dharma in the world when Dalits start demanding their rights. Boruah rightly says, "This happened as the oppressors always perpetrated the act of deliberate exploitation under the pretext of God's justification and adroitly made their deeds of coercion unobtrusive. As a result, Dalits could never perceive the real persecutor." (333)

Omprakash Valmiki's 'Salaam' shows how newly wedded Dalit boys and girls were coerced to go for Salaam (a customary salutation) in the high caste households especially where their parents worked. Though, the couples were given some clothes, grain and utensils but were shamed in numerous ways. Jumman, a village sweeper, for instance, has to face the wrath of Ballu Ranghar when his educated son-in-law, Harish refuses to go for Salaam: "Sensing the gravity of the situation Ballu Ranghar himself came to Jumman. As he arrived, he straightway reprimanded Jumman and his wife in front of the guests. 'Jumman, why hasn't your son-in-law come for Salaam so far? If it's your daughter's marriage, we too have our rights. Whatever is traditional will have to be practiced.'" (50) The story is the finest illustration of how the high caste used traditions to subordinate Dalits.

Every selected short story highpoints all forms of exploitation that Dalits undergo and also exposes the hypocrisy of the caste system and conception of purity and pollution. The 'Salaam' illustrates the rigid, complex multi-dimensionality of caste. Ironically, this story states how even high caste persons have to endure humiliation and discrimination if they ever had friendship or any kind of contact with the low castes. Kamal, who is actually a Brahmin by birth, has to face humiliation in the village tea shop. The high caste shopkeeper thinks him to be a low caste when Kamal tells him that he has come to the sweeper's wedding. The shopkeeper refuses to serve him tea to avoid pollution: "This is a village, not the city. . . Sweepers-cobblers don't get tea at my shop. . . Go elsewhere for tea." (42) Valmiki exposes the hypocrisy of caste through his ironical description of the general condition of the tea shop: "A big kettle of aluminium lay near the oven, which had got blackened. There were a few dirty glasses, cups and plates, and a glass jar containing some biscuits. The round cooking utensil was black from outside and brown from inside. The swarm of flies buzzed about nearby." (40) It is highly sarcastic that the high castes are more concerned about safeguarding their caste purity than personal hygiene and cleanliness. For instance, the high castes in the village tea stall admonished Kamal when he addresses them as brothers as it was insulting and degrading for them that a sweeper is addressing them as their kinfolk. (44) Valmiki reiterates that the high castes cannot accept Dalits as their equals as they are full of hatred and have a degrading attitude towards them. In the story, Kamal's mother drives Harish out of her house, heaping abuses on him. She washes her house and also sprinkles *gangajal* to sanctify the ground. Mother asks Kamal to stay away from Harish. (47)

In 'The Hide of an Ox,' Valmika scorns the hypocrisy of Hindus and their fanatical adherence to self-interested concept of purity: "As long as the Ox was alive, there was no problem.

The Ox that had helped to grow food till yesterday suddenly became impure on dying. Let alone touch it, even standing near it was no less than a sin." (55) It shows clearly that the narrative of purity and pollution is weaved to save the high castes from performing unhygienic tasks and to exploit Dalits under this guise. The observance of rules of untouchability and caste purity are not limited to illiterate villagers only, even the educated high castes are equally rigid, bigoted and fanatic. In 'Shavayatra' the high caste doctor refuses to investigate and touch Kallu's sick daughter Saloni. He simply prescribes her some pills after making some general enquiries. He refuses point blank when Kallu proposes that he should bring the patient to him. (218-19) In 'The Paddy Harvest' also it is because of caste prejudice that the high caste educated Deputy Commissioner ordered the police to use force and recover the paddy that Dalits had harvested from the encroached land. Chakravarti writes, "The Constitution has formally ended caste-based discrimination in public spaces, but it has neither broken the hold of the upper castes on material resources, nor their hold over the state machinery. Consequently, the enforcement of non-discriminatory provisions in public spaces remains a dead letter because the enforcers themselves, in many cases, subscribe to the ideology of caste." ("Through Another Lens..." 207) Powerful agencies such as police, law and media are also caste biased. In 'The Storeyed House,' Bayaji's house was burned by the high caste hooligans but after investigation the caste biased police reported that it was a simple incident of fire due to a petromax flare-up.

Caste is a complex, multi-layered phenomenon and requires a social transformation to eradicate it. The selected writers expose all kinds of discriminations in the name of caste and attack it as a repressive ideology. They maintain that Dalits themselves are not free from the prejudice of caste; they also practice untouchability in different forms and at different levels. Valmiki's 'Shavayatra' is the finest exposition of internal caste hierarchy prevalent among Dalits. In the story, the Chamars of the village refuse to help Kallu in the cremation of his daughter since Balhars are lower in hierarchy than Chamars. They refused to even arrange wood for the cremation and also did not allow Kallu to cremate his daughter on their cremation ground. (222) Valmiki highpoints that the internal caste hierarchy keeps Dalits divided and has a debilitating influence on their movement and struggle against the caste system. Making reference to Valmiki's hostility against the internal caste hierarchy, Naresh K Jain writes, "If Valmiki is ruthless in exposing Brahminism and the atrocities committed on Dalits, he is equally unsparing in his indictment of Dalits, particularly for practising untouchability within themselves." (Introduction 22) Dalits are not united and collective in their action and resistance against high caste perpetrators. This fact comes out best in 'The Storeyed House' when Bayaji's house was set on fire by the high castes because of jealousy and the low castes did not oppose or fight against the culprits. Bayaji's relatives who were present in his house for the house warming ceremony, cremated Bayaji without uttering even a single word about any kind of retaliation. In 'The Killing of a Cow' also Dalits did not object and protest when Sukka was accused of killing Mukhiyaji's cow and was punished unfairly.

In Mogalli Ganesh's 'The Paddy Harvest,' majority of Dalits are poor landless agricultural labourers, dependent on what they receive from the high castes for their labour. The high castes exploit them and do not pay them fairly so that they can stop them from becoming economically self-reliant. (258) It is because of starvation, landlessness and lack of employment opportunities that Dalits have to cut paddy from the encroached village land. They are insulted and tortured for this harvest as the high caste encroachers used their social power to impede Dalit efforts to procure food. Dalits are used as machines by the high castes without paying them proper wages and allowing them any rest or days-off. They are also coerced to work in hazardous sites and put their lives in danger.

In 'Oorakali,' the narrator has to undergo severe exploitation and work as a bonded labourer at Nattar's house: "I worked all day, repairing bunds, digging the sides of the canal, removing weeds from the fields. At night, I had to run the motor pump. On rainy days poisonous gases filled the open wells which were fitted with motor pumps. It was often necessary to go down such wells when a valve had to be rethreaded, or to change small parts when the bearing broke. In some households, they would first lower a hen into the well. Or, an open flame. In my master's house, they lowered me into the well, telling me to shake the rope if I felt breathless." (6) The narrator shows how the life of a Dalit labourer is more reviled and cheaper than animals or birds. (6) Thol Thirumavalavan writes that Dalits should be granted land rights for their economic development and progression as they remain poor and impoverished mainly because of lack of land. He advocates reservation for Dalits in taking government land on lease. (252-53)

Most of the selected writers maintain that Dalit women have to suffer more severely as compared to Dalit men and other non-dominant social groups. Dalit women are dehumanised and considered cheap labour and objects of sex by the high caste men. In 'Salaam,' Valmiki exposes the high caste men's attitude towards Dalit women when she shows Rampal talking degradingly about a Dalit girl: "The city people are taking such an attractive girl with them. Arey, if the girl had been married off in some village, it'd have benefited people like us." (44) In 'The Killing of a Cow' also Mukhiyaji asks Sukka to send his wife to his place when he hears about her youthful charm and beauty. (94) Valmiki maintains that wretched poverty and the outcaste status leads to the colonisation of Dalit women's bodies and also promotes their sexual exploitation. Uma Chakravarti writes, "Along with economic exploitation and the power to humiliate and degrade Dalits, the upper caste men also have the power to sexually exploit women of the lower castes." ("Mediated Narratives..." 256) This is also evident in 'Oorakali' where the narrator's mother was raped by some powerful high caste landlord while working in their fields. She dies in her attempt to abort the illegitimate child. (7) In the later part of the story, narrator's sister Pavunamma who was born from her mother's rape, was also cheated and raped by some high caste man when she begins working in Nattar's house. Pavunamma also dies in the course of abortion like her mother as it was not possible for her to either marry or disclose the name of the person who raped her. (7) Pavunamma chooses to die silently as she is aware that she cannot fight against the powerful high caste man who raped her. The author uses this instance to refer that most crimes committed by high caste men against Dalit women go unnoticed because of their caste power and influence. Dalit women do not speak about these crimes as they are not trusted either by police or law. (7)

Selected Dalit writers such as Valmiki, Karikalan, Ganesh and Abhimani attempt to address Dalit women's issues vocally and show changes in Dalit men's attitude towards women, but their standpoint and depiction of women are inadequate. Most Dalit women depicted in the selected short stories are passive recipients of violence and exploitation by the high caste men. They are not capable of action or fighting against their victimisers. Karuthayi in 'Ailment' could not retort even when she is insulted and rebuked by Manohari. This not only brings out the inadequacy of Dalit men's representation of Dalit women but also shows how Dalit women's voice, agency, autonomy and inherent power to fight back are deliberately and unfairly omitted. In addition, the selected writers depict Dalit women in terms of their relation to caste, class and sexual exploitation only. The internal patriarchal oppression that most Dalit women writers emphasise in their writing does not figure in these stories. They opine that Dalit men are as patriarchal and oppressive as non-Dalit men as they not only suppress Dalit women's individuality and identity but also thwart their efforts to grow and act autonomously. Gogu Shyamala argues that even the educated Dalit men are not free from gender biases and influences of Hindu patriarchal precepts such as chastity and purity. They educate their daughters not to empower and liberate them but simply because they want educated wives and daughters-in-law. They protect Dalit women from the high caste rapists not because they have respect for a woman's body, sexuality, will and agency but because they think it a challenge to their honour and masculinity. (Personal Interview)

The selected short stories expose the mechanism of Dalit

suffering and show how they are treacherously segregated by the hegemonic caste and class people. Most Dalit characters etched in the selected short stories lead lives of sub-human beings, despite which they exhibit Dalit consciousness and possess strength to articulate their issues and fight back. With the passage of time and spread of education Dalits not only assert their personhood, rights and dignity but also resist the oppression and exploitation unleashed on them.

In 'The Poisoned Bread' the young narrator, because of heightened Dalit consciousness, not only retaliates against Patil's scolding of Dalits but also rejects his views as hypocrisy and tactic to control Dalits and have authority over them: "Patil, will you kindly tell me what you meant when you accused us of forgetting religion, abandoning our caste and of polluting God? If a religion can't tolerate one human being treating another simply as a human being, what's the use of such an inhuman religion? And if our mere touch pollutes the Gods, why were Mahars and Mangs created at all? And who, may I know, created them? And would you please tell me the name of the God whom the Mahars and Mangs can claim as their own?" (168) The Narrator's questioning of religion is an act of open rebellion against the paraphernalia of caste and Dalits' subjection to it. Although, grandpa does not rebel against Patil when he scolds him and denies him wages but his Dalit consciousness and striving for dignity are evident when he praises the narrator for his courage and retaliation. (172) Besides, he advises the narrator to educate himself and break the constraints of caste and slavery. (174)

In 'The Storeyed House' also the writer aspires to establish that though Dalits are scolded, insulted, threatened and repressed frequently by the high castes, they still could not be trampled and silenced. It is true that Bayaji's house was burned by the high caste goons and Bayaji also dies during his attempts to extinguish the fire but his sons did not yield to the repressive high caste hooligans and resumed work to reconstruct the house soon after Bayaji's cremation. V Shivkumar and NK Jhota write that the determination of the six brothers to fulfil their father's dream is an expression of resistance and assertion of their rights. (928) Gauri Vishwanathan argues that the storeyed house can be seen as a metaphor suggesting Dalit pursuit of empowerment, assertion of fundamental rights, striving for humanity and a dignified life in a caste afflicted society where Dalits are coerced to live in mud huts. (216) Modern Dalits are aware that caste is a fraudulent and oppressive ideology and they must fight against it.

In 'The Hide of an Ox', Kale and Bhoore discuss strategies to elude caste and live a dignified life. Bhoore wants to educate his son (Chhutku) to counter and thrash caste whereas, Kale suggests that Dalits should leave the village and migrate to some big city like Delhi and Ghaziabad and work there in factories. In his opinion, the migration will not only give them an opportunity to improve their life conditions but will also lessen the caste based humiliation and exploitation. (60-61) Though, Kale and Bhoore are illiterate, they exhibit Dalit consciousness in an Ambedkarite way and subscribe to his views on Dalit liberation and annihilation of caste. Educated Dalits such as Mahadeva in 'The Poisoned Bread' and Harish in 'Salaam' are more overt and radical in the assertion of their rights and demands of equality and dignity. Harish's refusal to go for Salaam epitomises the Dalits' struggle for dignity and their rebellion against humiliation and dehumanisation in the name of traditions and customs. (49)

The voices of Dalit empowerment and resistance are also clearly audible in 'The Paddy Harvest.' The Dalit characters portrayed in the story are illiterate, poor landless labourers without access to resources but despite that they are not silent and inactive. Their struggle against starvation and the dominant socio-economic forces manifests in harvesting the paddy on the encroached land and also in their attempt to hide it. They were beaten and tortured by the police but many of them refused to surrender the paddy. The Dalit widow Thopamma fights back bravely against the perpetrators. She resists the policeman who enters her house by thrusting stinking bits of beef on his nose and also insults the Deputy Commissioner in a similar way while she spoils his white clothes. (22) Thopamma was beaten and arrested and tortured in the police station but she refuses to say anything about her connection to Ganeshwar Sangh and Naxalism. Finally, she flees from police custody and thus refuses to yield silently to the landlords and the caste biased police and administration. Her fighting back is significant not only because it indicates her strength and courage but also because it exhibits an awakened caste and class consciousness and an indomitable will.

It is true that Dalits are constantly despised and suppressed in almost every domain of life but despite all vulgarities and odds, they have an unprecedented capacity to love and appreciate. For instance, Mandayan's love for his illegitimate daughter shows his humanity and moral strength. Similarly, Kale and Bhoore also show humanity when they try to save the heifer struck by a truck on the road. Their humanity did not allow them to hurt the innocent animal for their livelihood. Finally, in conclusion it can be affirmed that the selected short stories attempt to awaken and mobilise Dalits against the hegemonic castes and classes who control the power structures and exclude Dalits from them. They demand justice and a viable space for themselves. There is hardly any repressive institution, tradition, law and custom that is not brought to scathing attack and scorn in these narratives. Dalit writers maintain that modern Dalits are aware of the roots of their suffering and are capable of action and fighting back against their victimisers.

Works Cited

- Abhimani. "Ailment." Translated by N Kalyan Raman, *The Oxford India Anthology of Tamil Dalit Writing,* edited by Ravikumar and R Azhagarasan, Oxford UP, 2012, pp. 101-106.
- Agrawal, Tarit. "Modern Sensibility: Meaning and Concept with Special Reference to the Poetry of Today." *Ashvamegh: Literary Flight,* vol. ii, no. xxii, 2016, n. page, ashvamegh.net/modern-sensibility-poetry-meaning-concept. Accessed 25 January 2020.
- Bandhu Madhav. "The Poisoned Bread." Translated by Ramesh Dnyate, *Poisoned Bread: Translations from Modern Marathi Dalit Literature,* edited by Arjun Dangle, new edition, Orient Black Swan, 2014, pp. 167-175.
- Boruah, Alimpa Bhuyan. "Bandhu Madhav's "The Poisoned Bread": A Mapping of Dalit Consciousness." *International*

Journal of English Language, Literature and Humanities, vol.iii, no. v, 2015, pp. 330-337, ijellh.com/papers/2015/June/37-330-337-June-2015.pdf. Accesed 21 January 2020.

- Chakravarti, Uma. "Mediated Narratives: Dalit Women in Miscellaneous Writings." *Re-searching Indian Women*, edited by Vijaya Ramaswamy, Manohar, 2003, pp. 251- 288.
- "Through Another Lens: Men, Women and Caste." *Translating Caste: Stories, Essays and Criticism*, edited by Tapan Basu, Katha, 2002, pp. 198-218.
- Ganesh, Mogalli. "The Paddy Harvest." Translated by Raghavendra Rao, *Translating Caste: Stories, Essays, Criticism*, edited by Tapan Basu, Katha, 2002, pp. 12-24.
- Gauthaman, Raj. "Dalit Protest Culture: The First Stage." Translated by S Theodore Baskaran, *The Oxford India Anthology of Tamil Dalit Writing*, edited by Ravikumar and R Azhagarasan, Oxford UP, 2012, pp. 263- 271.
- Hoval, Waman. "The Storeyed House." Translated by MD Hatkananglekar, *Poisoned Bread: Translations from Modern Marathi Dalit Literature*, edited by Arjun Dangle, new edition, Orient Black Swan, 2014, pp.176-184.
- Jain, Naresh K Introduction. *Amma and Other Stories*. Translated by Jain, Manohar, 2008, pp. 11-35.
- Joy, Meritta. "The Issue of Self-liberation in Waman Hoval's 'The Storeyed House.'" *Smiling Shadow*, n. page, 2016, merittajoy.blogspot.com/2016/03/the-issue-of-self-liberation-in-waman_18.html. Accessed 15 January 2020.
- Karikalan, Irathina. "Oorakali." Translated by Hephzibah Israel. *Translating Caste: Stories, Essays, Criticism*, edited by Tapan Basu, Katha, 2002, pp. 2-9.
- Khosla, GD Foreword. *Tamil Short Stories*, edited by Ka Naa

Subramanyam, Vikas Publishing House, 1980, pp. 3-6.

- Meenu, Rajat Rani. *Hindi Dalit Katha Sahitya: Avdharanayan Aur Vidhayan* (*Hindi Dalit Prose Literature: Concepts and Genres*) Anamika Publishers and Distributers, 2010.
- Mencher, Joan P "Caste System Upside Down." *Life as a Dalit: Views from the Bottom on Caste in India*, edited by Subhadra Mitra Channa and Mencher, Sage, 2013, pp. 3-34.
- Muktibodh, Sharatchandra. "What is Dalit Literature?" Transalted by Anil Raghunath Kulkarni, *Poisoned Bread: Translations from Modern Marathi Dalit Literature*, edited by Arjun Dangle, new edition. Orient BlackSwan, 2014, pp. 270 -273.
- Ravikumar, and R Azhagarasan. Introduction. *The Oxford India Anthology of Tamil Dalit Writing*, edited by Ravikumar and Azhagarasan, Oxford UP, 2012, pp.xv-xxxiii.
- Sanjana. "Resistance and Modes of Representation of Resistance in Omprakash Valmiki's Work *Amma and Other Stories.*" *The Criterion*, vol. 8, no. iv, 2017, pp. 97-102, www. the-criterion. com. Accessed 16 January 2020.
- Satyanarayana, K, and Susie Tharu. Introduction. *From Those Stubs, Steel Nibs are Sprouting: New Dalit Writing in South India Dossier 2: Kannada and Telugu*, edited by Satyanarayana and Tharu, Harper Collins, 2013, pp. 1-54.
- Shivkumar, V, and NK Jhota. "Asking for 'Social Consciousness' Against the Conventional Rules: A Study of Waman Hoval's Short Story – The Storeyed House." *Scholarly Research Journal for Interdisciplinary Study*, vol. i, no. iv, 2013, pp. 425-429, www.srjis.com/pages/pdfFiles/146685702920%20Vaishali%20 ShivKumar%20200113.pdf. Accessed 24 Jauaray 2020.
- Shyamala, Gogu. Personal Interview 10 July 2017.

- Singh, Jayshree."Dalits' Existance and Enviornment in the Literature of Margins: Poisoned Bread by Arjun Dangle." *Research Journal of English Language and Literature*, vol. 3, no. 2, 2015, pp. 128-131, www.rjelal.com. Accessed 16 January 2020.
- Subramanyam, Ka Naa. Introduction. *Tamil Short Stories*, edited by Subramanyam, Vikas Publishing House, 1980, pp. 7-16.
- Tharu, Susie, and K Satyanarayana. Introduction. *No Alphabet in Sight: New Dalit Writing from South India Dossier 1: Tamil and Malayalam*, edited by Tharu and Satyanarayana Penguin Books, 2011, pp. 1-69.
- The International Dalit Solidarity Network. *Report*, idsn.org/key-issues/manual-scavenging/ Accessed 15 November 2019.
- Thirumavalavan, Thol. "Land Rights." Translated by Meena Kandasamy, *The Oxford India Anthology of Tamil Dalit Writing*, edited by Ravikumar and R Azhagarasan, Oxford UP, 2012, pp. 252-256.
- Valmiki, Omprakash. "Salaam." *Amma and Other Stories*. Translated by Naresh K Jain, Manohar, 2008, pp. 37-53.
- "The Hide of an Ox." *Amma and Other Stories*. Translated by Naresh K Jain, Manohar, 2008, pp. 54-63.
- "Where Can Satish Go?" *Amma and Other Stories*. Translated by Naresh K Jain, Manohar, 2008, pp. 78-90.
- "The Killing of a Cow." *Amma and Other Stories*. Translated by Naresh K Jain, Manohar, 2008, pp. 91-101.
- "Amma." *Amma and Other Stories*. Translated by Naresh K Jain, Manohar, 2008, pp. 180-195.
- "The Homeless." *Amma and Other Stories*. Translated by Naresh K Jain, Manohar, 2008, pp.196-211.
- "Shavayatra." *Amma and Other Stories*. Translated by Naresh K Jain, Manohar, 2008, pp. 212-223.
- Vishwanathan, *Gauri. Outside the Fold: Conversion, Modernity*

and Belief. Princeton UP, 1998.

- Yadav, Aditi. "The Scourge of Manual Scavenging." *Oxfam India*, 31 July 2019, n. page, www.oxfamindia.org/blog/manual-scavenging-in-india. Accessed 18 January 2020.

CHAPTER 6

VOICES OF DALIT AWAKENING AND MOBILISATION

POETRY IS the most frequently practised and mediated genre by Punjabi Dalit writers. They used it not only to spotlight the social, economic and cultural distress, which they have to undergo, but also to bring out their burning indignation, mobilisation and uprising against every kind of exploitation, oppression, difference, and disparity prevalent in Punjab. Though many literary critics, historians and theorists are of the opinion that the tradition of Dalit poetry writing is just a few years old in Punjab but the early roots of Punjabi Dalit poetry can be located in the mystic verses of Sheikh Farid (1173-1265) in the twelfth and thirteenth centuries. Farid, who was essentially a Muslim Shaman, composed verses mainly on religious themes, moral purity, immortality of soul and the inevitability of death but they exhibit an acute social concern and a staunch humanist approach. They criticised all kinds of pretentions and duplicities in the name of religion and condemned the exploitation and humiliation of the poor and wretched by the elites in then Punjabi community. Farid's verses preached love and compassion for all living beings without any kind of discrimination. They declared that a person who distresses and troubles another cannot get the love and mercy of God since all living beings are an equal manifestation of His being.

Dalit literary historians and critics such as Rajkumar Hans, Bhagwant Rasulpuri, Mohan Lal Pholuria and others argue that the early spores of Punjabi Dalit poetry are found in the sacrosanct verses of the Sikh gurus. Hans says that Guru Nanak Dev, the first guru and founder of Sikh faith, wrote in the language spoken by the people and directed his writings not to amuse the elite but to expunge prevalent differences, uplift and awaken the depressed and deprived in society. (n. page) Since these features are very akin to modern radical Punjabi Dalit poetry, therefore, it can be argued that the tradition of writing poetry on Dalit issues with a sarcastic tone and reformist approach was initiated in the fifteenth century with the vocalisation of Guru Nanak Dev, who rejected caste as a hollow swaggering and called himself the lowest of the low:

> *"Neechan andar neech jati, Neechi hun ati neech*
> *Nanak tinke sang sath, Vadian siyon kya rees*
> *Jithe neech sanmalian, Tithe nadr teri bakhshish."*

(I am the lowest of the low castes; low, absolutely low I am with the lowest in companionship, not with the so called high. Blessing of God is where the lowly are cared for). (qtd. in Puri 193)

In addition to Nanak Dev, the corpus of writings produced by subsequent gurus also preached love and promulgated the idea of an equal and egalitarian society. They also held caste with equal contempt and allowed the so called low born access to education, knowledge and learning. Though, the socio-political and literary liberalisms of the Sikh gurus prepared grounds for the emergence of Dalit poetry but it cannot be termed as Punjabi Dalit poetry in the modern sense. It is because all gurus were of non-Dalit origin and their verses were religious and dedicated to God not solely to annihilate caste. Even the verses of protest and socio-political awakening composed by miscellaneous Punjabi poets of folk tradition cannot be categorised as Dalit poetry though they were very similar to modern Dalit poetry in terms of themes, styles and poetic techniques. The main reason for this exclusion is that these early poets did not depict caste as the root of all sufferings of Dalit masses and also did not exhibit an awakened Dalit consciousness.

Rajkumar Hans argues that "Punjabi Dalit literary tradition begins with Bhai Jaita alias Jiwan Singh (1655-1705) who was very close to the Gurus' household as he was the one who had carried the severed head of Guru Teg Bahadur from Delhi to Anandpur. Bhai Jaita composed a devotional epic 'Sri Gur Katha' in 1700 to describe and eulogise Guru Govind Singh's life and his efforts to being about socio-economic equality. He, thus initiated the tradition of Dalit writing in Punjab. There was no noted poet writing on caste issues specifically after the demise of Jiwan Singh in Punjab in the eighteenth century. Hans argues that Sadhu Wazir Singh (1790-1859) was the second Dalit saint poet who composed 'philosophical and cultural poetry' and wrote extensively on prevalent social issues. (n. page) His disciples Vir Singh Sehgal and Nurang Devi, also wrote radical poetry and revolutionised the anti-caste socio-political and literary movements in Punjab. Paramjit S Judge states that Giani Ditt Singh (1858-1901) and Daya Singh Arif (1894-1945) were two other significant poetic genius to lay the foundation of modern Punjabi Dalit poetry. (210) Daya Singh's verses exhibit contempt of caste, religion and Varna system and also radicalises the demand for a just and equalitarian social system.

Numerous modern Dalit critics and theorists are of the opinion that Punjabi Dalit poetry with an awakened Dalit consciousness and a revolutionary fervour began to appear after the advent of the Ad-Dharm Movement in Punjab in the 1920s. The Ad-Dharm movement provided a vital front for the proliferation of Dalit literary writings through the columns of their two weekly papers—*Adi-Danka* and *Ujala* initiated by anti-caste Dalit intellectuals and published by Ad-Dharm Mandal, Jalandhar. Punjabi Dalit poetic geniuses such as Gurdas Ram Alam and Chanan Lal Manak, some of the best products of the Ad-Dharm Movement, not only problematised the socio-political, economic and religio-cultural establishments but also revolutionised the demand for a just and equalitarian system. Poetry produced at that time was a mixture of the ideology of Bhakti saints such as Ravidas, Kabir and Nanak. It also evinces the influence of Sufism and Ambedkarism. It varied in literary techniques, representation of Dalit issues and treatment of themes but despite all these differences it abounded in caste and class consciousness and exhibits sustained opposition against prevalent social evils such as caste, untouchability and polytheism. Paramjit S Judge also writes that the verses of major Punjabi Dalit poets such as Charan Das Nidharhak, Gurdas Ram Alam, Chanan Lal Manik and Pritam Ramdaspuri, who emerged in the early twentieth century, radically interrogated caste and had an awakening and mobilising effect on Dalit masses in Punjab. (210)

The twentieth century Punjabi Dalit poets condemned Brahmanical Hinduism and proclaimed that all humans are equal. The activism of Mangu Ram and his Ad-Dharm Movement radicalised the caste question in both literary and non-literary spheres. But the Dalit literary fervour lost momentum in Punjab after the Ad-Dharm Movement lost force in the 1940s. It was through some non-Ad-Dharmis or non-Gadrite poets such as Hazara Singh Mushtaq (an activist of the Indian National Congress), Puran Singh, Mohan Singh and Dhani Ram Chatrik that Dalit literary traditions survived. It was with the rise of Naxalism in 1960s in Punjab that Dalit poetry once again gathered impetus. Showing the influence of Naxalism on Punjabi Dalit poetry, Hans writes that the Naxalism which reached Punjab in the late 1960s produced two vibrant Punjabi Dalit poets—Sant Ram Udasi (1939-1986) and Lal Singh Dil (1943-2007) who wrote not only with an unprecedented revolutionary zeal but also with a heightened Dalit consciousness. (n. page) The poetry of Udasi and Dil, who hailed from Dalit families, brought out social, economic, cultural and psychological distress and oppression of the deprived, depressed Dalits and voiced their revolt. Caste did not lose its intensity in their poetry despite their connection with far-leftism. Their poetry examined the leftist ideologies minutely and critically and exposed their inadequacies to address the Dalit issues. Udasi and Dil remained active and prolific for many decades and their poetry inspired many young Punjabi Dalit writers during the 1960s and 1970s. In the late 1980s or early 1990s many educated, vibrant Punjabi Dalit poets came to the fore and not only propounded a staunch Dalit point of view but also radicalised the demand for justice and equality for Dalits in Punjab.

In recent years, the Punjabi Dalit poetic output is multiplying and congregating maturity in terms of art and treatment of themes. Contemporary Dalit poets such as Balbir Madhopuri, Shri Ram Arsh, Sulakhan Mit, Gurmeet Kalarmajri, Madan Vira, Manjit Kadar, Bhagwan Dhillon, Buta Singh Ashant, Manmohan, Mohan Tyagi, Mohan Matialvi, Jaipal, Iqbal Gharu, Harnek Kaler, Sadhu Singh Shudrak and many others are writing adequately on interconnected issues of caste and class. These poets assert their personhood, identity and demand their dignity and rights in every sphere of life. The present chapter examines how the selected Punjabi Dalit poets—Madhopuri and Pall attempt to awaken Dalits, address their issues and mobilise them against the injustices and atrocities meted out to them. It also attempts to underscore the strategies and alternatives as suggested by them to annihilate caste, liberate Dalits from the constraints of caste, class and replace existing dominant institutions, hegemonic power relations and structures.

Pall and Madhopuri are representative voices in contemporary Punjabi Dalit literature. Dalit activist and poet, Kamal Dev Pall was born in 1957 in Hoshiarpur district of Punjab. He did his schooling from a village school. After completing his MA in Punjabi from Punjab University, he joined the Dalit movement. Influenced by Ambedkar's thought, vision and ideology, Pall came into contact with Dalit leader Kanshi Ram in the 1980s and remained active in Dalit socio-political movement till the mid-1990s. Though Pall migrated to America in 1995 and settled there permanently, he remained concerned with Dalit issues and their movement. He founded the International Bahujan Organisation in 1997 to unite and integrate immigrant Dalits in America and challenge caste at an international level. He has published two books of poetry and one book of Ghazals. *Days will Come Back* is his first collection of poetry translated into English. The poems in this collection delve into the lives of Punjabi Dalits and show their impoverished, pitiable life conditions. They also bring out the unrest and anger of Dalits and describe the poet's experiences as an immigrant in America.

Winner of many awards and honours, poet, prose writer, translator and editor, Madhopuri (born in 1955) is a representative figure of Punjabi Dalit literature. As a prolific writer, he has published three volumes of poetry: *Maroothal da Birkh* (1992), *Bhakhda Patal* (1998), *Meri Chonvi Kavita* (2011). In addition to poetry, Madhopuri has also written his autobiography, *Changiya Rukh* (2002), a travelogue *Samunder de Sung* (1996), novel *Mitti Bol Peye* (2020) and some critical works such as *Dilli Ik Virasat* (1998) and *Ad Dharam De Bani: Ghadri Baba Mangu Ram* (2010). *My Caste-My Shadow* (2020) is the English translation of his poems from *Meri Chonvi Kavita.* The poems in this collection problematise the existing system of inequality, bring out his smouldering anger and vocalise his protest against caste and class injustices. The present chapter details how Pall and Madhopuri bring out the exploitation of Dalit masses on account of caste, feudalism and gender through their poems in their respective collections, *Days Will Come Back* and *My Caste-My Shadow.* It measures the voices of their awakening. It also shows how they highpoint Dalits' optimism, their capacity to work hard, survive, rise and excel in different spheres despite constant opposition, numerous odds and injustices.

Days Will Come Back

Published in 2019 in English, *Days Will Come Back,* is a powerful articulation of Dalit issues and their voices of protest. It not only offers glimpses of Dalit lives in rural Punjab but also exposes their oppression in different spheres. In these poems the poet presents harsh and morbid realities of Dalit lives and exposes the prominent exploitative and discriminatory institutions such as caste, feudalism, religions and patriarchy. He maintains that these deceitfully architected institutions and customs operate exploitatively and keep the Dalits poor, deprived and dehumanised. Pall maintains that a huge part of natural resources and means of production such as land and industries are under the control of Jat Sikhs who also occupy the highest rung in caste hierarchy in Punjab. The dominant castes and classes exploit and dehumanise Dalits and use their influence and power to suppress them. Referring to this fact, Ronki Ram writes, "The centre of power in Punjab revolves around land. Most of the land is owned by Jat Sikhs. Although Scheduled Castes (SCs) in Punjab constitute a high proportion of the population (28.3 per cent) in comparison to the all-India average of 16.32 per cent, yet their share in ownership of land is negligible." (148)

Illustrating the landlessness of Dalit masses in Punjab, Harish K Puri also writes that Dalits and other agricultural castes were denied land ownership in Punjab under the Punjab Land Alienation Act 1901 till 1952. They were not allowed to buy and own land even if they had money to pay for it. (2695) Pall suggests that it is mainly because of landlessness that most Dalits are still poor and enslaved to the high caste landholding Jats, who possess huge tracts of land, exploit Dalit labourers and keep them poor and deprived. The landholding castes coerce Dalits to work as indentured labourers without paying them. Pall maintains that it is highly ironical and unjust that Dalits who work on the land and produce grains are still poor and hungry. The poet questions the hegemony of Jat Sikhs, their monocratic possession of land and their proprietorship of most of the mills and industries. In 'Real Face' he scornfully says,

"Come to Punjab sometime and watch
Those who kick hungry wombs
From farms to factories
They too are Sikhs with 5Ks." (19)

Pall argues that the landowning castes in Punjab enjoy all privileges and comforts of life whereas, poor Dalits who are mostly agricultural labourers, have to live like sub-human beings without access to even basic necessities of life. Sucha Singh Gill argues that the "largest number and proportion of SCs are employed in agriculture as labourers. In 1981 and 1991, 60 per cent of the total SC workforce belonged to this category. There are very few SC cultivators – only 6.7 per cent in 1981 and their number declined to 4.8 in 1991." (226) According to Census 2001, Scheduled Caste agricultural labourers constituted 66.97 per cent of the total 14.90 lakh agricultural labourers in Punjab. (n. page) According to Census 2011, most Dalit households and localities have no facility of drinking water, no latrines or proper supply of electricity in their houses. (n. page) Illustrating further on the deplorable and impoverished conditions of Dalit agricultural labourers in Punjab, Gurmanpreet Singh and Kamaljit Singh write that these labourers are poor, deprived, illiterate and socially, economically and culturally retrograded. They are mostly landless labourers and survive on seasonal employment in agriculture. They are impoverished and always indebted to the Jats who exploit them as they cannot find employment outside the agricultural sector because majority of them are illiterate and do not have any training or previous job experiences. (45) Pall writes,

> "From dawn to dusk
> The men and women of my village
> Get together in farms like a festival
> Now the farm owner, overwhelmed with happiness,
> Will rest and thank God
> After all the work is done, he will sell crops
> He will give two bunches to workers
> The rest he will sell and make money for his bank accounts." (44)

Poet maintains that illiteracy and wretched poverty also compel Dalits to work in unorganised sectors and coerce them to adopt perilous professions such as working in chemical factories, mines and excavations. (35) Additionally, the impoverished Dalits also have to work as manual scavengers for the high castes where they are humiliated and stripped of humanity. They have to compromise their dignity for survival. (39) The poet further shows that Dalits are also exploited within the high caste households where they work as domestic helps. They are made to work beyond their physical capacities and given just leftovers for rendering their services . (34)

Poems in this collection bring out the life condition of Dalits and expose every institution that exploits and discriminates against them. Like other Dalit writers, Pall also argues that Religion is the source of all disparities, injustices and exploitations that Dalits have to undergo. For Pall, religion is in no way less rigid, exploitative and oppressive than feudalism. In 'You Think Wrongly' the poet ridicules religion and warns Dalits against it:

> "This is what you think:
> That religion
> Is impartial to those who are discriminated
> Is less injurious than intoxicants
> Is more important than cattle food." (17)

Pall interrogates the predominance of Brahmins and opposes the privileges that they reserved for themselves. In 'Sons of Brahma' he launches a supercilious attack on Brahmins and Brahmanism and shows how they, who claim to be pure, superior and sons of God, are mere hypocrites and chief exploiters. He shows that Brahmins who are at the top of social hierarchy, exploit poor Dalits and live on their hard work without even thinking about their theory of *paap* and *punya* (sin and charity):

> "The sons of Brahma ask for grains
> From our infertile idle lands

The harvest has gone from our muscles
Into the wheat kernels
And we are sleeping now." (28)

In this poem, the poet shows that Brahmins want Dalits to be faithful and devoted to their religion that not only discriminates but also humiliates and dehumanises them. The poet exposes the whole mechanism of Dalits' subordination in conventional Indian societies and shows how they were not allowed to read Hindu religious books and how they were punished severely if they ever tried to even listen to the recital of holy mantras. 'Self-Respect' casts a searching spotlight on the atrocities inflicted on Dalits to break their spirit and perpetuate their position as ignorant and helpless:

"Centuries ago, you abused him
He remained silent
You became extremely happy
You tested the limits of his tolerance
Although you had forgotten
You yourself had poured molten lead into his ears
So that he couldn't hear anything
And you kept reciting Vedas and Smritis
And you kept devising new tools to enslave him." (20)

Ironically, Dalits are forced to obey the rules of the so called sacrosanct places of worship where even their shadow is not allowed. (28) Pall problematises Hindu Brahmanical concepts such as *karma*, *moksha* (salvation), *punrjanam* (rebirth), heaven, hell and gods for he is well aware that all these conceptions are part of Brahmins' treacheries to subjugate and dehumanise Dalits. The poet calls Brahmins capitalists and fraudsters as they swindle illiterate Dalit masses in the name of gods. They preach the concept of simple life, sacrifice, devotion, renunciation for others simply so that other castes cannot claim their right to better lives and they can earn unlawfully, and live unrestrained, luxurious lives. The poet appeals to Dalits that they should not accept their slavery in the name of notions such as dharma, bhakti, moksh and God. He wants Dalits to demand their rights without believing that their good deeds in this birth will be rewarded in the next birth. For him, the theory that Dalits are born from the feet of Brahma is a fraudulent tale consecrated and propagated by the high castes simply to ensure the service of *Shudras* and *Atishudras* to the remaining three Varnas. (12) The poet mocks temples, mosques, gurudwaras, gurus and saints as he believes that religion as a repressive ideology operates through them. He also criticises religious texts such as the Vedas and *Guru Granth Sahib* and opines that what is coded in these texts is not justifiable, unprejudiced and egalitarian in nature. Ironically, some of his poems on immigration show how the high caste immigrants who consider themselves pure and superior in India, work as labourers and domestic help for Americans. He maintains that they not only compromise their caste pride and assumed inherent purity but also dignity for survival in America. Pall argues that immigration, which gives Dalits an opportunity to lead a dignified life, makes non-Dalits feel a tinge of discrimination and humiliation. It makes them realise that they are not superior to the low castes in any way. His poem 'Pride' in this collection shows it vividly:

"The pride gets shattered
Outside grocery stores
Collecting cigarette butts
Moping shop floors." (47)

The poet holds religious pretentions with contempt and shows their hollowness. He criticises Sikhism for its caste biases despite its liberal ethos and claim of egalitarianism and non-discriminatory structure. Yogesh Maitreya aptly says that Pall's poems vocalise unheard and unspoken things about Punjab and the Dalits living there. (n. page) The poems in this collection break the long cherished myth that traditionally Punjabi societies were less casteist and Dalits enjoyed better socio-economic status as compared to other states in India. His poem, 'What a Paradox' is an overt and direct exposition of caste hierarchy prevalent in Sikhism:

"True Sikhs, after drinking the immortalizing nectar
Claim to be all equal
Possessing the five Ks
Caste still walks into all relations
What a paradox!" (50)

Pall shows that Sikhism is also as rigid and discriminatory as Hinduism. He argues that Sikhs show pseudo sympathy to the downtrodden, convert them to their faith, humiliate and exploit them in numerous ways. They interpret and practice religion in a way that suits them and excludes Dalits from all scopes of development and empowerment. The poet criticises the attitude of the high caste Sikh Jats towards low caste converts and divulges that they are not accepted as equals. Conversion is used to spread Sikhism and procure cheap labour:

"A few Dalits are baptized as Sikhs
Just to beat drums and play music
To be kept weak and lazy
What a paradox!" (51)

Jat Sikhs are hostile and discriminatory towards lower castes and because of these hostilities and prejudices Punjabi Dalits have started rejecting the orthodox Sikhism practiced and preached by Jat Sikhs. Dalits' rejection of traditional Sikh religiosity and their attempt to reconstruct an exclusive identity are reflected in their formation of separate gurudwaras, *deras*, sects and cremation grounds for themselves. The poet criticises Sikhs who not only follow Hindu religious practices but also establish political alliances with Hindus just for the sake of power. He ridicules the Sikhs' promise of *Khalistan* as utter dishonesty.

Pall also criticises Islam and Christianity and maintains that they are equally hostile and discriminatory towards Dalits. He maintains that though converted Dalits may not be discriminated against in Mosques and Churches as they are in Temples and Gurdwaras but they are not accepted as equals either.

Pall minutely examines caste, shows its every aspect and explains how it operates in the lives of Dalits. He mocks those high castes who call themselves secular but behave in a conservative, casteist, bigoted and inequitable way:

"He, as a secularist,
Criticizes racial discrimination
But he exploits the low caste downtrodden

Backward and homeless
He keeps them segregated in untouchable colonies
Practices untouchability
While he calls himself 'non-religious'." (35)

Pall maintains that Dalits are just used as a vote bank by high castes who hold the centre of political power. He criticises high caste politicians who remain indifferent to Dalit issues and their pain after they win elections and come into power. The poet regrets that despite numerous constitutional provisions and reservations Dalits are still on political margins. Even the elected Dalit representatives and leaders are not allowed to work independently; their work is always influenced by the high castes. Pall opines that Gandhi's invention of the word *Harijan* and its use to refer to Dalits was part of his strategy of Dalit placation and coaxing them to stay within Hinduism. In 'You Think Wrongly' Pall writes:

"This is what you think:
That Gandhi
Is such an actor who has not played the role of a scoundrel
Is never political when it comes to Dalit rights." (17)

Pall maintains that it is only Ambedkarism that can end caste conflicts and liberate Dalits. He also reveres and supports Buddhism. He glorifies Dalit culture, history and historical figures such as Buddha and refers to the Dalit agitation and political events such as the Mandal Commission. Pall also criticises the Communists for their standpoint on caste. He shows how violence (was) and is still used to thwart Dalits' attempt of progression and keep them silent and marginalised over centuries. The high castes are well aware that they will lose their socio-economic predominance and control of Dalits if they let them educate themselves and accumulate knowledge. Even government agencies such as police use violence to stifle Dalit voices. The poet uses the traditional symbol of 'eagle attacking swans' to bring out the intensity of violence against innocent and helpless Dalits and also represents the image of innocent blood flowing on the road:

> "You may not understand, but we do
> How swans are attacked by eagles
> How black roads laugh
> When the colour of the roads turns red." (37)

He further describes how powerful institutions and organisations such as National Human Right Commission (NHRC) also remain indifferent to the violation of human and fundamental rights of Dalits. Pall attempts to globalise caste and aspires to draw the attention of international communities, agencies and organisations to this worst system prevalent in India. He maintains that most crimes committed by the high castes against Dalits go unnoticed or unreported. Dalits are denied justice and the high caste perpetrators are acquitted simply because of their caste.

Pall vociferously addresses the issue of Dalit women's specific suffering and shows their three-fold marginalisation on account of caste, class and gender. He maintains that Dalit women who work for the high castes have to face humiliation, exploitation and frequent sexual assaults. In 'Daughter of

Forefather' the poet shows how rich non-Dalit men lure, rape and ultimately ruin poor Dalit women by praising their charm, beauty and by showing pseudo love:

> "The poor one's daughter-in-law is seen with lust
> While the whole city is scared of the rich one's
> daughter-in-law." (39)

The poet shows that Dalit women are denied even basic humanity and forced to compromise their dignity and bodily integrity to earn some money and support their starving families:

> "The whole family wanted to eat mustard stems
> Who paid the price of mustard with her body?
> Who knows?" (39)

Shalini Sharma and BK Agarwal write that Dalit women are discriminated against within their own families in terms of allocation of food, education and medical facilities. (268) They are assigned very less or no space within their households. They are treated as inanimate objects and considered the property of Dalit men. Pall shows sarcastically that Dalit men who consider Dalit women their property, impose numerous restrictions and prohibitions on them. They have to watch helplessly when their wives, daughters, sisters and mothers are sexually exploited by powerful high caste men:

> "Daughters are wealth to be owned by their husbands
> How will you tolerate
> When she comes pregnant from farms?" (39)

The poet exposes evils such as dowry and female infanticide prevalent in Punjab. Sharma and Agarwal also argue that incidents of female infanticide are increasing among Dalits with economic progression and spread of education. (266) The elite Dalits are increasingly adopting high caste culture and traditions not only to escape the stigma of caste but also to pass as high castes. Practices such as purdah, dowry and ascetic widowhood entered Dalit households from non-Dalit culture where women's subjection, suppression is directly associated with status and community honour. In 'Then and Now' Pall scorns the social attitude towards women and criticises their heinous and ruthless killing before birth:

"Who is born?
A girl?
They offered the midwife
New clothes, a stack of wheat
And buttermilk for one year
Go and dig the grave
Doctor, the result of ultrasound?
A girl
How much money?
Ten thousand
Will my wife be okay?
Don't worry." (42)

The poet locates the connection of female infanticide and dowry system and shows how this tramples women's dignity, breaks their spirit and makes them die untimely. In 'Dignity Dies Daily' Pall writes,

"My sister says she looks like a princess
Without dowry no prince wants to marry her." (39)

In addition, poor Dalits compromise their dignity to get their daughters married because of this evil of dowry. They borrow money from high caste landlords and money lenders who exploit, deceive and sometimes take away their precious keepings such as gold and lactating cows, buffalos. Pall articulates Dalit women's issues and emphasises the need for their empowerment and mobilisation to bring about justice and equity:

"Let us fill our daughters and sisters with courage
So that no tears fill in their eyes." (39)

The poems in this collection bring out the miseries of Dalit lives in Punjab and show their subordinated and miserable existence in a casteist, feudalist and hidebound society. Despite that these poems are not mere cries of pain and haplessness. They are powerful articulation of Dalit issues and exhibit an awakened caste and class consciousness. According to Yogesh Maitreya, "*Days Will Come Back* sings for us the songs of those who were deliberately not heard. It encapsulates the history of love and labour of Dalits, and a blueprint of their future." (n. page) According to Sirsa, this collection shows the boiling anger of Dalits which can burst any moment in the form of a revolt. (11) Pall maintains that modern Dalits are not passive recipients of humiliation, violence and atrocities meted out to them in the name of religion and social order. They are articulate, courageous, confident and well aware that they are capable not only of fighting back but also of winning. (21) In the poem, 'Burn This Down,' the poet declares that the silence that was imposed deceitfully on Dalits is a thing of the past as they are now cognisant of their oppression and position in hegemonic socio-economic order:

"It is rotten
The doctrine of work without payment
They ask for payment of their hard work
Those who have stained clothes and faces
They now understand the cost of hard work
The difference between *Karma* and hard work
They have started to understand
This cruel tradition is now rotten." (25)

The poet depicts that from their repression Dalits have learnt how they should fight back against their victimisers and how they can transform their pain into power. In 'Self-Respect' Pall says,

"Even then when you abused him
He captured in the depths of his mind
The movement of your lips and the expressions of your face
However, he never showed such expressions on his face
All the poison and anger he swallowed
Which after digestion entered his bloodstream
Ran into his veins rapidly and then
Entered the veins of his generations
That poison and that aggression
Has now entered inside me

It will heat up like lava
Inside the blood of countless oppressed people
And an explosion is possible any time." (20)

Showing the qualities of Pall's characters, Sirsa writes, "The central character of Kamal's poem is an enlightened man who comprehends the reasons behind his oppression and communicates his understanding to his fellow community members who too have been subjected to oppression." (12) They are strong and determined to actualise their dream of liberty and dignity. 'A Letter to a Brother' documents this promise:

"We have dreams in our eyes
And we walk on administrative streets
If they don't like this, we do not care." (31)

Pall maintains that Dalits are aware they have to struggle for a space in every sphere of life and have to undergo severe opposition and violence in their endeavours. (24) Bringing out Dalits' commitment to fight back and evoke a revolution Pall writes,

"In this war with oppressors
It is definite that common man will die
Then shouldn't we tell them:
When you have to die in any case,
Start cleaning the barrels of your rifles now
Turn your aim towards the brain of your oppressors,
Not towards the targets of paper made for shooting practice." (37)

Pall's poetry is a wake-up call for Dalits. In 'You Too Should Wake Up' the poet makes a virtual declaration of war against every exploiter and victimiser such as priests, landlords, factory owners, politicians, gods and religion. The poet is confident of Dalits' victory as he knows they are aware of their strength and weaknesses of their opponents:

"How long will you let this happen?
I will wake up; you, too, should wake up
After making money and eating
The priest will go to sleep
We will snatch the beaded garland from him
We will divide the beads amongst ourselves
Then we will shatter the beads into pieces
I will wake up; you, too, should wake up." (44)

The poet appeals to Dalits to revolt against the landlords who also exploit them:

"He is alone and we are eleven
Why do we fear him?
We will divide crop amongst ourselves
If anyone lays eyes on us
We will sharpen our sickles." (45)

Similarly, he wants Dalit workers to seize the factory and divide the profits among themselves. He also wants them to revolt against religious authorities which expose them to caste and class based exploitation. The poet is well aware that Dalits have to struggle for their rights, empowerment and dignity and their enemy is extremely strong but he is optimistic of a new dawn in their lives. (45-46) In his title poem (Days Will Come Back) the poet writes:

> That days will come back
> When we will fulfil our dreams
> We will grow the same roses in our backyards
> Then lawns will not only exist in palaces
> But also, in our courtyards." (52)

The poet uses the symbol of rose to indicate the proposed beauty in Dalit lives and uses lawn as a symbol to refer to prosperity that Dalits will bring in their lives through hard work and struggle. The poet writes that Dalits have an unprecedented capacity to work hard and survive despite severe repression, opposition and deprivation:

> "Our children try to locate gold medals
> In milk, yoghurt, buttermilk or in a cup of tea
> Our children leave homes
> Move towards Olympic grounds
> After only having drunk
> The milk from their mother's breasts." (43)

Pall also shows how Dalits are compassionate and considerate and respectful of others despite numerous odds, injustices and adversities in their lives. His poems attempt to awaken Dalit masses and mobilise them against injustices and exploitation unleashed on them.

My Caste-My Shadow

My Caste-My Shadow is Madhopuri's first collection of poetry to be published in English. The poems in this anthology are a powerful articulation of prominent issues ranging from social and religious disparities, caste, class, political oppression and marginalisation of Dalits. They also vocalise the issue of gender oppression and violence against Dalits in general and Dalit women in particular. They bring out their hopes, aspirations, desires, fears, anger, inner conflicts and tensions. The poet uses powerful images and symbols and refers to numerous mythological, historical figures such as Eklavya, Narad Muni, Shakuni, Abhimanyu, Rahu-Ketu, Dhanvantri Rishi, Sahiban-Mirza, Farhat, Banda Singh Bahadur, Pir Buddhu Shah, Salwan, Ichhran, Loona, Puran, Saddam, Tulsi, Manu and others to highpoint the plight and protest of Dalits over centuries.

Madhopuri is pained to see that in recent time poetry has lost direction, it has become insensitive and is far removed from the realities of life. He scorns contemporary poets as they have no courage to experiment with the form, content and themes of poetry. Consequently, their poetry is static in nature and limited in scope. For Madhopuri, poetry is a true expression of the lives of wretched masses, a medium to record and represent the cry of their anguish, discontent and anger. He employs poetry to organise and mobilise depressed and deprived masses against the hegemony of the high castes and classes. He attempts to induce a sense of self-respect among suppressed Dalits and encourages them to break their silence and fight collectively for their rights and dignity. He opines that it is better to die fighting against injustices than live as slaves of the high castes. In 'Poetry, Tell Them' Madhopuri appeals to Dalits to assert their dignity and rebel against them:

"Poetry,
tell those insects
it's better
to fly on rainy-season wings
and be burnt on flames
than to crawl and
be squelched under heels." (34)

The poet opines that literature is a voice of protest against injustice and discrimination that Dalits are subjected to for centuries. He reiterates that he does not want to write poetry to amuse the elite groups of society rather he dedicates it to social causes and to extol heroic, revolutionary figures such as Eklavya, Banda Bahadur, Pir Buddhu Shah and Pablo Neruda who spoke for humanism and equity and fought bravely against the perpetrators. The poet sings of those Dalits who are courageous to question and defy established conventions, laws and assert their rights vociferously:

"I want
my poems
to be dedicated to the birds
who in search of their feed
transgress the village bounds
and alight in this or that courtyard
unbothered by the high and low
rooftops of households." (35-36)

The poet places caste at the centre of his writing and exposes its mechanism. He revisits it from a staunch Dalit point of view, locates its embeddedness in Indian society and culture and highpoints how it operates in Dalit lives. Like other Dalit writers, Madhopuri also holds caste with contempt and condemns it as a source of dehumanisation and exploitation of Dalits. He maintains that the Hindu *Sanatana* Dharma, based on the four-fold Varna system, and lethal texts such as *Manusmriti, Naradsmriti* and Puranas like *Padma Purana, Agni Purana* and *Vayu Purana,* legitimises caste and naturalises oppression based on it. He writes,

"My caste is always with me
like my complexion
like my shadow.
We are so rolled into one
I'm nothing
except my caste,
in the city in the village
here or across the sea." (37)

Bringing out the perpetuity of caste, the poet further writes that though every animate and inanimate thing is destroyed by powerful natural hazards and calamities like earthquakes and Tsunamis but caste escapes all these and survives with all its features and codes. The poet scornfully writes that even death, the biggest leveller, cannot save Dalits from the stigma of caste:

"And in no time land became water;
in the blink of an eye

present became past.
People recalled:
'Death is a great leveller.'
Yet the survivors reversed the tune.
The living labelled the dead:
One high, the other low
one touchable, the other untouchable." (39-40)

Madhopuri reiterates that though the world is changing constantly but in India the system of caste is still observed chauvinistically. The poet regrets that the institution of caste is still so stringent that in India, even in the era of globalisation, humans are still categorised as high and low. Exposing the rigidity of caste as depicted in Madhopuri's poems, Hans says "Madhopuri has a clear idea about the deep-rooted nature of the hierarchal Indian social order and deep-seated prejudices of the oppressive castes towards Dalits and Adivasis." (Introduction 10) They are discriminated against and shamed not only in villages and small towns but also in big cities where they mostly move in search of their livelihood, and a dignified life:

"Many a time
This clayey body becomes thinner
than water;
words fall off the tongue
like leaves from a tree
in autumn; and
I feel I am drowning
and the earth doesn't open up to swallow me
when suddenly
someone wants to know
my caste." (43)

Madhopuri writes that Dalits are frequently told they are born to serve the high castes who use concocted religious theories such as *Karma* and *Purav Janma* (the previous birth) to persuade them to accept their subordinated position. Madhopuri exposes and condemns these black laws and shows how Dalits are not allowed to build permanent homes, earn money and even wear proper clothes. He criticises every institution and law that discriminates against Dalits. He maintains that Dalits' expression of autonomy, dignity, identity and their demands for rights are usually suppressed violently by the dominant castes and classes for they hold the centres of both social and economic powers:

"They don't want
they don't tolerate
coloured umbrellas over other's head
any warmth in the dead cold seasons
peals of laughter spilling in the *behadas*
They want
the rising waters
to recede like
the boil in milk
to nip the thought about to fertilize
They keep devouring the shades of trees
at noontide
the address
of the sons of this land." (80)

Madhopuri problematises the caste based feudalism and brings out the exploitation of Dalits under this system. In 'He Said' he says,

"He said
I am a blinkered ox
allow my weary limbs to rest
unblinker my eyes
They said
Your duty is not to see
But to shut your eyes after seeing." (46)

The poet says that most Dalits are landless agricultural labourers solely dependent on land owning Jat Sikhs who coerce them to work ceaselessly and do not pay properly. Most Dalits have to survive on the meagre quantity of grain they get as wages from their high caste employers. The poet uses the images of a 'yoked bull' and a 'tamed horse' that are put to work ceaselessly and are given no food. It is highly ironical that Dalits who are strong, hardworking, produce huge quantity of grains and have brought different revolutions such as "the green, the white and the blue revolutions" are strangely still subordinated to the high castes and are deprived and miserable. (55) He maintains that many of them have accepted caste slavery and have internalised the oppression as they think that being Dalit is their destiny. (55-56) Madhopuri maintains that Indian politics is controlled by the high castes and Dalits are swindled in the name of reforms by shrewd politicians who are proficient in their profession (politic) and in befooling people. The poet details ironically, that these politicians persuade Dalits to vote for them to win elections but do not work for them after they come to power. (81)

Madhopuri also writes about the tumultuous years in Punjab when numerous innocent Dalits were killed ruthlessly in the violence that broke out in 1979. Many were killed and many beaten, tortured and imprisoned for a long period. To bring out the terror, scare and suffering of innocent Dalit masses in Punjab, the poet refers to the historical ruthless massacre of Dalits in two villages Belchi and Pipran of Bihar in 1977:

> "Villages have become Belchi and Pipran
> O father
> Eagles besiege
> the girl-sparrows." (50)

The poet says that many families lost their sons and other male members during those years. There was no justice for the dead as proofs of their murders were destroyed by the powerful gun holding perpetrators:

> "Many eyes
> remained unrolled on deserted pathways
> to lovingly welcome someone
> But the pathways had devoured
> the footprints of the home-comers." (75)

Madhopuri maintains that the Dalit voices were stifled cruelly by the high caste Jat Sikhs who forced them into Khalistan Movement or the nauseated police who tortured them and made them suffer silently. Surinder S Jodhka argues that Bhindranwale recruited his soldiers from the marginalised classes and backward castes. Many of them were poor, workers and school dropouts who hardly knew how to hold a gun. Many of them were killed by police in "fake encounters, without charging them of any crime" and their names were buried. (1313) Bringing out the gravity and the consequences of the bloody violence that commenced in 1980s in Punjab, Simrat Dhillon says that "hundreds of people were killed, the majority being innocent pilgrims; (to the Golden Temple in Amritsar) Bhindranwale perished in the attack and the army succeeded in its operation, but the consequences were graver and triggered the assassination of Indira Gandhi" (4) the Prime Minister of India at that time. Madhopuri brings out the caste angle of the violence and reiterates that poor Dalits' dissenters having no caste power were brutalised more than the other rebels.

Madhopuri writes that Dalit women had to suffer more during the dark period of terror and violence in Punjab. Many of them were raped and murdered. The poet uses the image of eagles attacking sparrows not only to depict the killings of hapless Dalits but also to show the brutal rapes of Dalit women by gun holding Jat Sikhs. Here, Madhopuri refers to the historical reality that women have been molested and raped by male ruffians not only to gratify their sexual desires but also to avenge their rivals. Sanjay Srivastava says that "besides being an exercise of power by upper caste members, sexual violence is also a method used by the upper caste men to show the lower caste men that they were unable to "protect" their women." (qtd. in Sen n. page) They are also molested and raped by the high caste men who they work for either as agricultural labourers or domestic help. The poet writes that ironically the poor Dalit girls are made pregnant by these high caste men but they refuse to accept the children born from such rapes. Through his poems, Madhopuri refers to a dark reality that on an average more than four Dalit women are raped daily in India. Dipu Rai argues that "according to the latest data released by the National Crime Records Bureau (NCRB), India recorded 88 rape cases every day in 2019. Out of the total 32,033 reported rape cases in a year, 11 per cent were from the Dalit community." (n. page) Madhopuri maintains that the poor, young, innocent Dalit girls have to suffer silently as they are not powerful enough to resist their rapes or fight for their rights. Bringing out Dalit women's plight he writes,

"They went to mow the grass
And come back as mothers
O father the cow – like
Virgins." (49)

Madhopuri's gender sensibilities and sensitivities also clearly manifest in his depiction of his mother, wife and daughter. He acknowledges his mother's role in his upbringing and his journey as a Dalit towards liberation from the swamp of caste and poverty. The poet also writes about his wife and expresses his gratitude for her support and selfless love. In some of his poems he not only recognises his wife's role in his life but also depicts her as a courageous, patient and brave woman. He presents her as an ideal mate and a true friend. She always supports and encourages him to fight against all odds and injustices in life. Expressing his sense of appreciation and gratefulness to her in 'My Life' he writes,

"Ever since she has joined me
we are one-and-one eleven.
My feet sail above the ground

and I have left far behind
the jungle of deep sorrow,
piles of hatred.
I have laid down before her love
weapons of anger-resentments,
of animosities.
She has sowed
in my heart
the seeds of new revolt
just as she is nurturing
in her body
our heir to come." (65)

The poet is full of love and affection for his daughter also. He wants to protect her from all the evils and odds in life.

It is true that the poet offers space for his mother, wife and daughter but it is also equally true that his portrayal of them lacks authenticity. He represents them in relation to men and does not grant them individuality. For instance, his mother is just a shadow of her husband who is shown as a great achiever and a brave man. She happily tells her son (poet) how his father struggled during the course of his life without speaking much about herself. In a similar vein, he represents his wife as an ideal homemaker who surrenders her personhood and agency to her husband. The poet depicts her as a woman overburdened by the patriarchal concepts of wifehood and motherhood as she never strives for individuality and autonomy. (63; 65-66) The educated Dalit men may be full of love and respect for their wives, mothers and daughters but they still lack authenticity as they depict them within the framework of Hindu patriarchy and lack moral courage to support their agency, a separate personhood and identity. The womanhood that Madhopuri constructs is influenced by the Sanskritised Hindu culture where women are considered weak, sophisticated, honour of community, property of men or just objects to adorn their bedrooms.

Though most of Madhopuri's poems record the distress of suppressed Dalit masses but they are not merely a cry of helplessness. The poet argues that though most Dalits are victims of caste and class oppression, counterfeit religious ideologies and conventions but a huge section is being vocal on their issues and sufferings. Dalits as depicted in this collection, are strong and courageous who face every adverse situation bravely and do not surrender passively to the repressive socio-economic and political forces. Dalits have to survive on scraps as they cannot procure nutritious food but they are still strong and agile. They work more than the high caste people who are rich and eat wholesome and scrumptious food. (58) Despite numerous handicaps and limitations such as poverty and illiteracy, modern Dalits are capable not only of surviving but also of fighting back against hegemonic castes and classes. Modern Dalits do not surrender their rights and personhood to religious notions such as *tyag* (renunciation) and rebirth. To bring out the intensity of Dalit voices and their struggle to change this subordinated condition, the poet metaphorically refers to the divine bull of Hindu mythology, who is carrying the earth on his horn. (82) Madhopuri's Dalits not only question the unequal distribution of resources but also assert their right to property and demand an equal share in the means of economic production. In the 'Song of the Land' the poet says,

"Parrots nibble at milky corn
O Patwari
We can't tolerate this sin." (47)

Striking at the very roots of caste based bourgeoisie and unjust economic system the poet further states:

"The cropped hay puts out shoots again
O Patwari
Give us our share of three-arm length of space." (48)

The poet declares that modern Dalits are not simple and docile, they are aggressive and ready to fight for their rights. In recent years, they have begun to flout established caste laws and conventions and they resist everything that dehumanises and discriminates against them. (50) Madhopuri uses the images of birds flying against the wind and fish swimming against the current to show Dalits' defiance, mobilisation and uprising against the authority of high castes and classes. He claims that like the arrows of the great Dalit archer Eklavya, protesting Dalits are fighting to destroy the toxic system of caste and class and bring structural changes in the existing caste dominated social system. (49) The poet opines that contemporary Dalit literature can play a significant role to decimate discriminatory Sanatan traditions and establish the ideals of equality, liberty and fraternity. He appeals to his contemporary writers to produce a literature that exposes, despises and rejects Sanatan culture:

"Come my contemporary,
Let's sing, in the market place,

the death song
of the *sanatani* Sanskriti
that has divided mankind again and again
that is devoid of reason." (99)

The poet maintains that sanskritised culture is the root of Dalit sufferings in India as this culture, in the name of religiosity, promotes discrimination against Dalits and legitimises violence against them:

"Give up the Sanskriti of Sanskrit
Let's load with stones the boat
In which our life is living death." (100)

Though Madhopuri rejects the precept of caste and revolts against it he does not spread hatred against the high caste people and does not attack them personally. In 'Oasis' he appreciates his high caste friend Purshottum Sharma and expresses his gratitude to him for his compassion and support. He tells us that his friend is not blinded by the chauvinistic religious laws and caste abhorrence and always supported him selflessly in bad times:

"Whenever I descend
into dark endless caves
or boggy hells
he is visible as the steadfast polestar
Sometimes he is a brilliant sunshine
Sometimes an umbrella
Sometimes a protective sword

Sometimes the Lakshman Rekha
During a drought
he becomes a dew drop
In the desert
he becomes an oasis." (70)

The poet experiences severe caste and class based oppression and exploitation but it does not turn him harsh towards others or towards life. He exhibits a moral courage to love others and live life enthusiastically. In 'Life-II' he says,

"Life I wish to live with you
like a plant with mud
greenness with the leaf
the landscape with eye." (83)

Madhopuri is optimistic and believes that Dalits are strong with unprecedented physical and mental capabilities. His buoyant attitude towards life is evident in 'Consolation' in which he assures his wife that evil days will soon disappear and good times will come:

"Don't fear the water's rising waves
It will by itself
turn into eddy;
waters after all must flow
under the bridges,
my dear wife." (61)

Madhopuri writes to serve humanity and bring about

desirable changes in the lives of the depressed, deprived and other socio-economic groups. He is full of promises and attempts to democratise caste afflicted Indian society where Dalits can be treated equally. In 'Bring Back the Seasons' the poet says,

> "Bring back the seasons
> in which
> the grass trampled under feet
> can feel alive
> and grows tall during the night
> by four-fingers breadth
> bitter cucumbers remain no longer bitter
> sugarcane stalks become sweet
> and soap nuts too become sweet." (77)

Madhopuri's poetry, which strives to unfetter and empower Dalits is a skillful blend of various ideologies. He preaches humanism as the greatest religion. He advocates Buddha's philosophy of life, follows Ambedkar's visions and ideologies and endorses wholeheartedly what he suggested to annihilate caste, and liberate Dalits. Madhopuri also holds Marxism and Leninism with reverence as they speak of their economic exploitations and thus sympathize with them. His poem 'Red Speech' grieves the dissolution of Soviet Union and describes how the capitalist West danced and celebrated this collapse of the Union and how the East was sad. (95) He argues that though the Soviet is disintegrated but the ideology that it was founded on is imperishable:

"The flood waters can't be damned
howsoever hard they try
One day it will explode like a volcano
the fire that smoulders underneath the straw." (96)

In this collection, Madhopuri's poems speak collectively for the emancipation of Dalits and other non-dominant social, economic groups such as tribals and women and revolt against all that is discriminatory and suppressive. He deconstructs Hindu myths and scorns Hindu mythical figures such as Narad and Manu for their treacheries against Dalits. He uses Dalit figures such as Eklavya to bring out their oppression and remind them of their stigmatised past so they can mobilise themselves to fight for justice and equality. In addition to images and symbols, Madhopuri also uses unconventional diction and themes. He writes about the pain and suffering of impoverished Dalit masses. He also offers a peep into their minds and depicts their inner conflicts. Describing his own psychological anguish in the 'Waves' he writes:

"That moment is terrifying
When one is fighting Mahabharata within oneself:
one hears neither the sound of weapons
nor sees the flames issuing from the agnivaans;
at times one is crushed under time's chariot wheels
at others one is run over by the wheels of artha and kama." (89)

Bringing out his inner conflicts, dilemmas and psychological trauma, the poet compares himself with Abhimanyu, stuck in the *Chakravyuh* (squared planning done by Dronacharya in the epic battle of Mahabharata to defeat Pandavas) and striving to find a way out from this distress. (90) He maintains that it is always difficult to maintain mental peace when he is reminded of his past, especially, the days of poverty, suppression and humiliation and also of some broken relationships.

The selected poetry collections, *Days Will Come Back* and *My Caste-My Shadow* are powerful articulation of Dalit issues. They expose the mechanisms of Dalits' suffering and record militant voices of awakening and protest in contemporary Punjab. The selected poets, Pall and Madhopuri locate the root of Dalit anguish in Hindu religious beliefs, scriptures, and collectively revolt against them. They reject the notion of Hindu dharma and gods and attempt to devastate orthodox, discriminatory socio-cultural and religious conventions which subjugate Dalits and normalise their suppression. They oppose the dehumanisation of Dalits. Pall and Madhopuri vocalise the demand for fixed working hours and wages for agricultural and mill workers and strive for their education and property rights. The poems evince an awakened Dalit consciousness and attack every form of oppression and discrimination. They articulate the issues of gender discrimination and address Dalit women's specific suffering. In their opinion, it is mandatory to empower and liberate Dalit women to initiate a just and equalitarian socio-economic system, and eradicate all disparities and injustices prevalent in society.

In addition to thematic and strategic similarities, the selected poets are nearly alike in their poetic techniques and use of language, images and symbols. Both poets devote poetry to society and to give voice to those who have been muted treacherously for centuries. The subject of their poetry is a common man and they take their themes not from Hindu myths and legends but from the prominent social, economic and political issues. The selected poets reject the traditional images and symbols and devise their own that suit their language and subject matter. Besides Hinduism and Hindu religious texts, Pall and Madhopuri also reject Sikhism, Gurus and *Guru Granth Sahib* as they find them as discriminatory as Hinduism. They extol Dalit culture and celebrate Dalit figures such as Shambuk, Eklavya, Phule and Ambedkar. The poems in these collections are social in nature and speak collectively for the liberation of Dalits as a unit. Though, some of Madhopuri's poems evince a strong autobiographical element when he writes about his father, mother, wife, daughter, friend and village but the caste factor does not go out of focus. Underscoring the admixture of personal and communal in Madhopuri, Ghai rightly says, "This autobiographical element has a deep underlying connection with his caste and community. He is further able to connect his poetry to the broader world of his country and humanity at large. His dismay, not rage, is evident at what the Indian civilization has done to communities like his, and his deep concern that exclusion, discrimination and humiliations still continue both, at the obvious and subtle psychological levels." (24)

Finally, after an insightful study of selected collections, *Days Will Come Back* and *My Caste-My Shadow,* it can be inferred that they cover almost every aspect of Dalits' life and are significant articulation of Dalit awakening and mobilisation in contemporary Punjab. They not only report Dalits' sufferings, their anger and indignation but also show their activism, aim, vision and strategies to liberate themselves from slavery perpetuated by the edicts of caste, class and religion.

Works Cited

- Anand. "Life and Teaching of Guru Nanak." *History Discussion*, n. page, www.historydiscussion.net/history-of-india/life-and-teaching-of-guru-nanak/3178. Accessed 20 February 2020.
- *Census of India* 2001.
- *Census of India* 2011.
- Dhillon, Simrat. "The Sikh Diaspora and the Quest for Khalistan: A Search for Statehood or for Self-preservation." *Institute of Peace and Conflict Studies*, 2007, pp. 1-10, www.ipcs.org. Accessed 21 October 2020.
- Ghai, TC "Translating Balbir Madhopuri." (Translator's Note) *My Caste-My Shadow* by Madhopuri. Translated by Ghai, LG Publishers and Distributors, 2020, pp. 23-25.
- Gill, Sucha Singh. "Socio-Economic Transformation and Scheduled Castes in Punjab." *Dalits in Regional Context*, edited by Harish K Puri, Rawat Publications, 2004, pp. 225-240.
- Hans, Rajkumar. "Rich Heritage of Punjabi Dalit Literature and its Exclusion from Histories." *Academy of the Punjab in North America*, n. page, apnaorg.com/research-papers/ rajkumar-1/ Accessed 19 February 2020.
- Introduction. *My Caste-My Shadow* by Balbir Madhopuri. Translated by TC Ghai, LG Publishers and Distributors, 2020, pp. 7-17.
- Jodhka, Surinder S "Looking Back at Khalistan Movement: Some Recent Researches on its Rise and Decline." *Economic and*

Political Weekly, 2001, Republished Online in 2018, *Research Gate*, pp. 1311-1318, www.researchgate.net/publication/262121177_Looking_Back_at_the_Khalistan_Movement_Some_Recent_Researches_on_Its_Rise_and_Decline. Accessed 23 October 2020.

- Judge, Paramjit S "Existence, Identity and Beyond: Tracing the Contours of Dalit Literature in Punjabi." *Economic and Political Weekly*, 2014, vol. xlix, no. 29, pp. 209-216.
- Kumar, Pramod and Rainuka Dagar. "Gender in Dalit Identity Construction in Punjab." *Dalits in Regional Context*, edited by Harish K Puri, Rawat Publications, 2004, pp. 274-296. Madhopuri, Balbir. *My Caste-My Shadow: Selected Poems*. Translated by TC Ghai, LG Publishers and Distributers, 2020.
- Maini, Darshan Singh. *Studies in Punjabi Poetry*. Vikas Publishing House, 1979.
- Maitreya, Yogesh. "Dalit Writing, Global Contexts: In *Days Will Come Back*, Kamal Dev Pall Unmasks an Unseen, Unspoken of Punjab." *Firstpost*, 24 July 2020, www.firstpost.com/living/dalit-writing-global-contexts-in-days-will-come-back-kamal-dev-pall-unmasks-an-unseen-unspoken-of-punjab-7016061.html. Accessed 19 August 2020.
- Pall, Kamal Dev. *Days Will Come Back*. Translated by Rajinder Azad, Panther's Paw Publications, 2019.
- Puri, Harish K. "Scheduled Castes in Sikh Community: A Historical Perspective." *Economic and Political Weekly*, vol. 38, no. 2, 2003, pp. 2693-2701.
- "The Scheduled Castes in the Sikh Community: A Historical Perspective." *Dalits in Regional Context*, edited by Puri, Rawat Publications, 2004, pp. 190-224.
- Rai, Dipu. "No country for women: India reported 88 rape

cases every day in 2019." *India Today*, 30 September 2020, n. page, www.indiatoday.in/diu/story/no-country-for-women-india-reported-88-rape-cases-every-day-in-2019-1727078-2020-09-30. Accessed 18 October 2020.

- Ram, Ronki. "Limits of Untouchability, Dalit Assertion and Caste Violence in Punjab." *Dalits in Regional Context*, edited by Harish K Puri, Rawat Publications, 2004, pp. 132-189.
- Rasulpuri, Bhagwant. "Dalit Literature in Punjab." Translated by Rajinder Singh, *Journal of Literature and Aesthetics*, vol. 9, no. 1 and 2, 2009, pp. 131-135.
- Sen, Sumanti. "Four Dalit Women Raped Everyday: Why Caste Matters in Sexual Assaults." *The Logical Indian*, 13 January 2020, n. page, thelogicalindian.com/dalit-women-sexual-violence. Accessed 18 October 2020.
- Sharma, Shalini, and BK Aggarwal. "Educating Dalit Women for Development: A Study in Hoshiarpur District of Punjab." *Dalits in Regional Context*, edited by Harish K Puri, Rawat Publications, 2004, pp. 258-273.
- Singh, Gurmanpreet, and Kamaljit Singh. "Deplorable Conditions of Agricultural Labourers in Rural Punjab." *Journal of Economic and Social Development*, vol. xi, no. 2, 2015, pp. 44-48, www.researchgate.net/publication/307787185_DEPLORABLE_CONDITIONS_OF_AGRICULTURAL_LABOURERS_IN_RURAL_PUNJAB, Accessed 21 February 2020.
- Sirsa, Sukhdev Singh. "The Politics of Denial vs Eklavya." *Days Will Come Back*. Translated by Rajinder Azad, Panther's Paw Publications, 2019, pp. 9-14.

CONCLUSION

DALIT LITERATURE as an unconventional form of writing addresses Dalit issues and problematises existing caste based power structures and relations. It revolutionises Dalits' demand to transform every institution that dehumanises them, discriminates against and alienates them from economic resources, education and a dignified life. Dalit literature is marked by humanism as every Dalit writer speaks for humanity and strives to initiate a just and egalitarian system where Dalits may be treated as equal human beings without any consideration of caste, class and community. This book was an attempt to examine the textual representation of caste, class and gender identity in contemporary Dalit writings. It casts an authentic spotlight on how selected Dalit writers hailing from different regions, religions and belonging to diverse castes, cultures, economic and educational backgrounds understand, depict, represent and counter differences based on caste, class, gender and religion. It also underscores the similarities and dissimilarities if any, in different Dalit writers' representation of caste and their responses to it.

Before the critical analysis of selected texts, the word Dalit was defined and explained. The early roots, genesis, growth, nature, aim and aesthetic of Dalit literature were located to construct its historiography and examine its scopes. An insightful survey of history and concerned literature established that the earliest spores of Dalit literature were discernibly present in Buddhist literature. The literature composed by different Bhakti saints and cults, sects and religious movements such as Tantra, Natha, Sikhism, Arya Samaj and others also ridiculed caste and prepared grounds for the expedition of Dalit literature. In addition, the writings of radical Dalit intellectuals such as Jyotirao and Savitribai Phule, Muktabai, Iyothee Thass, Periyar, Ambedkar and many others also shaped Dalit literature and helped it to its present shape. These early intellectuals not only questioned the traditional divine view of caste but also devised radical anti-caste philosophy, vision and strategies to liberate Dalits and abrogate caste.

Most Dalit critics and writers opine that Ambedkar was the chief creative brainwave behind this literature. According to Rajat Rani Meenu, Marathi Dalit literature began with Ambedkar in the twentieth century. (36) Contemporary Dalit writers adhere to Ambedkarism and stand firmly for what Ambedkar preached and suggested to emancipate Dalits and annihilate caste. It is because of Ambedkar's philosophy that most Dalit writers hold caste with contempt and despise it as the source of all odds and injustices against them. Like Ambedkar, their writings also debunk the theory of divine origin of caste and Varna system and reject Hinduism. It is again because of Ambedkar's vision and influence that Dalit writers condemn the toxic religiosity preached by Hindu Brahmins and suggest either atheism or Buddhism as religious alternatives for Dalits.

In chapter one, the selected Dalit autobiographers, Valmiki, Biswas and Byapari, approach caste from a staunch Dalit point of view, expose the whole paraphernalia of caste and show how it operates in Dalits' lives. They argue that caste dehumanises Dalits and exposes them to severe exploitation. It was because of caste prejudices that Dalits had to live the lives of sub-human beings and they were deprived of education and property. Valmiki's description of his experiences at school and college authentically illustrates how Dalits' attempts to educate themselves and to lead a dignified life are thwarted by casteist forces that wanted Dalits to be in servitude to them. Valmiki shows that most Dalits (*chuhras*) used to work for the high caste, class Tagas and were given scraps for discharge of their duties.

In a similar vein, Biswas and Byapari also write that it was mainly because of caste that the lives of Namasudras was miserable both in colonial and post-colonial Bengal. Biswas writes that his community was ignored, suppressed and deprived in terms of education, means of transportation and health care services. Byapari also relates his experiences of suffering and maintains that the partition of the country further aggravated the lives of Namasudras who became citizens of nowhere living in tents in new India. He ridicules caste and argues that it was because of caste prejudice that Dalit refugees were discriminated against and alienated from rehabilitation and government welfare schemes. Every writer demonstrates a heightened Dalit conscious, speaks for community and eventually revolts against the prejudices of caste and class. Dalit autobiographers are not ashamed of their caste rather they vociferously assert their identities as Dalits and celebrate their culture. They suggest education to counter caste and advocate Dalit solidarity. They expose the intra-caste conflicts among Dalits and criticise them. The Dalit autobiographies attempt to awaken and mobilise silenced Dalit masses and appeal to them to respond to Ambedkar's call: 'unite, educate and agitate.'

Dalit writers expose and ridicule every institution that suppresses and discriminates against them. They write how Dalit women are the worst victims of gaze, molestation, rape and brutal killings by non-Dalit men. They advocate women's education and protest against evils such as devadasi, jogini, chira, naked worship and ascetic widowhood. They argue that Dalit community cannot be liberated without liberating Dalit women.

Chapter two brings out the inadequacies in Dalit men's representation of Dalit women. In *Baluta*, for instance, Pawar deserts his wife autocratically simply because of her rumoured love affair with a Muslim boy. It is because of his inherent patriarchal structure of thought that he could not allow even a bit of autonomy to his wife. Similarly, Limbale is also unable to understand what Masamai goes through as a deserted wife and a raped Dalit woman. He blames her for every wrong in his life. His attitude towards his mother shows that he was conditioned to behave within patriarchal structure. Limbale's attitude towards his mother proves that for Dalit men, the question of women is directly associated with community honour. So, they not only guard or rather repress their sexuality but also depict them as it suits them.

Madhopuri brings out his mother's suffering under her husband's authority and also acknowledges her role in his life but does not write much about his wife. He is not able to trounce this inherent stereotype in his latest poetic collection *My Caste-My Shadow*. His poems in this collection present her as a typical Indian housewife, an ideal homemaker who surrenders her personhood and identity to her husband, and lives for her children. In addition, Madhopuri is urbane in his depiction of his daughter; he wants to protect her from the struggles of life and does not want her to even know the bitter realities of Dalit life. His attitude towards Dalit women indicates that he attempts to represent them within the structure of traditional Hindu society. So, his portrayal of Dalit women is not authentic and explicit.

In addition, Dalit writers also blindspot internal patriarchy and Dalit women's subjection to it. The violence and gender discrimination that Dalit women undergo within their own household are not adequately depicted in Dalit male writings. In 'Oorakali,' for instance, Mandayan's wife and daughter are wooed, raped and eventually ravaged by the high caste landlords. Karikalan shows them both physically and emotionally weak and incapable of even resisting their rapes or advancements by the high castes. Valmiki's 'Killing of a Cow' also shows how beautiful Dalit women are considered their property by the high caste men and how they conspire to entrap, and then rape them. The Dalit women depicted by Kamal Dev Pall are also the worst victims of humiliation, violence and molestation by the high caste landholding Jat Sikhs. Although, he takes-up issues of Dalit women and criticizes evil practices such as dowry system and female infanticide, but it is equally true that like other Dalit male writers his portrayal of Dalit women is inauthentic, inadequate or rather counterfeit. Bringing out Dalit women's broken images as located in most Dalit male writings, Karan Singh says, "The domestic violence, inequality in matters of care and food never enters his vision. The obvious outcome is that the portrayal of women in male Dalit writers' novels suffers from surfeit and scarcity. Her concern as a human being and as a woman are subsumed in the larger and more apparent reality of being a Dalit." (68-69) The issues and sufferings of Dalit women are seen as just minor affairs and are usually overlooked. Dalit movements ranging in different regions of the country are male dominated. Similarly, the feminist movements are also high caste centric.

Dalit women's literature began to appear sustainably in the late 1980s or in the beginning of 1990s. It not only rejected Dalit male point of view but also challenged their deliberated exclusion from power structures and scope of reforms. Dalit women's autobiographies such as Shantabai Kamble's *Majya Jalmachi Chittarkatha*, Baby Kamble's *The Prisons we Broke*, Urmila Pawar's *The Weave of My Life*, Kumud Pawde's *The Story of My Sanskrit*, Bama's *Karukku* and many others vocalized Dalit women's issues. Modern Dalit women are aware how the patriarchal power operates in their lives. Bama's *Karukku* speaks explicitly not only of Dalit women's suppression and exploitation by the high caste rich landlords but also shows their sufferings within their own households and community. The high caste men not only use Dalit women as cheap domestic and agricultural labourers but also exploit them sexually. Besides, they are also scolded and dishonoured by the high caste women while giving them scraps for the discharge of their duties. Dalit women problematise the existing power structures and argue that government agencies such as police, media and law are also highly afflicted by the prejudices of caste, and gender. Even religions are gender biased or more discriminatory against Dalit women.

Bama shares her bitter experiences of caste and gender based discriminations prevalent in the convent and Church. Similarly, Baby Halder writes that within their homes or in private spheres the impoverished Dalit women have to endure verbal and physical violence at the hands of their fathers, brothers, husbands and even sons and in the public dominion they are further subjected to molestation, rape, forced and unpaid labour. In her life story *A Life Less Ordinary*, Baby maintains that it was mainly because of indifference of her father and brothers that she was pushed into an unmatched and unconsented child marriage. Again because of her husband's domination and hyper masculinity she had to leave her home and come to Delhi in search of job and a peaceful life. It is because of her bitter experiences and sufferings that she reiterates that Dalit women's exploitation and oppression is promoted by Dalit men themselves. Baby believes that Dalit women can lead a stable and dignified life if Dalit men encourage and cooperate with them.

The educated second generation Dalit women writers such as Meena Kandasamy, Mercy Margaret, Yashica Dutt and others are more uninhibited and explicit in their criticism and problematisation of caste, class, gender and religion. Kandasamy revisits Indian patriarchy and exposes the hypocrisy of those Indian men who claim to be educated and liberal. Her semi-autobiographical novel, *When I Hit You* shows graphically how her so called organic intellectual husband was exploitative, violent and dogmatic in his attitude towards her. He pressurises her to discontinue writing and calls her a shameless 'petit bourgeoisie whore' for writing on so called controversial issues such as sex. He monitors her mobile phone, pushes her off from social media and coerces her to surrender her email password to cut her connection with the world outside. She shows how women are still considered sub-human beings and how they are still denied personhood, agency and rights. She also shows that intellectual women such as Sylvia Plath and Kamala Das were also victims of patriarchal oppression. She refers to Plath and Das to prove that even learning, education and knowledge cannot win agency for women whereas, the power of knowledge grants men numerous unrestrained privileges.

Though, Dalit men and women writers are divided on the issue of Dalit women, internal patriarchy and gender oppression but they are almost same in their understanding and representation of caste, class issues and oppression. Like selected Dalit male autobiographers, Pawar, Limbale, Valmiki, Madhopuri, Biswas and Byapari the Dalit women's autobiographies such as Bama's *Karukku* and Halder's *A Life Less Ordinary* also criticise, antagonise caste and class and collectively revolt against them. In addition to self-writings, Dalit women and men's short narratives are akin in their depiction of caste and class such as Bama's 'Pongal' and Gogu Shyamala's 'Obstacle Race'.

Bandhu Madhav's 'The Poisoned Bread' not only brings out the throes and suffering of Dalits but also shows how the interaction of caste and class creates a gigantic mechanism that denies Dalits' humanity and coerces them to lead lives more despicable than animals. Other stories such as Hoval's 'The Storeyed House,' Valmiki's 'Salaam,' 'The 'Hide of an Ox,' 'The Killing of a Cow,' 'Shavayatra,' Karikalan's 'Oorakali,' Ganesh's

'Paddy Harvest' and Abhimani's 'Ailment' also portray caste and class oppression of Dalits and show how the so called high caste people conspire against Dalits and use different tactics to mute their voices. The exposition of the institutions of caste and class and a voice of protest against them is the basic thrust and character of Dalit literature.

Besides autobiographies and fiction, Dalit poetry also uses Dalits' suppression and uprising as leading themes. The selected Dalit poets – Pall and Madhopuri maintain that Dalits are poor because of their outcaste status and inferior socio-religious status imposed on them. Pall raises the issue of Dalit oppression within caste and feudalistic structures and argues that Dalits are denied access to education and a dignified life as they are despised and rejected in the Indian scriptures such as Vedas, Puranas and Smritis. Like Pall, Madhopuri also opines that Hindu religiosity is the source of all evils against Dalits so they should reject Hinduism to emancipate themselves and annihilate rampant caste and class based discriminations.

Finally, after having studied Dalit literature from a Dalit point of view it can be inferred that it addresses Dalit issues and aims to awaken suppressed Dalit masses. It demands Dalits' rights, their dignity and identity and attempts to raise a strong Dalit consciousness among them. It also appeals to Dalits to organise and mobilise themselves against dominant socio-economic forces. Dalit literature problematises existing power structures and questions Dalits' alienation from them. They reject and defy every institution and rule that discriminates against Dalits. Every Dalit writer holds caste with contempt and declares that caste dehumanises Dalits and exposes them to severe economic exploitation and physical abuse. Modern

Dalit writers are of the opinion that to liberate Dalits from the constraints of caste it is essential to devastate the conventional system of belief and orthodox Hindu religiosity as it discounts Dalits and legitimises injustices and discriminations against them. Most Dalit writers revile Hinduism as the root of caste and class based disparities and the marginalisation of Dalits. They reject Hindu Brahmanical virtues such as sacrifice and renunciation and demand their rights here on this earth only. They also revolt against Hindu gods as they find them anti-Dalit and discriminatory.

Byapari revolts against God for His indifference to the sufferings of Dalits and biases against them. Dalit literature celebrates and venerates Dalit heroic figures such as Bali, Ravan, Mandodari, Tarka, Shambuk, Shurpanakha and Eklavya who were victims of caste politics. Dalits condemn Dronacharya for deceiving Eklavya by asking for his thumb as *Gurudakshina* (fee and a sense of gratitude due to one's mentor). They also condemn Rama for cowardly severing the neck of shudra scholar Shambuk Muni, who accumulated the knowledge of Vedas and undertook penance. Most Dalit writers refer to the assassination of Shambuk to show that the high castes have always been scared of Dalits, their capacity to work hard, survive and grow powerfully despite numerous injustices. Dalit writers also denounce Hindu scriptures such as *Manusmriti*, *Naradsmriti*, Puranas and epics such as *Ramayana* and *Mahabharata* as they legitimise caste, justify discrimination and violence against Dalits. Besides scriptures, Dalit writers also rebuff Hindu religious festivals such as *Durga Puja* and Dusshera as they find them insulting for Dalits and a cheap exhibition of the high caste Hindus' arrogance, power and authority over them. Religious traditions such as burning the effigy of Ravana at Dusshera appear to be dehumanizing for Dalits as such conventions not only extol Aryan culture but also depict Dalits as wicked. (70)

Valmiki and Biswas in their respective life stories tell us that they were shamed by the high castes for eating pork. Dalit writers not only resist autocratic cultural imposition but also extol the golden heritage of their own culture. For them, Dalit culture is more inclusive, democratic and rich as compared to Brahmanical Hindu culture. Dalit writers appeal to Dalits to cast off Hindu religious hypocrisies, educate themselves and develop a scientific temper. Writers such as Daya Pawar, Sharankumar Limbale, Omprakash Valmiki, Balbir Madhopuri, Manohar Mouli Biswas, Manoranjan Byapari, Kamal Dev Pall and others are proud to be Dalits and they berate those who conceal their caste to pass as non-Dalits.

Though Dalit writers reject Hinduism as the root of casteism and Dalits' suffering but they find almost all religions biased against Dalits and are equally critical of them. For instance, Bama in *Karukku* criticises Christianity and exposes the rigid caste biases prevalent in the Church and convent. Similarly, Madhopuri and Pall also revolt against Sikhism and argue that Sikhs, who claim to be liberal and caste neutral, are as casteist as Hindus and the prejudice of caste is equally prevalent in Gurudwaras. Madhopuri writes that Dalits were not allowed in Gurudwaras and were given *Karah Prasad* from a distance. Pall also maintains that Dalits are treated as others even after conversion. Apart from Sikhism, Pall also condemns Islam for its inclusion of caste prejudice and scorns its philosophy of *Jannat* (heaven). (22) Most Dalit writers denounce religion as oppressive institutions and discard the existence of God. It is because of the discriminatory or inegalitarian nature of religions that most Dalit writers suggest atheism as a religious alternative for Dalits. Valmiki in his *Dalit Sahitya ka Saundaryashastra* says that Dalit literature follows Gautam Buddha's theory of atheism, scientific approach, and opposition to orthodox Hindu religious performances, rituals and traditions. (31)

Dalit literature which is marked by the spirit of rejection, resistance and innovation is unconventional and reactionary in its use of language also. Valmiki writes that Dalit writers use unconventional and agressive language to give a realistic description of the pain and anguish of impoverished Dalits. They use the language spoken by common Dalit masses in their everyday life. Since they are writing for commoners, they should be simple in their delineation of events and should not confuse their readers by using jargons and highly embellished language. They focus on the content and are least concerned about the form. For them, literature is not just a means of amusement but a tool to awake, unite and mobilise silenced and suppressed Dalits. So, naturally the images and symbols used in Dalit literature are distinctive and unconventional. Limbale says, "When Dalit writers employed religious symbols, it was to deconstruct them, infusing them with new meaning and purpose." (34)

Contemporary Dalit writers, critics and theorists maintain that the aim of Dalit literature is not to praise and eulogise what is pleasing and beautiful, rather it attempts to bring out the harsh realities of Dalit lives and advocates equality, justice and liberty. Dalit writers reiterate that the beauty of Dalit literature does not lie in the praise of gods, sensual description of women's body and the beauty of nature, the aesthetic of this literature lies in its rendering of reality, exposition of evil and realisation of truth. Dalit literature rejects many traditional aesthetical theories and concepts. Contemporary Dalit writers are conscious that the aesthetic of *Satyam, Shivam, Sundram* is nothing but a high caste strategy to exploit non-dominants and monopolise literary traditions. Dalit writers reject this consideration and demand a separate artistic yardstick for critical appraisal of this literature. Dalit literature propounds a staunch Dalit point of view and rejects an outsider perspective. They hate the sympathetic writings on Dalits by outsiders as such writings neglect their agony and discounts their personhood, dignity and identity. They aspire to awaken and mobilise Dalits against injustices and demand a just viable space in dominant social, economic, political, cultural and literary domains. Barring a few exceptions, Dalit literature exhibits the influence of Dalit intellectuals such as Kabir, Ravidas, Phule, Ambedkar, Thass, Periyar and others and reject the ideologies of Kandukuri Veeresalingam and Gandhi. They are also critical of Marxism as it does not adequately address caste issues. Every Dalit writer writes out of acute social commitment and their writing strives to transform existing power structures either by devastating or reforming them.

Works Cited

- Abhimani. "Ailment." Translated by N Kalyan Raman, *The Oxford India Anthology of Tamil Dalit Writing,* edited by Ravikumar and R Azhagarasan, Oxford UP, 2012, pp. 101-106.
- Arunima, G "Some Issues in an Analysis of Caste and Gender in Modern India." *Translating Caste: Stories, Essays, Criticism*, edited by Tapan Basu, Katha, 2002, pp. 219-233.
- Bama. *Karukku.* Translated by Lakshmi Holmstrom, Oxford UP, 2000.
- "Pongal." *Harum-Scrum Saar and Other stories.* Translated by N Ravi Shanker, Women Unlimited, 2006, pp. 1-6.
- Bandhu Madhav. "The Poisoned Bread." Translated by Ramesh Dnyate, *Poisoned Bread: Translations from Modern Marathi Dalit Literature*, edited by Arjun Dangle, new edition, Orient Black Swan, 2014, pp. 167-175.
- Biswas, Manohar Mouli. *Surviving in My World: Growing Up Dalit in Bengal.* Translated by and edited by Angana Dutta and Jaydeep Sarangi, Samya, 2015.
- Byapari, Manoranjan. *Interrogating My Chandal Life: An Autobiography of a Dalit.* Translated by Sipra Mukherjee, Sage/ Samya, 2018.
- Ganesh, Mogalli. "The Paddy Harvest." Translated by Raghavendra Rao, *Translating Caste: Stories, Essays and Criticism*, edited by Tapan Basu, Katha, 2002, pp. 12-24.
- Halder, Baby. *A Life Less Ordinary*. Translated by Urvashi Butalia, Zubaan, 2006.
- Hoval, Waman. "The Storeyed House." Translated by MD Hatkanangalekar, *Poisoned Bread: Translations from Modern Marathi Dalit Literature*, edited by Arjun Dangle, new edition, Orient Black Swan, 2014, pp. 176-184.

- Kamble, Baby. *The Prisons We Broke.* Translated by Maya Pandit, Orient Longman, 2008.
- Kandasamy, Meena. *When I Hit You: Or, A Portrait of the Writer as a Young Wife.* Juggernaut Books, 2017.
- Kardam, Jai Prakash. "*Dalit Sahitya aur Samaj Kuch Prashna.*" ("Some Questions on Literature and society"). *Dalit Chetna: Sahitya* (*Dalit Consciousness: Literature*), edited by Ramnika Gupta, Navlekhan, 1996, pp. 100-09.
- Karikalan, Irathina. "Oorakali." Translated by Hephzibah Israel. *Translating Caste: Stories, Essays and Criticism*, edited by Tapan Basu, Katha, 2002, pp. 2-9.
- Kumar, Raj. *Dalit Personal Narratives: Reading Caste, Nation and Identity.* Orient Black Swan, 2010.
- Limbale, Sharankumar. *Towards an Aesthetic of Dalit Literature: History, Controversies and Considerations.* Translated by Alok Mukherjee, Orient Longman, 2004.
- *The Outcaste: Akkarmashi.* Translated by Santosh Bhoomkar, Oxford UP, 2003.
- Madhopuri, Balbir. *Changiya Rukh (Against the Night: An Autobiography)* Translated by Tripti Jain, Oxford UP, 2010.
- *My Caste-My Shadow: Selected Poems.* Translated by TC Ghai, LG Publishers and Distributers, 2020.
- Namishray, Mohandas. "*Hindi Dalit Sahitya Samaj ka Sahitya Hai.*" ("Hindi Dalit Literature is the Truth of Society.") *Chintan ki Parampara aur Dalit Sahitya* (*The Tradition of Thought and Dalit Literature*), edited by Sheoraj Singh Bechain and Devendra Chaubey, Lata Sahitya Sadan, 2010. pp. 294-297.
- Omvedt, Gail. *Reinventing Revolution: New Social Movements and the Socialist Tradition in India*, East Gate, 1993.
- Pall, Kamal Dev. *Days Will Come Back.* Translated by Rajinder

Azad, Panther's Paw Publications, 2019.

- Pawar, Daya. *Baluta.* Translated by Jerry Pinto, Speaking Tiger, 2015.
- Satyanarayana, K, and Susie Tharu. Introduction. *The Exercise of Freedom: An Introduction to Dalit Writing*, edited by Satyanarayana and Tharu. Navayana, 2013, pp. 7-21.
- Satyapremi, Purshotam. "*Dalit Sanskriti ki Avdharana ka Pranadhar Dalit Sahitya.*" (Dalit Literature is the Life Spring of Dalit Culture"). *Dalit Chetna – Soch* (*Dalit Consciousness – Thought*), edited by Ramnika Gupta, Navlekhan, 1998, pp. 1-16.
- Shyamal, Gogu. "Obstacle Race." Translated by Uma Bhrugabanda. *Father May be an Elephant and Mother Only a Small Basket, But…* by Shyamala, Navayana, 2012, pp. 113-129.
- Singh, Karan. *Dalitism and Feminism: Locating Women in Dalit Literature*, Creative Books, 2011.
- Valmiki, Omprakash. *Joothan: A Dalit's Life*. Translated by Arun Prabha Mukherjee, Samya, 2003.
- *Amma and Other Stories.* Translated by Naresh K Jain. Manohar, 2008.
- *Dalit Sahitya ka Saundaryashastra* (*The Aesthetic of Dalit Literature*), Radhakrishna, 2001.
- Virdi, SL "Dalit Sahitya aur Punjabi Sahitya." ("Dalit Literature and Punjabi Literature") *Dalit Chetna: Sahitya* (*Dalit Consciousness: Literature*), edited by Ramnika Gupta, Navlekhan, 1996, pp. 95-99.